STUDIES IN BAPTIST HISTORY AND THOUGHT
VOLUME 40

To Express the Ineffable

The Hymns and Spirituality of Anne Steele

STUDIES IN BAPTIST HISTORY AND THOUGHT
VOLUME 40

A full listing of titles in this series
appears at the end of this book

Anne Steele's grave at St. Mary's Church, Broughton.

The grave is inscribed:
Silent the Lyre, and dumb the tuneful Tongue,
That sung on Earth her Great Redeemer's Praise,
But now in Heav'n, she joins th' Angelic Song,
In more Harmonious more exalted Lays.

STUDIES IN BAPTIST HISTORY AND THOUGHT
VOLUME 40

To Express the Ineffable

The Hymns and Spirituality of Anne Steele

Cynthia Y. Aalders

Foreword by D. Bruce Hindmarsh

WIPF & STOCK · Eugene, Oregon

Wipf and Stock Publishers
199 W 8th Ave, Suite 3
Eugene, OR 97401

To Express the Ineffable
The Hymns and Spirituality of Anne Steele
By Aalders, Cynthia Y.
Copyright©2008 Paternoster
ISBN 13: 978-1-60608-600-1
Publication date 4/15/2009
Previously published by Paternoster, 2008

This Edition reprinted by Wipf and Stock Publishers
by arrangement with Paternoster

STUDIES IN BAPTIST HISTORY AND THOUGHT

Series Preface

Baptists form one of the largest Christian communities in the world, and while they hold the historic faith in common with other mainstream Christian traditions, they nevertheless have important insights which they can offer to the worldwide church. *Studies in Baptist History and Thought* will be one means towards this end. It is an international series of academic studies which includes original monographs, revised dissertations, collections of essays and conference papers, and aims to cover any aspect of Baptist history and thought. While not all the authors are themselves Baptists, they nevertheless share an interest in relating Baptist history and thought to the other branches of the Christian church and to the wider life of the world.

The series includes studies in various aspects of Baptist history from the seventeenth century down to the present day, including biographical works, and Baptist thought is understood as covering the subject-matter of theology (including interdisciplinary studies embracing biblical studies, philosophy, sociology, practical theology, liturgy and women's studies). The diverse streams of Baptist life throughout the world are all within the scope of these volumes.

The series editors and consultants believe that the academic disciplines of history and theology are of vital importance to the spiritual vitality of the churches of the Baptist faith and order. The series sets out to discuss, examine and explore the many dimensions of their tradition and so to contribute to their on-going intellectual vigour.

A brief word of explanation is due for the series identifier on the front cover. The fountains, taken from heraldry, represent the Baptist distinctive of believer's baptism and, at the same time, the source of the water of life. There are three of them because they symbolize the Trinitarian basis of Baptist life and faith. Those who are redeemed by the Lamb, the book of Revelation reminds us, will be led to 'fountains of living waters' (Rev. 7.17).

Series Editors

Anthony R. Cross, Fellow of the Centre for Baptist History and Heritage, Regent's Park College, Oxford, UK

Curtis W. Freeman, Research Professor of Theology and Director of the Baptist House of Studies, Duke University, North Carolina, USA

Stephen R. Holmes, Lecturer in Theology, University of St Andrews, Scotland, UK

Elizabeth Newman, Professor of Theology and Ethics, Baptist Theological Seminary at Richmond, Virginia, USA

Philip E. Thompson, Assistant Professor of Systematic Theology and Christian Heritage, North American Baptist Seminary, Sioux Falls, South Dakota, USA

Series Consultant Editors

David Bebbington, Professor of History, University of Stirling, Scotland, UK

Paul S. Fiddes, Professor of Systematic Theology, University of Oxford, and Principal of Regent's Park College, Oxford, UK

† Stanley J. Grenz, Pioneer McDonald Professor of Theology, Carey Theological College, Vancouver, British Columbia, Canada

Ken R. Manley, Distinguished Professor of Church History, Whitley College, The University of Melbourne, Australia

Stanley E. Porter, President and Professor of New Testament, McMaster Divinity College, Hamilton, Ontario, Canada

To Dorene

Contents

Foreword by D. Bruce Hindmarsh	xiii
Figures	xv
Preface	xvii
Chapter 1	
Introduction	1
Sources and Method	4
A Biographical Sketch of Anne Steele	8
Family Life	10
Church Life	13
Education and Intellectual Stimulus	17
Social Stimulation and Support	20
Steele as Published Writer	23
Chapter 2	
"Sacred Poesy....in the Service of Religion":	
Anne Steele and Eighteenth-Century Hymnody	29
The Hymn as Literature and Theology	31
Anne Steele's Contemporaries	36
Isaac Watts	37
Charles Wesley	43
William Cowper	47
Elizabeth Singer Rowe and Anne Dutton	51
Baptist Hymnody	57

Chapter 3
"How Shall These Poor Languid Powers... / Display the Grace My Soul Adores?":
Anne Steele and the Problem of Language — 66
Anne Steele on Writing and Language — 67
Ineffability in Literature and Theology — 79
Ineffability and Anne Steele — 82
Tracing the Theme of Ineffability in Anne Steele's Hymns — 92
The Inexpressible and Silence — 99

Chapter 4
"Depress'd By Pain and Sickness, All My Powers / Are Dull and Languid":
Anne Steele and the Problem of Suffering — 102
Anne Steele on Suffering and the Silence of God — 103
Incomprehensibility and Anne Steele — 114
Tracing the Theme of Incomprehensibility in Anne Steele's Hymns — 123
The Incomprehensible and Silence — 131

Chapter 5
"Teach the Breathings of My Heart / Dependence and Desire":
Anne Steele's Faith in an Ineffable God — 136
Anne Steele and Resignation — 136
Anne Steele and Longing — 149
Tracing the Themes of Resignation and Longing in Anne Steele's Hymns — 159
The Word Breaks the Silence — 168

Chapter 6
Conclusion — 172

Appendices — 178
Appendix 1 Anne Steele's Family Tree — 178
Appendix 2 A Chronology of Anne Steele's Life — 180
Appendix 3 Anne Steele's Reading — 183

Bibliography 187

Index 203

Foreword

Anne Steele (1717-1778) is an important but understudied figure in women's history, in the history of poetry, and in evangelical and Baptist history. She was the first significant female hymn-writer in the modern period, and her hymns were regularly reprinted in hymnbooks through much of the nineteenth century in Britain and North America. Even today, there has been a small Anne Steele revival, with a number of recording artists and worship leaders rediscovering her hymns and their power. Her poignant, "Dear Refuge of my weary soul," is one such hymn to be revived and in common use once again.

Steele's personal papers only passed out of the family into institutional archives in Oxford relatively recently, and Cindy Aalders is among the first to use these materials to reconstruct and interpret the life and work of Steele. And she uses them to good effect in this book. She has not written a biography as such, though she has certainly done plenty of close historical reconstruction of disparate sources to create a portrait of Steele's life and milieu. But more than this, she has offered a sophisticated interpretation of Anne Steele's spirituality and poetics.

Steele's voice as a poet does not display the robust confidence of a Charles Wesley or the Augustan sobriety of an Isaac Watts, but rather the more chastened faith of one who has suffered much, who has her doubts, but who yet believes. In much of her verse Steele explores the inadequacy of language and incapacity of the poet to speak of God, and yet turns this very quandary into fine poetry and devotion. She uses more question marks than exclamation marks, so to speak, and this makes her an interesting figure in the eighteenth century, a period we think of as didactic more than romantic. Likewise, her profound acquaintance with loss and grief means that her insights into the life of faith are hard won and deeply personal. And so she cries, "Hast thou not bid me seek thy face? / And shall I seek in vain? / And can the ear of sovereign grace / Be deaf when I complain?" We hear in these honest questions not despair, but a deep faithfulness to a God whose ways can never be fully grasped.

This book offers many insights for the historian, the literary critic, and the student of Christian spirituality, but even more, it conveys something of the humility and grace of Anne Steele herself, whose faith was profound but never triumphalistic. If this book helps to revive scholarly interest in the life and work of Anne Steele, it will have performed a valuable role. If it inspires readers—as I think it should—to turn to Christ himself as refuge of their weary souls, it will have done even more.

Bruce Hindmarsh
Regent College, Vancouver

FIGURES

Figure 1 Map of Wiltshire and Hampshire — 11

Figure 2 Title page of *Poems on Subjects Chiefly Devotional* — 25

Figure 3 Advertisement for *Poems on Subjects Chiefly Devotional* — 27

Figure 4 Title page of Ash and Evans's "Bristol Collection" — 61

Figure 5 Frontispiece of the first volume of *Poems on Subjects Chiefly Devotional* — 73

Figure 6 Frontispiece of the second volume of *Poems on Subjects Chiefly Devotional* — 88

Figure 7 Frontispiece of the third volume of *Poems on Subjects Chiefly Devotional* — 133

Figure 8 Manuscript copy of "Dear Refuge of My Weary Soul" — 174

Preface

This book found its beginnings in a course I took with Bruce Hindmarsh in the spring of 2005. In a memorable lecture on eighteenth-century hymnody, Bruce introduced me to Anne Steele by playing a recording of one of her hymns. From that lecture, the idea for a thesis took shape, so that this book, in its original form, was a thesis written under Bruce's supervision for a degree from Regent College in Vancouver, Canada. It is fitting, I think, that a book on an eighteenth-century hymn-writer should have begun with hearing a hymn.

The eighteenth century saw an enormous outpouring of devotion in the form of congregational hymns, with such major contributors as Isaac Watts and Charles Wesley, as well as William Cowper, John Newton, and Philip Doddridge, among others. Notable and well-known figures, to be sure, but they were not the only participants in the proliferation of this important form of devotional expression. Rivaling the popularity of even the most accomplished eighteenth-century hymn-writers was the work of Anne Steele, a Baptist woman living quietly in Hampshire. Despite her impressive popularity throughout the eighteenth and nineteenth centuries, and in contrast to the many volumes devoted to her contemporaries, as I began my research I found that very little critical work had been done on Steele or her hymns.

Yet the story of Steele's life and contribution to eighteenth-century hymnody deserves to be told, not only to bridge a gap in our historical understanding, but because as my research progressed it became clear to me that Steele made not only an important contribution, as far as scope of influence goes, but also a unique contribution to eighteenth-century hymnody, and to the expression of eighteenth-century evangelical spirituality more generally. Here we do not find the enthusiastic confidence or stately eloquence of other, more well-known eighteenth-century hymn-writers, but rather an expression of faith that is personal and introspective, and that reveals a compelling depth of honesty regarding the common human experiences of suffering and doubt. Steele's particular sensibility resonated with worshippers throughout the eighteenth and nineteenth centuries and, while her hymns are rarely found in modern hymnbooks, many of those who are familiar with her hymns today continue to find in them a source of religious insight and spiritual encouragement. Then as now, Steele's hymns, like much of the best of eighteenth-century hymnody, speak to the very real hopes and fears and prayers of ordinary women and men, offering them words with which to respond to God in faith and love in the midst of a world that is marked throughout by sin and sorrow.

This book is not, strictly speaking, a biography, though the story of Steele's life will be told in its pages. Rather, it is an examination of the spiritual themes which emerge from a study of her life and, especially, her hymns. The approach I have taken is interdisciplinary, so that I consider Steele at once through the lenses of history, theology, and literary criticism. I have been helped significantly through the work of a number of scholars, and would like to mention J.R. Watson and Donald Davie in particular. As Professor Watson has himself pointed out, thus far there has not been enough serious attention given to the words of hymns, and so I am grateful for his work, and for that of the late Donald Davie, which have sharpened my thinking and provided models regarding modes of interaction.

While there has been little previous work done on Anne Steele in particular, in those instances where she is mentioned, the discussion is typically limited to pious reflection on various familiar and dramatic episodes in her life. Here, I have made an attempt to support my presentation of Steele with reference to her personal and family papers, now archived in the Angus Library at Regent's Park College, Oxford. I hope that the biographical sketch which follows in the Introduction, and that is developed in subsequent chapters, gives a more accurate picture of Steele than has been generally available until now. In addition, I hope that a truer picture of Steele will helpfully illuminate the chief themes to be considered in this book: her hymnody and spirituality. While this book was in the publication process, J.R. Broome's *A Bruised Reed* appeared as the first detailed life and times biography of Steele, and the reader is referred to it for a study of Steele's life in her local context.

As I come to complete this book, I am aware that I owe a great many debts of gratitude to those who have helped and encouraged me throughout its research and writing. I am mindful that I owe my most profound thanks to Bruce Hindmarsh, who welcomed me to eighteenth-century Britain and then acted as such a warm and generous host as I found my way around. I am richer for the example of his excellent scholarship, and for the way that he models the integration of intellect and affect in his work and life. He has read the words that follow more often than anyone other than myself, and his valuable feedback has made my work stronger (though the imperfections that remain are only my own). It is with a deep sense of gratitude that I call him my teacher and my friend.

I am grateful also for the contributions of Sarah Williams, who took a special interest in my preparations to research this book in Oxford, and played a significant role in making that trip a rewarding and memorable experience. Edith Blumhofer invited me to participate with her in a session on women hymn-writers at an American Society of Church History conference, and I am

Preface xix

grateful to her for giving me the opportunity to present some of my work there. Mary Louise VanDyke, of the Dictionary of American Hymnology at Oberlin College, was an impressive source of information, and I am thankful for her generous help in clarifying Steele's popularity in North America. I am likewise indebted to various helpful librarians, notably Sue Mills at the Angus Library at Regent's Park College, Oxford, and Cindy Derrenbacker and Joan Pries at the John Richard Allison Library at Regent College, as well as librarians at the Bodleian Library, the University of British Columbia Library, and Pitts Theology Library at Candler School of Theology.

Thanks also are due to my sister, Natalie Aalders, for help with Steele's family tree, and for patiently accommodating on its branches each new family member my research turned up. Additionally, she stepped in at the end to offer enthusiastic and welcome help with the map included here. Rosi Petkova similarly offered very capable technical assistance with the manuscript facsimile found in the Conclusion. As well, it has been a pleasure to work with Anthony Cross, at Paternoster, in bringing this work to press.

Friends also have left their mark on my work and on my life, and I am particularly grateful to Leslie Herrmann, Ellie McCullough, and Michelle Tittmar, who were near and constant sources of support throughout this project, and who nourished me with their food, drink, laughter, and prayers. And from a distance, Keith Grant blessed me with his camaraderie and care. Throughout her letters and verse, Anne Steele acknowledged the role that friendship played in her ability to write, and I have found that her words ring true. I am grateful for these friends.

Finally, I am glad to be able to thank Andrea Tisher, who took the texts with which I was working, set them to new music, and then recorded a CD—and in the process, became a very dear friend. There has been a great deal of pleasure and much to discover in this collaboration, and I am grateful to Andrea for giving life to Steele's texts in a way that I could not. This book began by listening to a hymn; what joy that there are now more of Anne Steele's hymns to hear, and to be sung.

Cindy Aalders
Vancouver, June 2008

O Thou who art beyond all—
Is this not the sum total of all that we can sing of Thee?
What hymn will human language raise to Thee?
  – Gregory of Nazianzus

CHAPTER 1

Introduction

On 25 January 1893, well over a century after Anne Steele's death, J. Cuthbert Hadden wrote a letter to Miss Bompas, a descendent of Steele's brother. Hadden, a noted Edinburgh organist and biographer, who was on the staff of the *Dictionary of National Biography*, was interested in writing an article about Steele for "a London magazine," and wrote to solicit information from Bompas, then in possession of many of Steele's surviving manuscripts.[1] In a subsequent letter, Hadden explains his interest in Steele's hymns: "I am not a 'reverend,' but being an organist it is my whim to consider myself very *near* a reverend! Playing the hymns Sunday by Sunday I always like to think of their writers, and there is no hymn I like better than 'Dear Refuge of My Weary Soul.'"[2] The hymn to which Hadden refers was given by Steele the title, "God the Only Refuge of the Troubled Mind," and begins with these words:

> Dear refuge of my weary soul,
>   On thee, when sorrows rise:
> On thee, when waves of trouble roll,
>   My fainting hope relies.
>
> While hope revives, though prest with fears,
>   And I can say, my God,
> Beneath thy feet I spread my cares,
>   And pour my woes abroad.[3]

---

[1] J. Cuthbert Hadden to Miss Bompas, 25 January 1893, STE 3/16 (x). The cataloguing system included here is that of the Steele Collection archived in the Angus Library, Regent's Park College, Oxford. Hadden (1861-1914) has written extensively on various composers and hymn-writers.

[2] In a postscript, Hadden adds, "I am on the staff of the 'Dictionary of National Biography' & when we get to the letter 'S' I will see that Anne Steele gets justice." J. Cuthbert Hadden to Miss Bompas, 1 February 1893, STE 3/16 (xi). Hadden himself later wrote an article on Steele which was published in the 1897 edition of the *Dictionary of National Biography*.

[3] Anne Steele, "God the Only Refuge of the Troubled Mind," *Poems on Subjects Chiefly Devotional, by Theodosia* (Bristol: W. Pine, 1780), I, 144 (references are to volume and page number).

This hymn effectively introduces the notes of introspection, spiritual hesitancy, and sensitivity to human suffering which distinguish Steele's hymns from those of many of her contemporaries. In it, Steele frankly confronts the reality of human sorrow, yet does so while affirming the love and sovereignty of God. And, more than a century after Hadden's letter to Bompas, the same hymn attracted me to this study of Anne Steele's hymns and spirituality, for in it I detected a surprising and appealing spiritual honesty, together with an acknowledgement of human loss and limitation, which are not often encountered in the church's hymnody.[4]

Anne Steele (1717-1778) was one of the most well-known and best-loved devotional hymn-writers of the eighteenth century. While the popularity of her hymns has certainly diminished in the last century, from the time of their publication in 1760 until late in the nineteenth century they were exceedingly popular. Steele has been lauded as both the "mother" of the English hymn and as a "laureate of hymnody" for the Baptist denomination.[5] Similar accolades abound. Writing in 1884, Edwin Hatfield remarks, "No one of the gentler sex has so largely contributed to the familiar hymnology of the church as...Anne Steele"; and in 1886, Samuel Duffield is more specific, claiming that Steele "stands fourth or fifth in the list of contributors to English hymnody, being outnumbered, usually, by Watts, Doddridge, and Charles Wesley; and, occasionally, by Newton."[6] When hymns began to be anthologized, Steele was well represented; Paul Richardson states that Steele's hymns "appeared more often than those of any other Baptist in the anthologies of all the dissenting churches for more than a hundred years."[7] And in 1892, when John Julian

---

[4] A recent recording of "Dear Refuge of My Weary Soul" by Sandra McCracken and Indelible Grace Music puts Steele's lyrics to new music in an effort to reintroduce her hymnody to the worship life of the church. I am grateful to Bruce Hindmarsh for introducing me to this hymn and thus to Anne Steele in a lecture he gave on eighteenth-century hymnody at Regent College on 9 March 2005.

[5] Erik Routley, *Hymns and Human Life* (London: John Murray, 1952), 206; Richard Arnold, "A 'Veil of Interposing Night': The Hymns of Anne Steele (1717-1778)," *Christian Scholar's Review* 18, no. 4 (June 1989): 384. Arnold argues that what Isaac Watts was for the Independents, Charles Wesley for the Methodists, and William Cowper and John Newton for the Evangelicals, Steele was for the Baptists; he judges her to be "really the *first* as well as the most significant hymn-writer of that sect." Ibid. (italics in original).

[6] Edwin F. Hatfield, *The Poets of the Church: A Series of Biographical Sketches of Hymn-Writers with Notes on Their Hymns* (New York: Anson D.F. Randolph, 1884), 570; Samuel Willoughby Duffield, *English Hymns: Their Authors and History* (New York: Funk and Wagnalls, 1886), 7.

[7] Paul Richardson, "Baptist Contributions to Hymnody and Hymnology," *Review and Expositor* 87, no. 1 (Winter 1990): 62. Albert Bailey states, "For nearly a hundred years Miss Steele's hymns were a good third to Watts's and Doddridge's in the hymnals of the

published his classic *Dictionary of Hymnology*, he noted more than seventy-five of Steele's hymns still in common use.[8] Notwithstanding this remarkable and enduring popularity, Steele has all but disappeared from modern hymnbooks and is little known today.

Despite this recent neglect, Steele's contribution to eighteenth-century English hymnody is worthy of the prolonged inquiry undertaken here for several reasons. Most fundamentally, this study will illuminate the life of a significant though, in the last century, largely ignored figure in the history of the church. Furthermore, as hymns are representative of the spiritual impulse of a particular time and place, this study will cast light on the devotional lives of eighteenth-century English Christians, and of Baptists more particularly.[9] The account of Steele's life and the example of her hymnody also represent an important episode in women's history, for she was the first notable woman hymn-writer, and therefore this study will clarify a narrative with, as yet, far too many gaps. More specifically, it will seek to elucidate Steele's unique expression of devotion via an exploration of the particular spiritual themes present in her hymnody.

The themes which emerge from a study of Steele's hymns are, at once, well represented in the history of Christian spirituality as well as remarkable within the context of eighteenth-century hymnody. Eighteenth-century devotional expression was typically confident and effusive, as through their hymns these writers hoped to encourage and edify worshippers, yet Steele self-consciously questioned her own ability—and, indeed, the ability of language itself—to praise God meaningfully. Unlike many other hymn-writers of that time, Steele

---

Dissenting Churches." Albert Edward Bailey, *The Gospel in Hymns: Backgrounds and Interpretations* (New York: Charles Scribner's Sons, 1950), 70.

[8] By way of contrast, observe that Julian counts sixty-one of John Newton's hymns and seventy of Philip Doddridge's hymns to be in common use in 1892. John Julian, *Dictionary of Hymnology: Origin and History of Christian Hymns and Hymnwriters of All Ages and Nations*, rev. ed. (London: J. Murray, 1907; reprint, Grand Rapids, MI: Kregel Publications, 1985), 2: 1089, 1: 804, 1: 306 (page citations are to the reprint edition). It is also interesting to note Steele's popularity in North America where, between 1791 and 1978, her texts were published almost 13,000 times in a wide variety of denominational hymnbooks, including Presbyterian, Methodist, Unitarian, Dutch Reformed, Moravian, and Mennonite, among many others. The Dictionary of American Hymnology, Oberlin College, Ohio.

[9] The significance of hymns and their relationship to the expression of popular piety is heightened in the eighteenth century by the fact that many people had few books other than perhaps a Bible and a hymnbook. For this reason, Ken Manley claims that "the devotional use of the hymnbook in both private and family prayers is perhaps far beyond much modern imagination." Ken R. Manley, "'Sing Side by Side': John Rippon and Baptist Hymnody," in *Pilgrim Pathways: Essays in Baptist History in Honour of B.R. White*, ed. William H. Brackney, Paul S. Fiddes, and John H.Y. Briggs (Macon, GA: Mercer University Press, 1999), 161.

did not focus on the comfort of knowing God's presence and then on praising God from that place of consolation. Instead, her experiences of earthly suffering and her perception of the absence of God prompted her to use her hymns as a means of probing and questioning the divine-human encounter. Whereas many eighteenth-century hymns are enthusiastic and robust, Steele's hymns are more often introspective, characterized by doubt and uncertainty, sometimes bordering on despair.

The prevalent themes in Steele's hymnody gesture toward two related problems: problems pertaining to language and suffering. They are related in that together they concern the limited human ability to comprehend God and then articulate meaning about him. That is, together they raise questions in relation to the classic spiritual theme of the ineffability of God. Throughout the history of the church, Christian writers have probed the boundaries of speech and silence as regards the human ability to convey meaning about God. Steele's letters and verse reveal a similar concern. Her understanding of the limitations of language and her experience of personal suffering might reasonably be expected to have resulted in her silence. Yet in faith, Steele persisted in her efforts to compose hymns, and in so doing has put words in the mouths of many thousands of Christians—men and women, inarticulate and educated, confident and troubled by spiritual doubts.

In the following pages, we will consider Steele's spirituality via an exploration of the tension between her successful and evocative devotional expression and her often painful efforts to articulate praise to God. We will ask how Steele overcame these potentially inhibiting difficulties—difficulties arising from self-doubt and struggles with inarticulacy, from her belief that language itself is powerless to offer meaningful praise to God, and from her questioning God's silence in the face of human suffering—such that she was able to make affirmations about God and the spiritual life. This book aims to demonstrate that Steele was able to overcome those problems pertaining to language and suffering which might have prevented her from articulating praise to God because her spirituality was marked by a sustained hope in the midst of doubt and uncertainty: she longed for the knowledge of God's presence even while sensing his absence, she allowed her experiences of pain to be transfigured by her resignation to God's will, and she anticipated the eschatological perfection of her voice.

Sources and Method

In 1760, Steele published two volumes of hymns, poems, and versified psalms under the title *Poems on Subjects Chiefly Devotional, by Theodosia*.[10] In 1780,

---

[10] [Anne Steele], *Poems on Subjects Chiefly Devotional, by Theodosia* (London: J. Buckland and J. Ward, 1760). The first volume contains 105 hymns and 28 "occasional

two years after Steele's death, these volumes were republished, and to them was added a third volume, *Miscellaneous Pieces, in Verse and Prose*.[11] This third volume, of poems and prose reflections, was prefaced by an "Advertisement," or biographical sketch of Steele, written by Caleb Evans.[12] These two early English editions—which were published under a pseudonym, Theodosia (though the 1780 edition identifies Steele as author in the prefatory "Advertisement")—were followed by an edition in America, where Steele's popularity rivalled that in England. In Boston in 1808, the three previous volumes were published as two volumes entitled *The Works of Mrs. Anne Steele*.[13] Another English edition followed in 1863, when Daniel Sedgwick published *Hymns, Psalms, and Poems, by Anne Steele*.[14] This volume omitted some of the poems as well as all of her prose meditations, and was prefaced by a memoir written by John Sheppard, which provides some useful biographical information about Steele gleaned from his personal friendship with Steele's

---

poems," while the second volume contains 52 "occasional poems" as well as 47 "psalms attempted in verse."

[11] [Anne Steele], *Poems on Subjects Chiefly Devotional, by Theodosia* (Bristol: W. Pine, 1780). The additional volume contains 71 "miscellaneous poems" and 21 "miscellaneous pieces in prose"—it should be noted, however, that many of the "miscellaneous poems" could arguably be classified as hymns.

[12] Evans's "Advertisement" is followed by a lengthy poem mourning the death of Steele. The poem is anonymous, but Hugh Steele-Smith, a twentieth-century ancestor of Steele's brother, identifies the author as Steele's niece, Mary Steele Dunscombe (1753-1813). See Hugh Steele-Smith's research files on Anne Steele, STE 11/1.

[13] Anne Steele, *The Works of Mrs. Anne Steele, Complete in Two Volumes. Comprehending Poems on Subjects Chiefly Devotional: and Miscellaneous Pieces in Prose and Verse: Heretofore Published under the Title of Theodosia* (Boston: Monroe, Francis and Parker, 1808).

[14] Anne Steele, *Hymns, Psalms, and Poems, by Anne Steele, With Memoir by John Sheppard* (London: Daniel Sedgwick, 1863). In 1859, Daniel Sedgwick (1814-1879) began publishing reprints of works by seventeenth- and eighteenth-century hymn-writers under the general title of Library of Spiritual Song. He became "the foremost living hymnologist" when an enlarged second edition of his *A Comprehensive Index of Many of the Original Authors and Translators of Psalms and Hymns* was published in 1863. His manuscripts were used by John Julian in the compilation of his *Dictionary of Hymnology* in 1892. G.C. Boase, "Sedgwick, Daniel (1814-1879)," rev. Megan A. Stephan, *Oxford Dictionary of National Biography* (Oxford: Oxford University Press, 2004 [http://www.oxforddnb.com/view/article/25013, accessed 23 October 2006]). Sedgwick was, according to Louis Benson, "the first to make a collection and systematic study of English hymn books." Louis F. Benson, *The English Hymn: Its Development and Use in Worship* (New York: Hodder and Stoughton, 1915; reprint, Richmond, VI: John Knox Press, 1962), 260 (page citations are to the reprint edition).

niece, Anne Steele Tomkins (1769-1859).[15] In 1967, a small volume of Steele's hymns was published in England, including a preface by J.R. Broome, in which is given significant background regarding the Steele family's early history as well as the church in which Steele worshipped throughout her life.[16] In this volume, Steele's hymns were republished as in the 1863 edition, but her psalms and poems were omitted. In researching this book, each of these five editions has been consulted. In the pages that follow, however, I have cited chiefly the 1780 edition.

In addition to these published works, a significant collection of Steele's manuscripts, including correspondence and unpublished hymns and poems, is archived in the Angus Library at Regent's Park College, Oxford. The Steele Collection in the Angus Library also contains poetry and correspondence written by various other members of the Steele family, as well as books belonging to the family and miscellaneous documents related to Steele's life and work. This rich repository of unpublished material has been researched and will inform this book and its conclusions. The collection was preserved within the Steele family until 1992, when it was given as a gift from Hugh Steele-Smith, a descendent of Steele's brother, to the Angus Library. Steele-Smith engaged in a lengthy inquiry into his family's history and the Steele Collection contains his extensive research notes and files, along with his collection of early printed material on the Steele family, which also have been consulted. Records from the Broughton church, likewise archived in the Angus Library, have been used to substantiate details related to the Steele family's involvement in that church and the community.

Following the present introductory chapter, the second chapter will take a broad view of eighteenth-century hymnody, considering the landscape within which Steele lived and worked, and asking particular questions about the hymn as a work of both literature and theology. In the third and fourth chapters, we will consider the problems of language and suffering which might have prevented Steele from being able to praise God, as they highlight God's ineffability and the limitations of human articulation, specifically as related to speech about God. In the fifth chapter, I will attempt to resolve those problems and suggest how indeed Steele was able to overcome the problems of language

---

[15] For Anne Steele Tomkins's correspondence with Sheppard, see STE 6/5. The difficulty of distinguishing between Steele's hymns and poems is highlighted by Sedgwick's reclassifying some of Evans's "miscellaneous poems" as hymns.

[16] Anne Steele, *Hymns by Anne Steele*, preface by J.R. Broome (London: Gospel Standard Baptist Trust, 1967). More recently, Broome expanded his research into a biography of Steele, which further clarifies Anne Steele's place within a large family of significant local influence; the various business interests and considerable wealth of the Steele family; as well as the origins and activities of the Particular Baptist churches in Hampshire and Wiltshire, and the Steele family's place within those churches. J.R. Broome, *A Bruised Reed: The Life and Times of Anne Steele* (Harpenden, UK: Gospel Standard Trust Publications, 2007).

and suffering in order to make affirmations about God and the spiritual life, despite her belief that God was both ineffable and incomprehensible. In the final chapter, I will bring together the various themes considered in the previous discussion in order to draw conclusions about Steele and her particular spiritual vision.

Chapters Three through Five will follow a consistent pattern. In each chapter, the primary sources just noted, and in particular the correspondence and poetry, will be used as a point of entry into an exploration of Steele's reflection on various spiritual themes. Snapshots will be taken of significant events or exchanges in Steele's life in order to illuminate her devotional experience and, simultaneously, to bring her to life as a real person who lived in a particular time and place. Noteworthy relationships, with both family and an array of influential friends, will also be considered, since Steele's work was always undertaken within the context of these associations. Attention to these connections will help to develop a clearer picture of eighteenth-century Baptist life, and of Steele's place within it.

From these initial vignettes, the scope of each chapter will broaden out to consider the image of Steele which emerges when she is observed within her particular context. The approach taken will be both historical and literary, with points of contact to classic works of Christian spirituality.[17] Without this contextual consideration, Steele will appear distorted by an overemphasis on, for example, her sense of melancholy, whereas an understanding of her writing within the Age of Sensibility will clarify her sometimes gloomy choice of language. Attention will therefore be given to such traditions as eighteenth-century Baptist Calvinism, the beginnings of evangelicalism, and early

---

[17] The study of hymns will be necessarily interdisciplinary, as the genre exists at the intersection of theology, poetry, and music. J.R. Watson likewise indicates that hymns are, "more obviously than most poetry, image—music—text." J.R. Watson, *The English Hymn: A Critical and Historical Study* (Oxford: Oxford University Press, 1997), 22. In this book, I will not consider the element of music. Steele herself only wrote hymn texts which, for much of the eighteenth century, were then sung to a variety of tunes, as was common with hymn-writing and hymn-singing during the period.

For a comprehensive and systematic guide to English-language hymn tunes, including those tunes to which Steele's texts were sung, see Nicholas Temperley, *The Hymn Tune Index: A Census of English-Language Hymn Tunes in Printed Sources from 1535 to 1820* (Oxford: Oxford University Press, 1997). This index is also available on-line: Nicholas Temperley, *The Hymn Tune Index* (http://hymntune.music.uiuc.edu, accessed 13 January 2007). The on-line database is an updated version of the printed index, and contains "all hymn tunes printed anywhere in the world with English-language texts up to 1820, and their publication history up to that date." For a helpful discussion of hymn tunes, see also John Wilson, "Looking at Hymn Tunes: The Objective Factors," in *Duty and Delight: Routley Remembered: A Memorial Tribute to Erik Routley (1917-1982), Ministry, Church Music, Hymnody*, ed. Robin A. Leaver and James H. Litton, 123-152 (Carol Stream, IL: Hope Publishing, 1985).

Romanticism, all of which were refracted in Steele's personality and writings. It is hoped that by bringing Steele's character into clearer focus through this contextual analysis, we will be able to garner deeper insight into her hymnody and spirituality.

Having thus widened the perspective, each chapter will then refocus, though now on the specifics of Steele's hymnody. The final section of each chapter will be comprised of an analysis of hymns representative of key spiritual themes that emerge from a study of Steele's hymnody. Where appropriate, her hymns will be brought into sharper relief through comparisons made with the work of other eighteenth-century hymn-writers. As well, the last generation has witnessed a renewed academic interest in the study of eighteenth-century congregational hymns, resulting in a number of key texts which will be brought to bear on the present discussion of Steele's hymnody. It is hoped that this analysis of Steele's hymns will illuminate not only her unique spirituality, but will shed light on the reasons for her extraordinary popularity in the eighteenth and nineteenth centuries, as well as her continuing appeal to those familiar with her hymns today. But prior to turning to an in-depth exploration of Steele's spirituality as it is revealed in her hymnody, it will be helpful to sketch an outline of her life, which will then be given texture and depth through the subsequent discussion.

A Biographical Sketch of Anne Steele

J. Cuthbert Hadden's comment, recorded earlier, "Playing the hymns Sunday by Sunday I always like to think of their writers," signals a sentiment that appears to have motivated much inquiry into hymns and their writers from the late nineteenth century through the middle of the twentieth century. Prior to recent scholarly advancements in the study of hymnody, hymns were treated as a kind of folk genre; writing about hymns typically was limited to stories related to the circumstances or personalities behind the composition of particular hymns. For this reason, perhaps, the biographical stories typically relayed about Steele tend to capitalize on the dramatic, despite dubious archival evidence.

Most stories told about Steele turn on her experiences of acute personal suffering. The events most often relayed include the early death of her mother, her fall from a horse as a teenager which left her a life-long invalid, and the death of her fiancé by drowning just a few hours before their intended wedding. However, while Steele's mother did die when she was three years old, there is little to support the veracity of the stories regarding her injury and fiancé. Still, the stories are pervasive. The image of Steele which has emerged from these accounts is of a reclusive, sensitive, and melancholic woman of extreme piety whose verse rose naturally from her experiences of personal loss. See, for example, Edwin Hatfield's depiction of Steele:

> Heart-broken at her grievous loss [that is, the loss of her fiancé], she cherished his memory through life, and entertained no similar proposals from any other person. She gave her days to works of piety and benevolence, diffusing throughout her neighbourhood the sweet savor of godliness, and attaching to herself, and more to her Saviour, the hearts of the sick, the sorrowing, and the needy.
>
> The hours of her sorrow were often relieved by the composition of a hymn, expressive of her own spiritual condition and aspirations.[18]

It is not uncommon for Steele's character and motivation as a hymn-writer to be reduced to a simple statement, such as, "Many of her hymns, written to lighten her own burdens, give beautiful expression to the sweetness of her Christian character, and the depth of her Christian experience."[19] Similarly, "She poured out her grief in her hymns and poems and the sweetness they embody is in direct contrast to the bitterness of her heart-break," or "The grief-stricken young woman with heroic faith nevertheless rose above her afflictions and found solace in sacred song."[20] However, such statements appear to be based primarily on an emotional reading of the events just noted—events which evoke an affecting image of Steele that intensifies the experience of singing her hymns by inducing particular emotions in the singer. At the same time, an emphasis on the dramatic inspiration of her hymns effectively removes Steele from the ranks of ordinary Christians in their pews, as they attempt to articulate their devotion to God in faith and song. It would seem that the approach most often taken toward the telling of Steele's life story has had more to do with hagiography than biography.

Steele's biographical story is far from mundane, but neither is it as sensational as frequently depicted. Most previous writing about Steele's life appears to recycle stories of questionable validity, sometimes embellishing those stories in order to highlight her extreme piety. While the effect may

---

[18] Hatfield, *The Poets of the Church*, 571. Stirring accounts of Steele's purported loss of her fiancé abound. Emma Pitman's version of the event suggests embellishment, but is not out of keeping with many similar stories:
> Early on that morning the intending bridegroom had gone to the river to bathe, and had sunk never to rise again. Some one who knew he had gone to bathe went to look for him, and aided in recovering his lifeless corpse. At the very time when, according to the nuptial arrangements, he would have been uttering the sacred vows, his lifeless body was brought home. The sight of the beloved dead almost made her brain reel, and it was hours and days before she could even think of submission. It was a tempest of sorrow at first; then it subsided, and she penned one of our sweetest hymns.

Emma R. Pitman, *Lady Hymn Writers* (London: T. Nelson and Sons, 1892), 67-68.

[19] Henry S. Burrage, *Baptist Hymn Writers and Their Hymns* (Portland, ME: Brown Thurston and Company, 1888), 46.

[20] Ernest Emurian, *Living Stories of Famous Hymns* (Grand Rapids, MI: Baker Book House, 1955), 40; E.E. Ryden, *The Story of Christian Hymnody* (Rock Island, IL: Augustana Press, 1959), 299.

encourage devotional reflection, it does little to increase our knowledge of Steele or our understanding of her spirituality. Therefore, an effort here will be made to relay events in Steele's life with reference primarily to letters, diaries, and other verifiable sources. For the purposes of this study, I will focus on those aspects of her life which encouraged her reflection on the themes of language and suffering, as well as those events and relationships which supported her writing efforts.

Family Life

Anne Steele was born in 1717 in the small village of Broughton, in Hampshire, England (see Figure 1), the second child of William Steele (1689-1769) and Anne Froude Steele (1684-1720) (see Appendix 1). William Steele was a successful timber merchant who, according to J.R. Broome, "supplied the timber for the warships in Portsmouth Dockyard," resulting in the family's comparative wealth.[21] The Steeles lived in a comfortable home, christened "The Grandfathers," which was amiably surrounded by an expanse of trees and gardens. Anne, known within the family circle as Nanny, had an older brother, William (1715-1785), and would later gain, though only briefly, a second brother, Thomas. Thomas Steele died as an infant and was buried on 1 July 1720; Anne Froude Steele's own burial on 7 May 1720 alludes to the likelihood of her death in childbirth. And thus the themes of illness and death, which would recur with notable frequency as she aged, were introduced in Anne's young life.

Anne's father remarried within three years so that in May 1723, Anne Cator Steele (1689-1760) became her stepmother, and on 29 June 1724, the family celebrated the birth of Anne's half-sister, Mary (1724-1772). Extant letters and diaries indicate that these five surviving members of the Steele family enjoyed friendly and supportive relationships. Substantial surviving correspondence between Steele and her sister and between Steele and her brother reveal affectionate relationships characterized by mutual concern for the physical, intellectual, and spiritual well-being of the other. Steele was also clearly devoted to her father. While none of their letters survive, Steele did dedicate to

---

[21] Broome, preface to *Hymns by Anne Steele*, xvii. On the wealth of the Steele family, see also John Sheppard's memoir of Steele in *Hymns, Psalms, and Poems, by Anne Steele*, v-vii. Karen Smith, who has done significant archival research on the lives of eighteenth-century Baptists in Hampshire and Wiltshire, notes, "a small indication of [the Steele family's] increasing wealth and status in rural society may be found in the trust deeds of the Whitchurch Baptist Church when in 1743 William Steele is simply listed as a carpenter, but by 1757, he and his son are listed 'gentlemen.'" Karen Elizabeth Smith, "The Community and the Believer: A Study of Calvinistic Baptist Spirituality in Some Towns and Villages of Hampshire and the Borders of Wiltshire, *c.* 1730-1830" (DPhil diss., University of Oxford, 1986), 13, n. 27, quoting Trust Deeds for 1743 and 1757, Hampshire Records Office (MS 46M71 T3 and T4).

Introduction

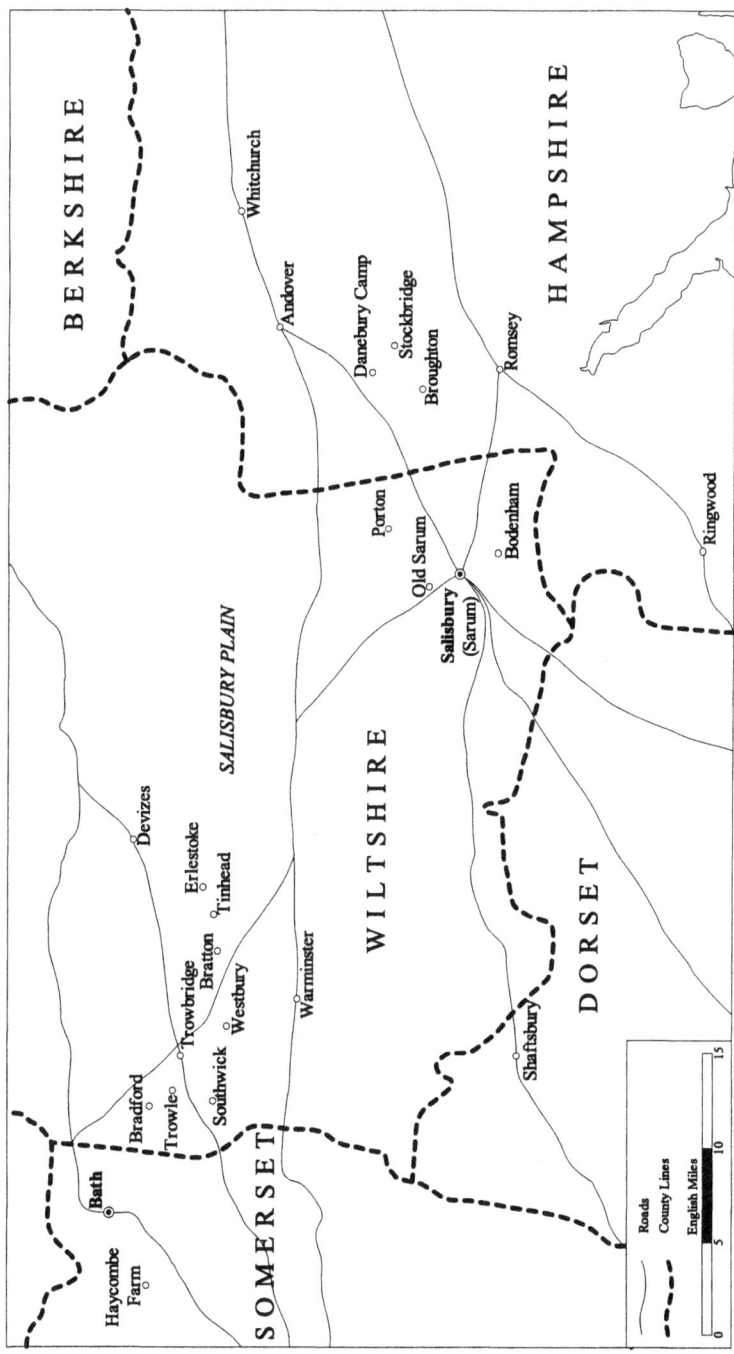

Figure 1: Map of Wiltshire and Hampshire

him the 1760 edition of her hymns and poems, acknowledging that it was at his "kind approbation" that she consented to their publication; her dedication reads, in part, "I have now at your desire collected [my verse] into a little Book which I beg leave to present to you as a humble acknowledgement of the grateful sense I have of your paternal affection and the benefit I have received from your instructions."[22] The bond between Steele and her family was forged further by physical proximity: she lived with her father and stepmother until her father's death in 1769, after which time she moved to "Broughton House," the home of her brother, where she remained until her death in 1778.

The ties of significant familial relationships extended beyond the walls of home, however, as Steele had a place in a network of families united by marriage and a commitment to the Dissenting cause. Marjorie Reeves shows how both Anne Froude Steele and Anne Cator Steele were connected to leading Baptist families: the Froude family, near Devizes, "had been active in promoting the Baptist cause since the mid-seventeenth century," while the Cator family, living near Trowbridge, was similarly committed to the denomination.[23] Anne Cator Steele's sister, Jane, married John Gay of Haycombe, "thus linking the Steeles with yet another strongly Dissenting family."[24] Despite the fact that Steele has customarily been depicted as

---

[22] Draft dedication of Steele's hymns and poems to her father, c. 1760, STE 3/5.

[23] Anne Froude Steele was the daughter of Edward Froude, the first Particular Baptist minister at Erlestoke, a village near Devizes, where Steele on occasion stayed with relatives. Reeves notes, "The beginnings of a Baptist group at Erlestoke can be dated to c. 1662." Marjorie Reeves, *Pursuing the Muses: Female Education and Nonconformist Culture, 1700-1900* (London: Leicester University Press, 1997), 2. J.R. Broome records that Edward Froude, Steele's grandfather, was in attendance at the 1689 Assembly of Particular Baptist ministers, where "he was in the company of William Kiffin, Hansard Knollys, Benjamin Keach, Andrew Gifford and many other Particular Baptist ministers from all over England and Wales—over one hundred and fifty in number, who had assembled to consider the rebuilding of the denomination after the years of persecution." Kiffin, Knollys, Keach, and Gifford were prominent Particular Baptist ministers in the late seventeenth century. Broome, preface to *Hymns by Anne Steele*, ix, xi. For further information on the Froude family as Nonconformists, see Marjorie Reeves, *Sheep Bell and Ploughshare: The Story of Two Village Families* (Bradford-on-Avon, UK: Moonraker Press, 1978), 17-18, 28-31.

Reeves explains that William Steele's second marriage "brought him into another Nonconformist connection." Anne Cator was "the younger daughter of Thomas Cator, a glazier of Trowle, the rural area between Trowbridge and Bradford; he actually lived in the parish of Bradford-on-Avon. Cator, it seems, was also connected with the Baptist cause, for in his will he left £5 to the minister of the Bradford Baptist Church. The Cators had connections with Trowbridge Baptists as well, for Anne was baptized there." Reeves, *Pursuing the Muses*, 2-3.

[24] Reeves traces the Gay family back to the seventeenth century: "In the middle of the seventeenth century a Richard Gay owned land at Haycombe. His son was almost certainly the Richard Gay, living at Haycombe, who was imprisoned in Ilchester gaol as

reclusive, loath to leave her home in Broughton, letter and diary accounts attest to her recurring presence in Trowbridge and Haycombe, as well as in Ringwood at the home of the Manfields, a family similarly linked to the Steeles through marriage. Letters further illuminate the measure of affection between Steele and her aunts and cousins, confirming the significant part Steele's extended family played in her social sphere.

While Steele's life is marked throughout by supportive and affectionate relationships, and with genuine joy and love, it was marred just as often by illness and premature death. Steele herself was troubled by the debilitating symptoms of chronic illness. Death also played a recurring role in her life. In 1729, she lost both an uncle, John Gay, and an aunt; smallpox claimed the life of her cousin, Richard Gay, in 1736; she lost her uncle, Henry Steele, in 1739; in 1743, her cousin, Elizabeth Gay, died, most likely also of smallpox; and in 1758, her aunt, Jane Gay, died. More painful losses were yet to come. In 1760, her stepmother, Anne Cator Steele, died; she lost her young nephew, Samuel Wakeford, in 1767; in 1772, her sister, Mary Steele Wakeford, to whom she was particularly devoted, died at the age of forty-eight. The death of her father in 1769, after years of her caring for him at "The Grandfathers," appears to have come as a particular blow. This litany of loss is included in order to introduce the theme of suffering in Steele's life; while it is treated only cursorily here, it will be the subject of more sustained reflection in subsequent pages.

Church Life

In her study of eighteenth-century Calvinistic Baptist spirituality, Karen Smith notes, "the Steele family of Broughton in Hampshire....had an important place in the history of the growth and development of the churches in Hampshire and Wiltshire."[25] This significant role dates from 1699, when Henry Steele (1654-

---

a Nonconformist minister in the reign of Charles II. If this is correct, Richard the minister's son was the John Gay of Haycombe who, by marrying Jane Cator of Trowbridge, also became linked with the Steele family at Broughton." Ibid., 3.

[25] Smith, "The Community and the Believer," 12. J.R. Broome observes that the Particular Baptist group into which Steele was born "dates in the Hampshire/Wiltshire area from about 1640-50....they first appear at Devizes about 1646, Porton, near Salisbury, about 1653, and at Southwick, near Trowbridge, about the same period....a Particular Baptist Church was formed at Porton on 3rd April 1653. This was the founder Church of the one of which Anne Steele became a member...it having transferred its centre from Porton to Broughton in 1710." Broome points out that "From these early Churches (we use the term in relation to people rather than buildings) at Devizes, Southwick and Porton, there grew in Wiltshire a number of smaller causes at Westbury, Erlestoke and Bratton." Steele's grandfather, Edward Froude, was the pastor at Erlestoke and her uncle and then father pastored the Porton/Broughton church. Broome cites as reference "an excellent piece of historical research, which is now rare and

1739), Anne Steele's great-uncle, agreed to pastor the Broughton church; he served the congregation until his death in 1739. From 1709, his nephew and Steele's father, William Steele, assisted him, assuming the primary pastoral role in 1739 and maintaining it until his own death in 1769. As was common at the time, both Henry Steele and William Steele held secular positions in addition to their spiritual roles as Dissenting pastors: they were both successful timber merchants. Smith observes that "in addition to nearly seventy years of pastoral oversight which they gave to the Broughton church, they were able to provide financial support for the Baptist cause more widely."[26] Certainly their support of the Broughton church was significant. Steele's niece, Mary Steele Dunscombe (1753-1813), notes that "by the blessing of Providence" both William Steele and Henry Steele "possessed a comfortable independence" and that therefore their "labours in the ministry were all gratuitous."[27] Furthermore,

---

almost unobtainable," *Twenty Golden Candlesticks*, published by W. Doel in 1890. Broome, preface to *Hymns by Anne Steele*, viii-ix. The Broughton church was established during the years of persecution in which Dissenting churches were restricted; repeatedly during the 1670s and 1680s, Edward and Elizabeth Froude, Steele's maternal grandparents, were reported for non-attendance at the parish church. On one of these occasions, Edward Froude was identified as "a Nonconformist Anabaptist preacher." Ibid., xi. Nonconformists rejected the right of the Established Church to determine how and where they should worship. They "developed the notion of the voluntary or 'gathered' church." Jane Shaw, "Introduction: Why 'Culture and the Nonconformist Tradition'?" in *Culture and the Nonconformist Tradition*, ed. Jane Shaw and Alan Kreider, Religion, Culture, and Society (Cardiff: University of Wales, 1999), 2. For a comprehensive treatment of the origin and nature of Dissent, see Michael R. Watts, *The Dissenters*, vol. 1, *From the Reformation to the French Revolution* (Oxford: Clarendon Press, 1978).

The Steele family belonged to the Particular Baptist denomination. Particular Baptists were Calvinistic in theology, believing that Christ died for the elect, or for particular people; General Baptists, on the other hand, were Arminian, believing that Christ's death was for all men and women. The significance of this distinction with regard to Steele's hymnody will be discussed later in this book.

[26] Smith, "The Community and the Believer," 13.

[27] Mary Steele Dunscombe, quoted in John Sheppard's memoir in *Hymns, Psalms, and Poems, by Anne Steele*, v. Sheppard further notes how William Steadman records in his diary that Henry Steele gave "cottages and a burying-ground to the church, and fitted up their place of worship in a very neat substantial manner." Steadman, quoted in Sheppard's memoir in *Hymns, Psalms, and Poems, by Anne Steele*, v. William Steadman (1764-1837) accepted a call to the pastorate of the Broughton church in 1789 and remained there for eight years. He is better remembered as the president of Horton Academy, which trained ministers for the Baptist church in the north of England, as the Bristol Baptist Academy did in the south. Sharon James, "William Steadman (1764-1837)," in *The British Particular Baptists, 1638-1910*, ed. Michael A.G. Haykin (Springfield, MO: Particular Baptist Press, 2000), 2: 162-181. The Broughton church did not have to raise support for a pastor until after William Steele's death in 1769, but even

the Broughton church book records that the two men consistently donated to the church considerably more than any other member of the congregation.[28]

The Broughton church certainly occupied a focal point in the lives of the various members of the Steele family.[29] Anne Cator Steele's diary records a tally of church membership, noting baptisms, deaths, and transfers from other churches, and alternately praising God for his "late mercy in reviving our church" and lamenting the need for the church to "set apart each Wednesday before church meeting for prayer on account of our low estate."[30] Anne Cator Steele's concern for the Broughton church extended to a concern for the spiritual health of her own family. Her prayer that God "begin to work upon the souls of our children" was answered in 1732, when young Anne went with her stepmother to the home of Henry Steele, then minister of the Broughton church, to give an account of her soul and her desire to be baptised.[31] Anne Cator Steele

---

after this, when Josiah Lewis assumed the pastorate, the burden of raising his annual wage was carried primarily by the Steele family. Smith, "The Community and the Believer," 213-214.

[28] Broughton Church Book, 1730-1756, Broughton 1/3. The cataloguing system included here is that of the Broughton Baptist Church Records archived in the Angus Library, Regent's Park College, Oxford.

[29] Even Steele's various illnesses were catalogued by her stepmother with reference to Steele's ability or inability "to go to Meeting." See, for example, Anne Cator Steele diary, 7 October 1753, 11 May 1755, 21 November 1756, STE 2/1/3. Anne Cator Steele appears to have kept a diary throughout her adult life, though only three volumes survive, which are labeled, by her, "Book the Second," "Volume V," and "Volume VI"; respectively, these volumes cover the years 1730-1736, 1749-1752, and 1753-1760. For the most part, Anne Cator Steele's diary is a record of her spiritual concerns—for herself, her family, and the community of the Broughton church. The diary also fills in some detail regarding her stepdaughter's daily life since, apart from intermittent times away at school between 1729 and 1733, and part of a year spent living with her brother in 1757 and 1758, Steele lived with Anne Cator Steele from 1723 until her stepmother's death in 1760.

Where excerpts from letters and diary accounts have been included in this book, variations in spelling, including errors, have been preserved; to avoid frequent interruptions, "[sic]" will be included in moderation. However, to alleviate difficulties with regard to reading, punctuation has been standardized.

[30] Anne Cator Steele diary, June 1732, STE 2/1/1; March 1749, STE 2/1/2.

[31] Anne Cator Steele diary, 2 March 1732, STE 2/1/1. Earlier, on 3 January 1732, Anne Cator Steele records "joyning in prayer with Mr Steele this morning, he being drawn out to beg earnestly for the conversion of our children." Anne Cator Steele diary, 3 January 1732, STE 2/1/1. On 27 May 1732, Anne Cator Steele records the visit of her stepson, William Steele, and a cousin, Sarah Ethridge, to Henry Steele, noting, "they both talk'd with him in order to give in their Experience." Anne Cator Steele records Anne's reaction to the events: "Nany was troubled & seem'd very much cast down." Anne Cator Steele worries about the state of Anne's soul, praying that "God would subject her will & bring her into his house," but concludes that day's reflections, "hopeing God has

records the visit of 10 June 1732, as well as her experience leading up to it:

> I have been drawn out earnestly to desire assistance and direction for Nanny, thinking she is willing, God assisting and directing her, to give in her experience tomorrow. I have had very encouraging Scriptures and have talked with her and find God have been very Gracious to her in that way also that was on my mind....I went with Nanny to Uncle Steele where I had great cause to rejoice in beholding the goodness of God to her.[32]

The following day, Anne gave an account of her experience of salvation, "to the full satisfaction of the church."[33] And on 9 July 1732, at the age of fifteen, she was baptised.[34]

Steele's place in this notable Particular Baptist family certainly brought religion and the church to the centre of her awareness, as she observed her father's commitment as a pastor and as she witnessed her stepmother's concern for the spiritual health of the church. There is evidence also of other Particular Baptist ministers staying at "The Grandfathers" with the Steeles: in 1735, following the meetings of the Western Association of Particular Baptist Churches, which William Steele attended, Anne Cator Steele records in her diary, "Four ministers to lodge."[35] Anne was eighteen years of age at the time.

---

design'd her for some great work he having given her a good capacity." Anne Cator Steele diary, 27 May 1732, STE 2/1/1.

[32] Anne Cator Steele diary, 10 June 1732, STE 2/1/1.

[33] Anne Cator Steele diary, 11 June 1732, STE 2/1/1. On the practice of requiring prospective church members to give a public account of God's work upon their souls, particularly in the context of the eighteenth-century Dissenting church, see D. Bruce Hindmarsh, *The Evangelical Conversion Narrative: Spiritual Autobiography in Early Modern England* (Oxford: Oxford University Press, 2005), 287-320.

[34] The church book records, "July 9th 1732 was Baptised John Parsons, Mrs [sic] Ann Steele & Eliz. Green, afterward at the next Church meetting [sic] gave themselves members of this Church." Broughton Church Book, 1730-1756, Broughton 1/3.

[35] Anne Cator Steele diary, 2 June 1735, STE 2/1/1. The Western Association of Particular Baptist Churches met from 27 May 1735 to 31 May 1735. As the meetings were held in the next village to Tinhead, the former home of Anne Froude Steele, J.R. Broome surmises that William Steele likely stayed at the home of Anne Froude Steele's brother. According to Broome, when William Steele returned to Broughton on 31 May 1735, he brought a minister, "Mr. Fosket," with him. J.R. Broome, *The Friendly Companion* (February 1984): 25. This Mr. Fosket may have been Bernard Foskett (1685-1758), a Particular Baptist minister who, from 1727, was pastor of the Broadmead church in Bristol and president of the Bristol Baptist Academy. From 1734, Foskett was assisted at the academy by Hugh Evans, father of Caleb Evans, who would become a particular friend of Steele's later in life. Under the leadership of Foskett and Evans, the academy would train such key leaders among the English Particular Baptists as John Collett Ryland, John Ash, and Benjamin Beddome. Michael Haykin notes the important role Foskett played in urging a confessional basis for the Western Association of Particular Baptist Churches, adding that this work "bore rich dividends in the decades to

This pattern of significant ecclesial connections established early in life would be repeated in her later life, as we will see. The prominent role of the church in Steele's life would significantly influence her efforts as a hymn-writer, as the practice of worship assumed a central role in her consciousness.

Education and Intellectual Stimulus

Steele's education, both formal and informal, was notable for a girl growing up in early eighteenth-century England. Whereas toward the end of the eighteenth century, efforts were made to improve formal education for girls, incorporating subjects such as reading, writing, and arithmetic while maintaining an emphasis on polite accomplishments such as dancing, drawing, and music, earlier in the century, the formal education of girls was sporadic at best and more often nonexistent.[36] Steele did benefit from a formal education, though how great a benefit this was is certainly debatable. One letter survives from Anne's time at a boarding school in Trowbridge; this letter from a twelve-year-old Anne to her stepmother reads, in part, "I suppose you know my mistress is an odd tempered Woman but she is as kind to me as to the rest, our work is most on headcloaths, and I hope I shall Learn very well."[37] Despite the innocuous nature of the curriculum, the decision to send Anne and her sister, Mary, to school was problematic, reflecting a hesitancy relating to girls' education more generally. On 20 February 1733, Anne Cator Steele records in her diary her concerns

---

come, as a considerable portion of the vitality of English Baptist life in the late eighteenth century can be traced to the west country Baptists." Michael A.G. Haykin, "Foskett, Bernard (1685-1758)," *Oxford Dictionary of National Biography* (Oxford: Oxford University Press, 2004 [http://www.oxforddnb.com/view/article/71073, accessed 19 June 2006]). Roger Hayden comments on Foskett's contribution to the writing and singing of hymns in English Baptist churches: "He encouraged the development of congregational hymn singing in Baptist churches, even writing some of his own hymns for use in worship at Broadmead. The occasional hymn writing of Foskett and others—such as Joseph Stennett, Benjamin Wallin, and Foskett's protégé, Benjamin Beddome—in turn encouraged John Ash and Caleb Evans, students at Bristol Academy, to produce the first Baptist hymnbook in 1769 as an alternative to Watts's, a collection supplemented with many hymns by Baptist authors." Roger Hayden, "The Contribution of Bernard Foskett," in *Pilgrim Pathways: Essays in Baptist History in Honour of B.R. White*, 189. The Steele Collection at the Angus Library contains a booklet of verses in Benjamin Beddome's hand, which includes five hymns by Bernard Foskett. See STE 3/17/1. Beddome and Steele were well acquainted with each other, as we will see later in this chapter.

[36] On the improvement of girls' education in the late eighteenth century, see Susan Skedd, "Women Teachers and the Expansion of Girls' Schooling in England, *c.* 1760-1820," in *Gender in Eighteenth-Century England: Roles, Representations and Responsibilities*, ed. Hannah Barker and Elaine Chalus (London: Addison Wesley Longman, 1997), 101-125.

[37] Steele to Anne Cator Steele, 26 September 1729, STE 3/7 (i).

"about putting our daughters out to bording scool [sic]. I had many doubts about it."[38] These doubts may have originated from Henry Steele's apparent disapproval of sending Anne and Mary Steele away to school. On 9 June 1733, Anne Cator Steele records the condemnation of "Uncle Steele" who "took this time to reprove me concerning our daughters going to scool charging it upon me as sin. I defended myself as well as I could in such a doubtful case but my thoughts were pretty much ruffled about it."[39] Whatever Anne Cator Steele anticipated that the Steele girls would gain from their education, her concern for their spiritual welfare remained paramount: she hoped that "they might be preservd & kept from learning vain words & other vanitys with which the world aboundeth."[40]

Steele herself argues vigorously for the education of girls in an unpublished and undated poem addressed to her brother, William Steele. In it, she protests against the injustice of men considering women unable "to converse, to think or act with judgement," when she deems any feminine failures in these matters to have more to do with lack of education than lack of natural capacity.[41] She asks:

> But shou'd we not were education given
> Be wiser? were our young and tender minds
> But cultivated well with useful Learning
> If—Learning, what have girls to do with learning?
> Their minds be cultivated well worth while
> Teach them to darn & stitch & make a pudding
> And if they must to dance & sing and curtsie
> This is enough for them.[42]

---

[38] Anne Cator Steele diary, 20 February 1733, STE 2/1/1. While Anne and Mary Steele's education began at Trowbridge, it was continued at Salisbury. On 2 April 1733, Anne Cator Steele writes in her diary, "My desires being drawn out concerning the children going to school, desiring it may yet be prevented if the Lord saw it best, yet I have often tho't the providence of God did direct in it...which made me think as I have before whither God has not design'd some work for this his young servant....Getting things in order and putting up Nany and Molly's cloes they being to go tomorrow to one Mrs. Connors of Salisbury a bording scool [sic] in the Close." Anne Cator Steele diary, 2 April 1733, STE 2/1/1. Mary Steele was known within the family circle as Molly.

[39] Anne Cator Steele diary, 9 June 1733, STE 2/1/1. Further insight into Steele's education is found in a surviving notebook of handwriting exercises, dated 1728, when Anne was eleven years of age. The phrases which Anne was made to duplicate include, "Eternity is a horrid prospect to a dying sinner," "Good manners are an excellent ornament to youth," and "Rule your passions and in all things act according to reason." See STE 3/14.

[40] Anne Cator Steele diary, 29 March 1731, STE 2/1/1.

[41] Steele, untitled, STE 3/3/6, no. 28.

[42] Ibid.

Setting aside an uncharacteristic sarcasm, Steele states her case more directly, but with equal fervour:

> Ah why is Woman thus depress'd and scorn'd
> By tyrant Man? if we're less wise then they
> 'Tis their own fault who cramp our education
> Nature has given us Souls as Large as theirs
> As much our minds deserve to be improv'd
> We are as capable of learning all
> That's worthy knowledge.[43]

Clearly, despite the deficiencies of her schooling (or perhaps due to them), Steele possessed a keen desire for the benefits of learning so often withheld from her sex.

Steele's formal education, admittedly limited, was supplemented by the intellectual stimulus she received through reading and through the relationships she enjoyed with educated men in her life. The Steeles were a remarkably literary family; in an unpublished poem, Steele records an image of the family spending an evening around "a good Fire of odiferous Peat":

> When one of the Company reads to the rest
> Grave Author or Poet or what we like best
> All soft and harmonious the hours glide along
> Conversing with Pope or with Thompson or Young[44]

The poets Steele identifies are, according to James Sambrook, the writers of "the three best-known religious poems of the century, the *Essay on Man* (1733-34), the *Seasons* (1726-44), and *Night Thoughts* (1742-46)."[45] Steele was

---

[43] Ibid.

[44] Steele goes on to reveal her humour as well as a penchant for versification:
> But to the Sublime we cant always attend
> I mean Polly & I for we sometimes descend
> To capping of Verses for Varietys Sake
> And laugh at the whimsical Mixture we make
> Or if Rhyming should happen our fancy to hit
> Quick flows the extempore Nonsense or Wit

Steele, untitled, STE 3/3/1, pp. 3-4. Polly was a familial name for Steele's niece, Mary Steele Dunscombe.

[45] James Sambrook, *The Eighteenth Century: The Intellectual and Cultural Context of English Literature, 1700-1789*, 2nd ed., Longman Literature in English Series (London: Longman Group, 1993), 44. Steele's inclusion of "Thompson" in this list of favourite authors almost certainly is meant to refer to James Thomson (1700-1748), the popular author of *The Seasons*. The other authors mentioned by Steele, Alexander Pope (1688-

clearly well read and enjoyed the stimulation of reading and conversation relating to the works of favourite authors. The breadth of her reading, as can be determined from her poetry and letters, included well-known religious writers, both Baptist and otherwise, as well as classical writings not necessarily religious (see Appendix 3).

A great deal of Steele's intellectual stimulus likely was acquired through her ongoing relationships with educated men in her life. In fact, Marjorie Reeves argues that Steele was indebted to these men for "much of her real education."[46] While we have seen that Steele was introduced early in life to various prominent Baptist figures, by the 1750s, when she was in her thirties, she had developed personal friendships with men such as Caleb Evans, John Ash, Philip Furneaux, and Benjamin Beddome—leading religious figures who we will consider in greater depth later in this book.[47] These men were all educated for the ministry, and most were involved in the practice of hymn-writing, either for the use of their own congregations or intended for a wider circulation. The theological exchange which must have ensued will have influenced the content of Steele's hymnody, but perhaps just as important, these men encouraged the use of her poetic gifts in a religious culture that did not normally welcome the voices of women writing on sacred subjects, thus facilitating her development as a hymn-writer.

Social Stimulation and Support

Steele had a certain affinity for living a quiet life, removed from the "continual

---

1744) and Edward Young (1681-1765), the authors of *An Essay on Man* and *Night Thoughts*, respectively, will be further considered in subsequent pages.

[46] Reeves, *Pursuing the Muses*, 26.

[47] Of particular interest on this subject is Steele's relationship with John Ash who, in 1777, published *Sentiments on Education*, which included a chapter entitled "On Female Accomplishments." The chapter begins with a quotation from *The Spectator*: "In our daughters we take care of their persons, but neglect their minds." Ash begins the chapter with pointed censure: "The solicitude of parents, especially of mothers, to make their daughters fine ladies…is truly ridiculous." Despite this suggestive beginning, Ash soon clarifies his conviction that, while women should not be groomed merely to be fine ladies, there remain certain achievements of which women are capable, while others are beyond their purportedly limited capacities. Ash approves of teaching women writing, geography, and astronomy, along with music, needlework, and drawing; he hopes that "the fair pupil will find sufficient leisure for books, and an inexhaustible fund of rational and refined pleasure in reading." He disapproves, however, of women's reading of philosophy and romance, quoting the French bishop, François Fénelon (1651-1715): "the one may perplex your thoughts, the other infect the innocence of your mind." John Ash, *Sentiments on Education Collected from the Best Writers, Properly Methodized, and Interspersed with Occasional Observations* (London: Edward and Charles Dilly, 1777), 2: 7-9.

din of a noisey town."[48] In several unpublished poems, she refers to herself, in jest, as a "poor solitary Nun," living a life of "Lone quiet in an humble Cell." Yet this is the life she preferred, she explains, as it "suit[s] my temper full as well."[49] The quiet, bucolic life she chose served to support her writing endeavours, as she repeatedly locates her inspiration to write in natural beauty.[50] But Steele's reference to herself as nun should also be understood as an allusion to her remaining single, despite as many as three marriage proposals, including one from the Baptist pastor and hymn-writer, Benjamin Beddome.[51] While Steele chose a life of limited social stimulus, the friendships she did nurture were particularly supportive of her writing efforts.

Marjorie Reeves locates Steele at the centre of a writing circle which

---

[48] Steele to William Steele, 27 June 1736, STE 3/8 (i).

[49] Steele, "To Melinda," STE 3/3/1, pp. 10-12. The identity of Melinda cannot be determined. The "Cell" to which Steele refers may have been a free-standing structure at "The Grandfathers," to which she made a habit of retreating. In a letter to her sister-in-law in 1750, Steele writes, "my Cell too has its charms, the Honeysuckle at my window is in full bloom and I am sometimes entertain'd with the soft warbling of a neighbouring Nightingale." Steele to Mary Bullock Steele, 7 May 1750, STE 3/9 (i).

[50] See, for example, the series of letters between Steele and her sister, Mary Steele Wakeford: STE 3/10 (ii), (iii), (xiii).

[51] Steele's reference to herself as a "poor solitary Nun" is located in a light-hearted poem in which she refers to Melinda's "Victorious" return from town where she "subdu'd" "Three Hearts"; Steele bemoans the fact that she, "Moping at home cant rise to one." Steele, "To Melinda," STE 3/3/1, pp. 10-12.

The most well known of Steele's proposals may have come from James Elcomb, who reportedly drowned mere hours before their intended wedding. Another proposal, from an unnamed man, can be discerned in correspondence between Steele and her sister, Mary Steele Wakeford. Both of these offers of marriage will be considered in greater detail later in this book. A third proposal, from Benjamin Beddome, is preserved in a letter in which he makes a passionate declaration of his love for Steele. The letter reads, in part:

> If continued Thoughts of you & a disrelish to everything besides may be consider'd as Arguments of Love surely I experience the Passion, & if the greatness of a Persons love will make up for the Want of Wit, Wealth & Beauty, then may I humbly lay claim to your Favour....Mad'm give me leave to tell You that these Words speak the very Experience of my Soul, nor do I find it possible to forbear loving You. Would You but suffer me to come & lay before You those Dictates of a confused Mind which cannot be represented by a trembling Hand & Pen. Would You but permit me to cast my self at your Feet & tell You how much I love, Oh What an easement might you thereby afford to a burdend Spirit.

Benjamin Beddome to Steele, 23 December 1742, STE 3/13 (i). Steele's response has not survived, yet she could not have given her consent as in 1749 Beddome married Elizabeth Boswell (1732-1784), while Steele remained single.

included literary family and friends.[52] While she would become the most accomplished writer in the family, many family members, both immediate and more distant, tried their hands at writing verse—further demonstrating the importance of language and literature in the Steele family. There is evidence, in letters and poetry, that this verse was shared and discussed, and that Steele's opinion was solicited.[53] The Steele Collection in the Angus Library contains the surviving poetic efforts of not only Steele, but her sister, Mary Steele Wakeford, her brother, William Steele, and various younger members of the family. Steele appears to have offered inspiration and encouragement to this younger generation of writers, including her niece, Mary Steele Dunscombe, and her younger cousins, Marianna, Caroline, and Jane Attwater.[54]

Steele's participation in poetic dialogue extended beyond her family, however, and included various leading Baptist pastors and writers, as has been noted. Letters and poetry survive which cast light on the intellectual interchange and mutual encouragement which took place between Steele and these influential friends. Particularly interesting, as they illuminate Steele's own thoughts on the act of writing, are her poems which appear in the form of dialogues between herself, her sister, and her friend, the Independent pastor, Philip Furneaux. These dialogues often centre on their inspiration to write and their effort to articulate thought in verse, and locate the act of writing within the context of close personal friendship.[55] In addition to this personal support,

---

[52] See Reeves, *Pursuing the Muses*, 61-84; Marjorie Reeves, "Literary Women in Eighteenth-Century Nonconformist Circles," in *Culture and the Nonconformist Tradition*, 10-17.

[53] See, for example, Steele's response to a letter in which the verse of two aspiring poets was sent to her for comment. Steele replies, "The pieces you sent me wrote by a Lady are indeed excellent," and then goes on, "you desire my opinion of your own verses. It is this: the tho'ts are good, the language not unpractical, but they want a little correcting and deserve it." The "Lady" referred to here is Hannah Towgood Wakeford, the first wife of Joseph Wakeford, then married to Steele's sister, Mary Steele Wakeford. Steele to anonymous man, undated, STE 3/13 (vi).

[54] Mary Steele Dunscombe assumed the familial pseudonym, Silvia, while Marianna, Caroline, and Jane Attwater were, respectively, Maria, Dorinda, and Myrtilla. Late in Steele's life, the poet, Mary Scott Taylor, a close friend of Mary Steele Dunscombe, began to join in the literary conversations taking place within the Steele family circle; within this circle, Scott adopted the pseudonym, Myra. For further information on the writings of Jane Attwater, see Marjorie Reeves, "Jane Attwater's Diaries," in *Pilgrim Pathways: Essays in Baptist History in Honour of B.R. White*, 207-222; Reeves, "Literary Women in Eighteenth-Century Nonconformist Circles," in *Culture and the Nonconformist Tradition*, 18-21.

[55] See, for example, Steele, untitled, STE 3/3/1, pp. 20-24; Steele, "A Dialogue," STE 3/3/1, pp. 25-37. The voices participating in these dialogues are those of Silviana, Amira, and Lucius, pseudonyms for Steele, Wakeford, and Furneaux. This convention, of writing lengthy versified dialogues using classical pseudonyms, was typical eighteenth-century practice.

Steele's efforts as a writer likely were bolstered by a more fundamental identification with the Dissenting church, which was characterized by a common sense of oppression. According to N.H. Keeble, "communication and writing were essential to the continuance of nonconformity."[56] That is, the Dissenting church needed to communicate their beliefs and experiences in order to survive, and this was born out in a disproportionate number of literary successes among Dissenters. This mutual sense of difference amongst Dissenters would lead to "supra-local allegiances between members of the same denomination"—allegiances such as that between Steele and various leading Baptist figures, near and far, which would prove to be significant in the publication of Steele's hymns and poems.[57]

Steele as Published Writer

We have noted that in the middle of the eighteenth century it was still relatively uncommon for women to publish works on religious subjects, so one might wonder how Steele was able to publish *Poems on Subjects Chiefly Devotional* in 1760. In his "Advertisement," appearing in the 1780 edition of Steele's verse, Caleb Evans notes Steele's long-time practice of writing poetry and hymns for her family and friends, adding, "it was not without extreme reluctance she was prevailed on to submit any of them to the public eye."[58] But submit them she did. In May 1755, we find the first reference to Steele discussing with Philip Furneaux the possibility of publishing her poems and hymns, and by November 1757, Furneaux and Joseph Wakeford, Steele's brother-in-law, began to bring parts of her verse to London for printing.[59] Finally, in October and November 1759, the Steele family celebrated the

---

[56] N.H. Keeble, *The Literary Culture of Nonconformity in Later Seventeenth-Century England* (Leicester, UK: Leicester University Press, 1987), 82.

[57] Rosemary Sweet, *The English Town, 1680-1840: Government, Society and Culture* (New York: Pearson Education, 1999), 189.

[58] Caleb Evans, "Advertisement," in *Poems on Subjects Chiefly Devotional*, III, vii.

[59] In a letter to her brother, Steele writes, "Mr. Furneaux came yesterday a little before noon, preach'd in the evening & return'd to Andover this morning. We had a great deal of chatt intermingled with reading my papers & canvassing the printing affair in which his opinion corresponds to yours." Steele to William Steele, 16 May 1755, STE 3/8 (vi). Her stepmother, with her customary sense of spiritual gravity, records in her diary the event of sending the manuscript to London: "This day Nanny sent a part of her composition to London, to be printed. I entreat a gracious God who enabled and stirred her up to such a work, to direct in it, and bless it for the good and comfort of many." Anne Cator Steele diary, 29 November 1757, STE 2/1/3. From October 1757 to May 1758 Steele lived with her brother at "Broughton House"; Hugh Steele-Smith surmises that her stay there may have been related to the preparation of her poems for printing. Hugh Steele-Smith's research files on Anne Steele, STE 11/1.

publication of her hymns and poems (see Figure 2).[60]

Steele herself attributed her success as a writer to the influence of her friends. In an unpublished poem, entitled "Reviewing My Verses for Publication," Steele expresses doubt regarding the quality of her verse, and concludes, dejected, "Let Lines so spiritless as these / To Dark Oblivion be consign'd."[61] The tenor of the poem alters when "Friendship" is introduced, for friendship has the power to encourage her and to dispel "Chagrin," which would convince her of her inadequacies as a writer.[62] Friendship declares, "I to the Press the Work consign."[63] In another poem, "To Lysander," in which Steele disparages her verse as "artless," and in which she self-consciously remarks that the muse that inspires her is "in learning's arduous toil unskill'd," she again credits friendship's role in recognizing the worth of her verse and in stimulating her success as a writer:

> Indulgent Friendship, listening, caught the strain,
>   And fondly fancy'd it was tun'd to move;
> Then, smiling, bore it to the distant plain,
>   Far, ah how far beyond its native grove!
> But say, Lysander, can such notes as these
> Amid politer scenes expect to please?[64]

We have already noted that it was Philip Furneaux and Joseph Wakeford

---

[60] In October 1759, William Steele returned from London with a set of books from the printers, though they were not yet bound. On 24 October 1759, Anne Cator Steele records in her diary that she has been reading Steele's poems, and praises God "for his distinguishing favours to our family." She continues, "I earnestly desire the blessing of God upon that work that it may be made very useful....I have now been reading our daughter's printed books, which I have earnestly desired might be accompanied with the Divine Spirit in the perusing." On 25 November 1759, Anne Cator Steele records that Mary Steele Wakeford spent the evening reading her "Sister's Hymns just printed," and on 27 November 1759, Anne Cator Steele records Joseph Wakeford's "commendation of [Steele's] Books of Poetry that came from London last Saturday." Anne Cator Steele diary, 24 October 1759, 25 November 1759, 27 November 1759, STE 2/1/3.

[61] Steele, "Reviewing My Verses for Publication," STE 3/3/1, pp. 1-2.

[62] Ibid.

[63] Steele classifies good verse as that which gains the approval of Piety, Virtue, and Friendship. The poem concludes:
> The Lay which Piety approves
> Which Virtue guides & Friendship loves
> That asks no Smile of flattering Fame
> Oblivion cannot dares not claim.

Ibid.

[64] Steele, "To Lysander," *Poems on Subjects Chiefly Devotional*, I, 189-190. For a slight variant of this poem, see Steele, "To Lysander," STE 3/3/3, no. 1. Lysander was a pseudonym for John Lavington.

POEMS,

ON

SUBJECTS

CHIEFLY

DEVOTIONAL.

IN TWO VOLUMES.

A NEW EDITION.

To which is added, A THIRD VOLUME, confifting of
MISCELLANEOUS PIECES.

By THEODOSIA.

―――――――― *He tunes*
My voice (if tun'd) ; the nerve that writes, fuftains.
                                        Night-Thoughts.

―――――――――――――

BRISTOL:

Printed by W. PINE. Sold by T. CADELL, T. MILLS, and T. EVANS;—and by J. BUCKLAND, *Pater-nofter-Row*, and J. JOHNSON, *St. Paul's Church Yard*, LONDON, 1780.

Figure 2: Title page from *Poems on Subjects Chiefly Devotional* (2nd ed., 1780)

who "bore [Steele's verse] to the distant plain" of London for publication, and Steele appears to have been gratefully conscious of their assistance. Later, Caleb Evans would assist Steele in the sale of the second edition of her hymns and poems, by placing an advertisement in the circular letter for the Western Association of Particular Baptist Churches (see Figure 3).[65]

While Steele's success is partially attributable to her friendships with encouraging and well-connected pastors and writers, the wealth of her family certainly eased the difficulties she might otherwise have experienced in securing a publisher. On 9 August 1777, Steele's brother, William Steele, writes from London to his daughter, Mary Steele Dunscombe, informing her, "I have left Sisters Manuscript with Messrs Dilly & am to call again Monday."[66] It would seem that at the end of Steele's life there was an effort to publish more of her verse, though it is unclear whether this is the initial effort leading to the second edition of *Poems on Subjects Chiefly Devotional*, or an effort to publish a new volume of her verse. On 14 August 1777, William Steele again writes to his daughter:

> I have promis'd Mr Dilly to dine with him tho' I cant say I have much inclination to it, as I presently found that nothing can be done with him about Sisters Books, "the Poems are very good some of them sublime, but Poetry sells the worst of any works, because there are but few that read it or indeed understand it"—true enough indeed...I think there is no other way of publishing Sister's works but as done before by taking the whole on our Selves for the Booksellers will run no risques....He talks of Poetry like a Man of Trade that knows no more of it than belongs to his business.[67]

---

[65] Western Association of Particular Baptist Churches, *The Elders and Messengers of the Several Baptist Churches, Meeting at Exon, Prescott, Wellington, Bridgwater,...Being Met in Association at Frome,...the 17th and 18th days of May, 1780. To the Several Churches They Represent Send Christian Salutation....*[Bristol: n.p., 1780].

[66] William Steele to Mary Steele Dunscombe, 9 August 1777, STE 4/5. Edward and Charles Dilly were booksellers and publishers in London who primarily published literature of a theological nature. They also published John Ash's *A New and Complete Dictionary of the English Language* (1775). Their home "became one of the most noted meeting-places of literary men in London. Both Boswell and Johnson frequently dined there." The 1780 edition of Steele's hymns and poems would be published by William Pine, a printer in Bristol who also, between 1767 and 1771, published several editions of Wesley's *Hymns*. Pine also published Ash and Evans's "Bristol Collection," which will be considered in more detail in the following chapter. H.R. Plomer, G.H. Bushnell, E.R. McC. Dix, *A Dictionary of the Printers and Booksellers Who Were at Work in England, Scotland and Ireland from 1726 to 1775* (Oxford: Bibliographical Society at the Oxford University Press, 1930), 74-75, 199.

[67] William Steele to Mary Steele Dunscombe, 14 August 1777, STE 4/5. Two weeks later, William Steele again writes from London, indicating that he is agreeably

This Day is published,

Adorned with elegant Frontispieces,

A NEW EDITION OF

THEODOSIA's POEMS,

On Subjects chiefly Devotional:

TO WHICH IS NOW ADDED

A THIRD VOLUME,

CONSISTING OF

MISCELLANEOUS PIECES.

Price 10s. 6d. handsomely bound in Calf and lettered.

The Third Volume may be had separate by those who purchased the first Edition, upon an early Application to the Editor, Price 3s. 6d.

☞ Those who take six Sets will be allowed a Seventh gratis.

The Proprietor of these Volumes having devoted the Profits which may arise from the Publication of them, to the Benefit of The BRISTOL EDUCATION SOCIETY, the Editor takes this Method of informing his Friends of this Circumstance, that they may favour him without Delay with their Orders either for whole Sets or the third Volume only, in order that the Institution designed to be promoted by this Publication may receive as much Benefit from it as possible.

Bristol, May 27, 1780.   CALEB EVANS.

Figure 3: Advertisement for *Poems on Subjects Chiefly Devotional*

---

entertained by "Dr Ash's Friends." William Steele to Mary Steele Dunscombe, 27 August 1777, STE 4/5.

Here we learn that the costs of publishing Steele's 1760 edition of hymns and poems were assumed by the Steele family, who had the means to sustain the necessary expenses on account of their flourishing timber business. Indeed, Caleb Evans records that Steele "was placed by providence in a state of independence" and adds that the profits from the sale of the first and second editions of her verse were donated to charity.[68]

In 1777, when William Steele was in London pursuing the publication of Steele's hymns and poems, Steele herself was confined to a room in his house, where she had spent much of the previous eight years, suffering from debilitating chronic illness that would lead to her death on 11 November 1778, at the age of sixty-one. Caleb Evans would later record her deathbed scene:

> When the interesting hour came, she welcomed its arrival, and though her feeble body was excruciated with pain, her mind was perfectly serene. She uttered not a murmuring word, but was all resignation, peace and holy joy. She took the most affectionate leave of her weeping friends around her, and at length, the happy moment of her dismission arriving, she closed her eyes, and with these animating words on her dying lips, "I know that my Redeemer liveth," gently fell asleep in Jesus.[69]

Following a life in which she had known more illness than health and in which she laboured to use her poetic gifts to offer praise to God, Steele entered the rest she had long anticipated.

Contrary to the image of Steele most often portrayed—that of a reclusive, melancholic, and extremely pious woman—the image that has begun to emerge here is, not surprisingly, more complex. At the outset, any attempt to understand Steele must give due consideration to the network of relationships that supported her. She was a member of a prominent, wealthy, and remarkably literary family with strong connections to the Particular Baptist denomination, and likely as a result of those connections she was able to establish lasting friendships with an array of influential pastors and writers. As well, while Steele's experience of life contained constant reminders of human frailty, her letters and verse reveal a habitual good humour, and Caleb Evans tells us that "she possessed a native cheerfulness of disposition."[70] Following his moving, if stylized, depiction of Steele's deathbed scene, Evans remarks that though Steele had died, through "Her excellent writings...she still speaketh."[71] It is these writings that will form the focus of this book, in which we will attempt to define the nature of Steele's spirituality as it is revealed in her life and expressed in her hymnody.

---

[68] Caleb Evans, "Advertisement," in *Poems on Subjects Chiefly Devotional*, III, x.
[69] Ibid.
[70] Ibid., ix.
[71] Ibid., x.

CHAPTER 2

"Sacred Poesy....in the Service of Religion": Anne Steele and Eighteenth-Century Hymnody

Anne Steele's hymns represent one voice in an important new outpouring of poetic devotion that took place during the eighteenth century. In a century that sometimes has been judged as socially decadent and spiritually dry, the impressive popularity of the hymn is one way to substantiate the existence of a devotional impulse at work in the lives of faithful English women and men. Donald Davie contends that, unless it is acknowledged that during the eighteenth century England was not "an irreligious nation," "the great hymns which are a glory of that period will seem to float unanchored, in a sort of historical limbo."[1] For during the eighteenth century, the congregational hymn reached dramatic new heights of popularity, effectively transforming both the form and substance of Christian worship. Consequently, the century during which Steele was at work has been called, by George Sampson, "the century of divine songs."[2]

This transformation of worship was stimulated by the work of a variety of hymn-writers labouring in isolation or networks, working anonymously or to great acclaim, intending their compositions for private or public use. In this chapter, we will survey the landscape of eighteenth-century hymnody, within which Steele played a significant role, considering the pioneering hymn-writing efforts of Isaac Watts and Charles Wesley, as well as the work of lesser-known, though also significant, men and women such as Benjamin Beddome and Anne Dutton. Throughout, we will pay particular attention to what these representative figures convey regarding their understanding of their tasks as hymn-writers, as well as what their writing reveals about the distinctive style and substance of their hymns.

In considering the style and substance of a hymn—or, put another way, its form and content—we recognize that the hymn has a double nature. That is, the hymn can be understood as a work of both literature and theology, and it

---

[1] Donald Davie, *The Eighteenth-Century Hymn in England*, Cambridge Studies in Eighteenth-Century English Literature and Thought, no. 19 (Cambridge: Cambridge University Press, 1993), 8.
[2] George Sampson, "The Century of Divine Songs," in *Proceedings of the British Academy*, vol. 29 (London: Oxford University Press, 1943), 37.

therefore should be analyzed accordingly. Madeleine Forell Marshall and Janet Todd's definition of the hymn accounts for this double nature; they identify hymns as "artful expressions of religious truths."[3] According to Marshall and Todd, hymns must be "doctrinally correct and spiritually edifying," but at the same time must "certainly remain poetry."[4] Before turning to survey the landscape of eighteenth-century hymnody, it will be helpful to consider the significance of understanding the hymn as both literature and theology, since our subsequent analysis of the eighteenth-century hymn, and of Steele's hymnody more specifically, will be given scope and direction by probing both the form and content of particular hymns.

---

[3] Madeleine Forell Marshall and Janet Todd, *English Congregational Hymns in the Eighteenth Century* (Lexington, KY: University Press of Kentucky, 1982), 2. There have been many attempts to define the hymn, from Augustine's "singing to the praise to God" to Carl Price's "lyric poem, reverently and devotionally conceived, which is designed to be sung and which expresses the worshipper's attitude toward God or God's purposes in human life. It should be simple and metrical in form, genuinely emotional, poetic and literary in style, spiritual in quality, and in its ideas so direct and so immediately apparent as to unify a congregation while singing it." Augustine, note to Psalm 148, quoted in Watson, *The English Hymn*, 2; Carl F. Price, "What is a Hymn?" Paper 6 of the Hymn Society of America (1937): 8, quoted in Harry Eskew and Hugh T. McElrath, *Sing with Understanding: An Introduction to Christian Hymnology* (Nashville, TN: Broadman Press, 1980), 7.

[4] Marshall and Todd, *English Congregational Hymns in the Eighteenth Century*, 1, 2. There is some debate, particularly among early hymnologists, regarding whether hymns should properly be defined as poetry. In his classic study, *The English Hymn*, Louis Benson, for example, considers the reasons that the hymn may have been "studiously ignored in the manuals of English Literature." He concludes, "The truth is that if the methods of the literary historian are not misapplied to Hymnody, they are at least inadequate. A hymn may or may not happen to be literature; in any case it is something more. Its sphere, its motive, its canons and its use are different. It belongs with the things of the spirit, in the sphere of religious experience and communion with God. Its special sphere is worship, and its fundamental relations are not literary but liturgical." Benson, *The English Hymn*, viii. Marshall and Todd object to Benson's desire to examine hymns "only devoutly"; they write, "However profound the religious experience conveyed by the hymn, however inspired the form by its spiritual content, the diction, figurative language, and verbal design of the hymns are human creations dependent on the literary tradition within which the poet is working." Marshall and Todd, *English Congregational Hymns in the Eighteenth Century*, 5. J.R. Watson judges the argument regarding whether hymns are indeed poetry to be "old-fashioned and unnecessary." He considers there to be "no reason why a good hymn should not be one kind of poetry" and in his work attempts to demonstrate "what kind of poetry hymnody is, its characteristics as a genre with its own rhetoric and language." Watson, *The English Hymn*, viii.

The Hymn as Literature and Theology

When we consider the hymn as literature, we take seriously the way in which language is used by the hymn-writer in order to convey meaning.[5] We consider the form of a hymn: the way in which it is presented on the page, and the techniques the hymn-writer uses in order to convey meaning. We are able to analyze a hymn with reference to the literary devices deployed by its writer. The precise use of chiasmus, for example, may heighten the effect of a particular verse, just as careful and controlled repetition may intensify the sense of a line. In addition, eighteenth-century hymn-writers used a limited number of hymn metres, sometimes to great effect. Early in the century, most hymns were written in one of only three metres—Short, Long, or Common Metre—yet J.R. Watson shows that each of these metres "has its own character, which shapes the material and becomes part of the meaning."[6] While matters of literary devices and metre certainly contribute to the meaning of a hymn, on a more fundamental level a hymn-writer's diction, or choice of language, is used to communicate meaning.

Donald Davie, himself a poet as well as literary critic, considers that good poetry takes seriously "what its words say, *each* of those words, severally and together."[7] He relates this careful attention to words to the language of the

---

[5] Various attempts have been made to study the hymn as literature. See, for example, Donald Davie, "The Language of the Eighteenth-Century Hymn," in *Dissentient Voice: The Ward-Phillips Lectures for 1980 with Some Related Pieces*, University of Notre Dame Ward-Phillips Lectures in English Language and Literature, vol. 11 (Notre Dame: University of Notre Dame Press, 1982); M. Pauline Parker, "The Hymn as a Literary Form," *Eighteenth-Century Studies* 8 (1974-1975): 392-419. For an early attempt to consider the literary value of hymns, see Jeremiah Bascom Reeves, *The Hymn as Literature* (New York: Century Company, 1924). And, for a recent effort, see J.R. Watson's very helpful and comprehensive *The English Hymn: A Critical and Historical Study*. Watson classifies his book as a work of literary criticism, indicating that in previous studies of the hymn, "the texts of hymns have received little serious critical study from students of English Literature." Watson, *The English Hymn*, vii.

[6] Short Metre (S.M.; 66.86.) "specializes in the sharp, neat, well-focused use of biblical texts." Common Metre (C.M.; 86.86.) "allows a much more flexible and expansive pattern" than S.M. Long Metre (L.M.; 88.88.), with its longer lines, "changes the whole range of possibilities, because each line is now long enough to take a proposition by itself." Ibid., 32-33. For further discussion of the possibilities and meanings of these metres, see Austin C. Lovelace, *The Anatomy of Hymnody* (New York: Abingdon Press, 1965), 24-43.

[7] Davie, "The Language of the Eighteenth-Century Hymn," in *Dissentient Voice*, 71 (italics in original). Elsewhere, he explains that "good diction comes from making a selection from the language on reasonable principles and for a reasonable purpose. All poets when they write have one purpose. They want to create an effect upon the mind of the reader." Donald Davie, "The Diction of English Verse," in *Purity of Diction in English Verse* (New York: Schocken Books, 1952), 6.

eighteenth-century hymn, claiming that the best hymns are those which use language to effect a clear, even a "transparent," means by which to express Christian devotion and experience.[8] By this, Davie does not mean that the best hymns convey a simplistic rendering of the Christian experience, since many hymns confront paradoxes central to the Christian faith, but rather that their language is carefully simplified to translate meaning quickly, and to a diverse assembly of worshippers. Indeed, according to Pauline Parker, one of the distinguishing characteristics of a hymn is that it "must instantly convey a meaning, and its development must follow lucidly from point to point without any necessity of harking back."[9] These constraints are prescribed by the intended use of the hymn, which is to be sung congregationally and therefore must be understood immediately.

Hence, the form of the hymn is circumscribed by particular conventions, as is true of any art form and, in particular, any classic art form. Formal constraints—that is, constraints with regard to form—have caused some to argue that the hymn is not poetry in the same way that free verse is poetry. As a result, for many years the hymn has been castigated as an inferior kind of poetry, characterized by limitations and obligations.[10] But Donald Davie objects, arguing that it is a matter of hymn-writers choosing one style, the plain style, over against another style: "subtlety is not everywhere nor at all times an artistic virtue, and certainly mildness is not—a bleak boldness is just as legitimate a formal effect for a poet to aim at, and indeed it is one of the effects particularly aimed at by the plain style."[11] Plainness, then, became a stylistic ideal to which many hymn-writers aspired, as it enabled their words to be understood quickly by congregants, thereby easing an entrance for those congregants into worship and facilitating an encounter between God and the

---

[8] Davie, "The Language of the Eighteenth-Century Hymn," in *Dissentient Voice*, 76.

[9] Parker, "The Hymn as a Literary Form," 401-402.

[10] Donald Davie observes that the eighteenth-century congregational hymn is "a body of poems hedged about with restrictions such as—so we are invited to think by current and long-established opinion—no 'true' poet could or should tolerate....this is a body of poetry that challenges at nearly every point those influential theories of poetry which take off from the assumption that the poet has no responsibility except to his own sensibility, his own 'vision.' And so it is easy to see why these writings are commonly excluded from the category of poetry, or are included there only on sufferance, as so many marginal or delimiting cases." Davie, *The Eighteenth-Century Hymn in England*, 17.

[11] Donald Davie, introduction to *The New Oxford Book of Christian Verse*, ed. Donald Davie (Oxford: Oxford University Press, 1981), xix. Similarly, Jeremiah Bascom Reeves, citing William Cowper's lines, "There is a fountain filled with blood, / Drawn from Immanuel's veins," writes, "Excessive mildness is not an inherent trait of the hymn as a literary form." He concludes, "The best hymns, indeed, are notable for boldness and animation of style, and always of course under artistic control." Reeves, *The Hymn as Literature*, 45.

human soul. Indeed, Davie identifies this poetic style as an act of service on the part of hymn-writers such as Isaac Watts, Philip Doddridge, and Charles Wesley, all "sophisticated and learned men," who "deliberately purged their language of everything that would make it inaccessible to men and women who were less sophisticated and less learned than they were. And in the process, as they must have realized, they denied themselves the Shakespearean or Popian splendors that depend upon allusion and mysterious resonance and obliquity."[12]

Just as a hymn should be understood as a work of literature, its effectiveness contingent on how it functions within the bounds of a specific genre, it likewise represents a particular theology. Eighteenth-century hymns reveal something of the religious climate of their time, elucidating the theology and spirituality of their writers and singers; they provide, according to Marshall and Todd, a "great quantity of information about popular religious feeling that is inaccessible elsewhere."[13] Ernest Payne claims that in "the Free Churches a hymn book takes the place occupied by the Prayer Book in the devotional life, public and private, of the Anglican," while George Sampson considers hymns to be "the ordinary man's theology."[14] As theology, the hymn is made to express religious doctrine, which then "echoes in the heart" as it is repeated in church or at home.[15] In this way, the hymn becomes a means by which believers are made to rehearse a particular theology. When we consider the hymn as theology, we take seriously the message the hymn-writer has laboured to convey. In this capacity, we are able to analyze the hymn according to the doctrine that has been expressed therein.[16]

And just as the hymn is constrained in matters of form, so it is in matters of

---

[12] Davie, "The Language of the Eighteenth-Century Hymn," in *Dissentient Voice*, 76-77. Elsewhere, Davie writes, "The great hymn-writers...applied themselves to perfect for their hymns a style that should not be subtle but plain—and this for the good reason that they wanted to speak plainly to plain men and women, to the unlettered but devout worshippers in the pews." Davie, introduction to *The New Oxford Book of Christian Verse*, xix.

[13] Marshall and Todd, *English Congregational Hymns of the Eighteenth Century*, 2. J.R. Watson indicates that hymns "are a part of popular culture, and yet also part of a religious and literary culture." Watson, *The English Hymn*, 5.

[14] Ernest A. Payne, *The Free Church Tradition in the Life of England* (London: SCM Press, 1944), 79; Sampson, "The Century of Divine Songs," in *Proceedings of the British Academy*, 37. Sampson also considers the hymn to be "the poor man's poetry, the only poetry that has ever come home to his heart." Ibid.

[15] Ibid.

[16] Various attempts have been made to study hymns with a view to elucidating their theology. See, for example, Lowell B. Harlan, "Theology of Eighteenth Century English Hymns," *Historical Magazine of the Protestant Episcopal Church* 48, no. 2 (June 1979): 167-193; J. Ernest Rattenbury, *The Evangelical Doctrines of Charles Wesley's Hymns* (London: Epworth Press, 1941); J. Ernest Rattenbury, *The Eucharistic Hymns of John and Charles Wesley* (London: Epworth Press, 1948).

content. J.R. Watson qualifies this constraint, indicating that for many

> the hymn is not expected to sow doubt in the mind of the singer, or produce complex and contradictory emotions, or express frustration, anxiety or confusion....instead they express assurance and banish doubt....Apart from the portrayals of the Crucifixion, there does not seem much awareness, in hymnody, of misery and suffering, of the great dilemmas of the human situation, of the most serious problems of tragic art and human life, of the greatness and wretchedness of the human condition.[17]

Again, because the hymn is thus limited with regard to content, it sometimes has been declaimed as an inferior kind of poetry. Donald Davie protests against Lord David Cecil's indictment that "Hymns are a second-rate type of poetry" because "they do not provide a free vehicle for the expression of the poet's imagination, his intimate soul."[18] Davie counters that "we may agree that there are first-rate and second-rate poems, without conceding that there are first-rate and second-rate *types* of poetry, least of all when the distinction turns on the expression or non-expression of 'the poet's...intimate soul.'"[19] Hymns certainly are devotional verse, expressing emotion that is, ideally, representative rather than private or individual, but the "peculiar glory" of hymns, according to Davie, is that "at their best they are doctrinally exact, scrupulous and specific."[20]

While the eighteenth-century hymn can be understood in terms of either literature or theology, and will be discussed with reference to both its style and substance in the ensuing pages, its real power is recognized when the form and content of a hymn are considered in concert. In fact, Watson refers to "the inseparability of form and content" in the discussion of hymns, and by this he means that how a hymn-writer expresses a theme will affect the hymn's meaning and, in turn, will direct the devotional experience.[21] Both style and substance serve the intention of the hymn, which is to direct praise to God by expressing what is in the human heart.[22] Donald Davie reflects on the dual nature of hymns as both literature and theology: "Theological niceties are *not* sterile—not so long as they can be translated into worshipping experience.

---

[17] Watson, *The English Hymn*, 4.
[18] Davie, *The Eighteenth-Century Hymn in England*, 155, quoting Lord David Cecil, introduction to *Oxford Book of Christian Verse* (1940).
[19] Davie, *The Eighteenth-Century Hymn in England*, 155 (italics in original). Watson agrees, stating, "There is no reason why poetry which has been written for a purpose or an occasion should be less effective than expressions of private emotion." Watson, *The English Hymn*, 12.
[20] Davie, *The Eighteenth-Century Hymn in England*, 14.
[21] Watson, *The English Hymn*, 15.
[22] Here, the heart is used, in Watson's words, as a "metonymy for the whole person, spiritual, emotional, physical, the feeling and thinking human being." Ibid., 4.

When that happens, their logical niceties can be translated into experiential niceties and, when verbal expression is in question, into linguistic niceties also."[23] Thus, words, meaning, and religious experience are united in the singing of a hymn. Literature and theology, the form and the content of the hymn, together become a conduit for devotional experience, the mysterious meeting of God and the human person.

Eighteenth-century hymn-writers were conscious of this relation between literature and theology, of the ways in which their poetic efforts were made to serve the expression of doctrine and, ideally, to enable devotional experience. Marshall and Todd note that in the congregational hymn one finds evidence of the eighteenth-century poetic ideal which aspired to a "careful alliance of poetic delight and instruction."[24] That is, eighteenth-century hymn-writers were concerned that their compositions were, at once, both instructive and pleasing.[25] This twin concern can be traced in the poetic theory of various hymn-writers. In *Horae Lyricae* (1706), for example, Isaac Watts writes of his desire to create a "Composition of Virtue and Delight."[26] John Wesley, in his preface to *A Collection of Hymns, for the Use of the People Called Methodists* (1780), a book he describes as a "little body of experimental and practical divinity," casts poetry in the role of "the handmaid of piety."[27] Wesley argues that in hymns there is "both sense and poetry," and that this allows the Christian "to sing praise to GOD...with the spirit and with the understanding also."[28] Anne Steele, for her part, likewise reflects on the nature of poetry and on its role in the expression of religious meaning. In response to a letter from an unnamed woman who wrote to complement her verse, Steele declares that "sacred Poesy" is best employed "in the service of Religion."[29] Steele's letter includes a

---

[23] Davie, *The Eighteenth-Century Hymn in England*, 14 (italics in original).

[24] Marshall and Todd, *English Congregational Hymns in the Eighteenth Century*, 149. N.H. Keeble relates this "careful alliance" to the hymn-writing efforts of Dissenters. He indicates that Dissenting hymnody "is a particular example of the general determination of nonconformist writers to profit their readers by, as Bunyan put it, 'aluring' them. They recognized that the edificatory and the enjoyable were not inimical; the one might serve the other." Keeble, *The Literary Culture of Nonconformity in Later Seventeenth-Century England*, 155.

[25] This dual artistic intention was not only the province of hymnody, as it can be traced in other eighteenth-century artistic forms. The art of William Hogarth (1697-1764), for example, is artistically pleasing even as it makes pointed social comments. Hogarth was a popular painter who is best remembered for those paintings in which he satirized eighteenth-century social and religious culture.

[26] Isaac Watts, preface to *Horae Lyricae*, 9th ed. (Boston: Rogers and Fowle, 1748), xviii.

[27] John Wesley, preface to *A Collection of Hymns, for the Use of the People Called Methodists* (London: J. Paramore, 1780), iv, vi.

[28] John Wesley, quoted in Davie, *The Eighteenth-Century Hymn in England*, 24.

[29] Steele to anonymous woman, 8 August 1761, STE 3/13 (vii).

verse in which she acknowledges the potential of her hymns to both "profit" and "please":

> If ought you find in Theodosia's Lays
> To profit or to please, transfer the praise
> To him whose bounty ev'ry gift bestows;
> Since all unmerited that Bounty flows.[30]

Having thus deflected human praise, Steele returns to the motivation stirring her poetic efforts: "the praise of the Almighty Donour."[31]

Thus, eighteenth-century hymnic efforts took place during a time when the prevailing aesthetic sensibility held that art could both edify and delight, a fact that requires the hymn to be considered as a work of both theology and literature. Consequently, in the following discussion we will consider the specific ways in which the form and content of a hymn, together and separately, are employed to create meaning and to enable religious experience. Ideally, the singing of hymns will give voice to a worshipper's heartfelt devotion to God, and for this reason alone they have great value. But as a work of literature by which, in its singing, the faithful are made to rehearse a particular theology, it is instructive to consider how hymns are composed and made to convey meaning and enable religious experience. Prior to turning to an in-depth study of Steele's hymnody it will be helpful to take a broad view of eighteenth-century hymnody and to consider how these themes are represented in the work of her contemporaries.

Anne Steele's Contemporaries

To place Steele in her particular theological and literary landscape, we will briefly survey eighteenth-century hymnody, touching down on various key hymn-writers, and considering examples of their hymnody with an eye to the particular style and substance of their hymns. Certainly the two most significant contributors, as far as scope of influence, to the burgeoning field of hymnody in the eighteenth century, were Isaac Watts and Charles Wesley. Indeed, their combined work effectively transformed public worship. For this reason, and because they have left record of their own thoughts on hymns as an artistic and theological form, they will be considered here in some depth. In addition, their hymns, and the hymns of other hymn-writers included in this chapter, will be

---

[30] Ibid. See also Steele's draft dedication of her poems to her father, where she similarly writes, "If you think they are capable of affording pleasure or proffit you may if you please communicate any of them to friends or fellow Christians." Draft dedication of Steele's hymns and poems to her father, c. 1760, STE 3/5.

[31] Steele to anonymous woman, 8 August 1761, STE 3/13 (vii).

used as sources of comparison in our subsequent discussion of Steele's hymnody.

Isaac Watts

When Anne Steele was born in 1717 in Hampshire, Isaac Watts (1674-1748) was forty-three years of age, living in nearby Hertfordshire, and well established in a productive career as a writer of hymns and prose.[32] He had already published two of his great works in verse: *Horae Lyricae* in 1706 and *Hymns and Spiritual Songs* in 1707. *The Psalms of David Imitated in the Language of the New Testament* would follow in 1719. Dissatisfied with the contemporary state of worship, Watts aspired to change the experience of worship for those in the pews, creating possibilities for more authentic corporate worship. The form of congregational worship had been constrained within the bounds of the customary practice of singing psalms in a few conventional metres—the standard versions of psalms being those of Sternhold and Hopkins (*The Whole Booke of Psalmes, Collected into Englysh Metre*, or the "Old Version," published in 1562) and Tate and Brady (*New Version of the Psalms of David, Fitted to the Tunes Used in Churches*, or the "New Version," published in 1696).[33] Watts challenged the monopoly of psalmody, encouraging the writing and singing of hymns. Whereas Watts was not the first to begin to

---

[32] Isaac Watts was an Independent minister at the prominent Mark Lane Church, which later became Bury Street Church, in London. Though often in poor health, his ministry there flourished. In addition to his pastoral employment, Watts had a successful career as a writer. He published numerous works of verse and prose, including various volumes on education and philosophy. His greatest impact, however, would be felt through his poetic and hymn-writing compositions. Watts's verse inspired the work of many subsequent eighteenth-century hymn-writers. His hymns were heavily anthologized, and featured prominently in John Wesley's *A Collection of Psalms and Hymns* (1737). Watts was also well connected with numerous prominent eighteenth-century religious figures, including Philip Doddridge, John Wesley, George Whitefield, Selina Hastings, the Countess of Huntingdon, and Elizabeth Singer Rowe. Isabel Rivers, "Watts, Isaac (1674-1748)," *Oxford Dictionary of National Biography* (Oxford: Oxford University Press, 2004 [http://www.oxforddnb.com/view/article/28888, accessed 17 April 2006]).

[33] Metrical psalmody was deemed by many to be the proper measure of congregational singing, as it versified the Bible, which was inerrant, rather than giving expression to fallible human thought and emotion. William Romaine, for example, in his apologia for psalmody, considered the matter easily closed. To those who argued for the right to introduce hymns into public worship, Romaine countered, "This should silence every objection—*It is the word of God*." William Romaine, *An Essay on Psalmody* (London: n.p., 1775), 136 (italics in original). Romaine (1714-1795) was a Church of England clergyman who was a popular, if sometimes controversial, preacher. He argued earnestly for the primary role of psalms in Christian worship, publishing *An Essay on Psalmody* in 1775, in which he mocked Watts's hymnic efforts as "Watts whyms" and "Watts jingle." Ibid., 137.

experiment with the composition of hymns, his work was extraordinarily successful and did much to stimulate an increased acceptance of hymns in public worship.[34] Others, including Anne Steele, would follow Watts's leading and in so doing, according to Horton Davies, would restore "to the people the right to sing the praise which either the clerk or the choir had filched from them."[35] Donald Davie measures the significance of Watts's efforts:

> There is quite clearly *prima facie* quantitative evidence for supposing that Watts's *Hymns and Psalms* ("Watts Entire," as it came to be called) has been more influential than any of the works of its century that we think of as most popular— more than Johnson's *Dictionary*, more than *Robinson Crusoe* or *Gulliver's Travels*, more even than *The Seasons* or "Ossian."[36]

In his preface to *Hymns and Spiritual Songs*, Watts identifies the unsatisfying recitation of psalms in corporate worship as the motivation for his publication of hymns and psalms cast in the light of Christian experience. Watts argues that psalmody is often met with "dull Indifference," and he observes that when singing psalms, "the Minds of most of the Worshippers are absent or unconcern'd."[37] He judges the manner in which psalmody is practiced as "Evil," indicating that while it "should elevate us to the most delightful and divine Sensations," instead it makes "flat our Devotion" since it is "foreign to the State of the New Testament, and widely different from the present Circumstances of Christians."[38] That is, in singing psalms, the Christian recites

---

[34] For a helpful introduction to the history of the congregational hymn in England, see Richard Arnold's introduction to *English Hymns of the Eighteenth Century: An Anthology*, American University Studies, series 4, English Language and Literature, vol. 137 (New York: Peter Lang, 1991), 1-27. Arnold notes that, following the Reformation, England followed Calvin on the issue of psalm-singing, believing that it was a more appropriate means by which to praise God, as opposed to hymn-singing, which was encouraged by Luther. Ibid., 1.

[35] Davies adds that eighteenth-century hymn-writers "brought back lyricism in praise and gave a place to the religious affections in an age of rationalism and formalism." Horton Davies, *Worship and Theology in England*, vol. 3, *From Watts and Wesley to Maurice, 1690-1850* (Princeton: Princeton University Press, 1961; reprint, Grand Rapids, MI: Eerdmans, 1996), 234, 235 (page citations are to the reprint edition).

[36] Donald Davie, *A Gathered Church: The Literature of the English Dissenting Interest, 1700-1930*, The Clark Lectures 1976 (New York: Oxford University Press, 1978), 33-34.

[37] Isaac Watts, preface to *Hymns and Spiritual Songs* (London: J. Humphreys, 1707), iii-iv.

[38] Ibid., iv. Watts offers a more complete argument for the reformation of traditional psalmody in his essay, "A Short Essay Toward the Improvement of Psalmody: Or, An Enquiry how the Psalms of *David* ought to be translated into Christian Songs, and how lawful and necessary it is to compose other Hymns according to the clearer Revelations of the Gospel, for the Use of the Christian Church," in *Hymns and Spiritual Songs*, 233-

the experience of Old Testament believers rather than the experience of those living after Christ. Watts felt that the effect of thus introducing Old Testament characters and events into contemporary worship could be disorienting and intrusive, detracting from the possibility of authentic worship. He writes, "When we are just entering into an Evangelic Frame, by some of the Glories of the Gospel presented in the brightest Figures of *Judaism*, yet the very next Line perhaps which the Clerk parcels out unto us hath something in it so extremely *Jewish* and cloudy that darkens our Sight of God the Saviour."[39] He suggests that there is a better way to touch and move the heart, claiming that poetry, encouraged by a divinely-inspired imagination, has the power to "convey Piety in resisting Nature, and melt the hardest Souls to the Love of Virtue."[40] And so he wrote hymns which gave new expression to devotional experience. Largely through the efforts of Watts—his "Attempt for the Reformation of Psalmodie"—the form of singing in public worship was transformed from the previously predominant psalm to the innovative new hymn.[41]

The particular form that Watts's hymns took has been described, variously, as "dramatic," "ceremonious," and "austere."[42] He endeavoured to express religious sentiment in readily accessible language and correspondingly writes, "It has been my Labour to promote the pious Entertainments of Souls truly serious even of the meanest Capacity, and at the same time (if possible) not to give Disgust to Persons of richer Sense and nicer Education."[43] That is, he attempted to write, at once, in a way that would be acceptable and meaningful to both popular and élite audiences. To this end, Watts established a set of guidelines to direct his hymn composition. He writes in the preface to *Hymns and Spiritual Songs*:

> The whole Book is confin'd to three Sorts of Metre, and fitted to the most common Tunes. I have seldom permitted a Stop in the middle of a Line, and

---

276. See also his preface to *The Psalms of David Imitated in the Language of the New Testament, and Apply'd to the Christian State and Worship* (London: J. Clark, R. Ford, and R. Cruttenden, 1719), iii-xxxii.

[39] Watts wanted to see "*David* converted into a Christian." Watts, preface to *Hymns and Spiritual Songs*, v, x (italics in original). Watts's reference to the clerk parceling out lines refers to the then-current practice of the church clerk reading out a line to have it sung back to him by the congregation. Singing proceeded in this way and has been blamed, in part, for the lifeless manner in which songs were sometimes sung. Watts himself lamented the "unhappy Mixture of Reading and Singing." Ibid., viii.

[40] Watts, preface to *Horae Lyricae*, xiv.

[41] Watts, preface to *Hymns and Spiritual Songs*, xiii.

[42] Marshall and Todd comment on Watts's inclination to create dramatic tableaux in his hymns. Marshall and Todd, *English Congregational Hymns in the Eighteenth Century*, 34, 64; Davie, *The Eighteenth-Century Hymn in England*, 149, 57.

[43] Watts, preface to *Hymns and Spiritual Songs*, 2nd ed., corrected and much enlarged (London: J. H[umphreys], 1709), ix.

seldom left the end of a Line without one....The Metaphors are generally sunk to the Level of vulgar Capacities. I have aimed at ease of Numbers and Smoothness of Sound, and endeavour'd to make the Sense plain and obvious; if the Verse appears so gentle and flowing as to incur the Censure of Feebleness, I may honestly affirm, that sometimes it cost me labour to make it so: Some of the Beauties of Poesy are neglected, and some wilfully defaced: I have thrown out the Lines that were too sonorous, and have giv'n an Allay to the Verse, lest a more exalted Turn of Thought or Language should darken or disturb the Devotion of the plainest Souls.[44]

The form of Watts's hymns is thereby seen to be highly structured, and this intentionally, so that he might "aid the Devotion of Christians," which he identifies as his "whole Design."[45] Watts curtailed his full poetic potential in order to offer hymns to the church which would be understood by the broadest base of worshippers, and understood quickly as they were being sung. Harry Escott refers to this curtailing as an "artistic *kenosis*," adding, "Watts had to lay his poetic glories aside and dress the profound message of the Gospel in the homespun verse and language of the people."[46] Indeed, Watts acknowledges these difficulties in his essay, "A Short Essay Toward the Improvement of Psalmody"; he writes, "'Twas hard to restrain my Verse always within the Bounds of my Design; 'Twas hard to sink every Line to the Level of a whole Congregation, and yet to keep it above Contempt."[47] Donald Davie indicates that Watts "practised what Pope and the Scriblerus Club called 'the art of sinking,'" and that he "did so deliberately, after counting the cost."[48]

---

[44] Watts, preface to *Hymns and Spiritual Songs* (1707), viii-ix.

[45] Ibid., x.

[46] Harry Escott, *Isaac Watts Hymnographer: A Study of the Beginnings, Development, and Philosophy of the English Hymn* (London: Independent Press, 1962), 26 (italics in original).

[47] Watts, "An Essay Toward the Improvement of Psalmody," in *Hymns and Spiritual Songs*, 276.

[48] Davie, *A Gathered Church*, 24. The Scriblerus Club was an eighteenth-century literary club whose members included Alexander Pope, Jonathan Swift, Thomas Parnell, and John Gay. The club's objective was to mock false learning, and did so through the writings of a fictional character, Martinus Scriblerus.

See also John Hoyles's analysis of Watts and the "art of sinking." John Hoyles, *The Waning of the Renaissance 1640-1740: Studies in the Thought and Poetry of Henry More, John Norris and Isaac Watts* (The Hague: Martinus Nijhoff, 1971), 175-189, 233-250. Hoyles shows how Watts's poetic efforts issued from his theological belief that the language of religion, and, as it relates to language, religious experience, should be accessible to a broad audience: "Watts's ideal was a plain style in religion and in poetry. He worked hard and consistently to sink metaphysical quirks in both spheres. A non-mystical piety went hand in hand with purity of diction. Watts's work in the fields of aesthetics and prosody provides eloquent confirmation of the moral premise which informs his religious thinking." Ibid., 189.

Throughout his hymns, Watts displays a careful control, as he labours to make the gospel both clear and meaningful to the ordinary worshipper in the pew.

As to the content of his hymns, Watts is thoroughly scriptural. Born into the Dissenting tradition, he exhibits a commitment to the essential role of Scripture in worship, as well as the transformative role of doctrine in the Christian's life. Many of his hymns are therefore didactic in nature, as he articulates his doctrinal beliefs and attempts to instruct his congregants in matters of theology and religious devotion.[49] As a hymn-writer, he aimed to make religion readily accessible, without compromising any of the depth of the Christian faith. While the content of his hymns is not rendered simplistic, it is presented in careful, clear verse in order to be articulated meaningfully by his congregants. The substance is largely theological and is matched by formal qualities that are restrained and dignified. J.R. Watson interprets Watts's desire for clarity and simplicity in worship: "in addition to recommending ordinary language, Watts wishes to banish uncertainty, muddle, imprecise thinking, and superstition."[50]

In order to appreciate the distinct style and substance of Watts's hymnody, consider his hymn, "Man Frail and God Eternal," which begins with these words:

> Our God, our Help in Ages past,
>   Our Hope for Years to come,
> Our Shelter from the stormy Blast,
>   And our eternal Home.
>
> Under the Shadow of thy Throne
>   Thy Saints have dwelt secure;
> Sufficient is thine Arm alone,
>   And our Defence is sure.
>
> Before the Hills in order stood,
>   Or Earth receiv'd her Frame,
> From everlasting Thou art God,
>   To Endless Years the same.[51]

---

[49] Donald Davie refers to the axiomatic character of some of Watts's hymns. Davie, *The Eighteenth-Century Hymn in England*, 27-38. Marshall and Todd explain the didactic nature of Watts's poetic expression: "He took the singers and their feelings by the hand and led them along an instructive pathway....The desired end of a hymn thus became the education of religious sensibility by means of the supervised refinement of human feeling into devotional response, with the help of the Blessed Spirit." Marshall and Todd, *English Congregational Hymns in the Eighteenth Century*, 33.

[50] Watson, *The English Hymn*, 141.

[51] Watts, "Man Frail and God Eternal," *The Psalms of David Imitated in the Language of the New Testament*, 229. The substitution of "Oh" for "Our," in the first line—a

The language is strong and dignified, the vocabulary simplified; the sense, throughout, is "plain and obvious." The overall effect is one of austerity. There is, nowhere, a stop in the middle of a line, but each line instead completes a thought or phrase. The hymn is written in Common Metre, and features the iambic foot, whose movement, according to Austin Lovelace, "is stately and noble and is best used for those texts which are propositional."[52] As well, the message is thoroughly scriptural, as its text is based on that of Psalm 90, though it is rewritten in such a way as to increase its relevance for contemporary Christians. Donald Davie explains that in this hymn, Watts gives us "a psalm, not translated, but paraphrased and modernized, and yet in no sense 'freely adapted,' but modernized according to a very strict method."[53]

While psalmody featured the experiences of those Old Testament believers long dead, Watts, by making the language of worship pertinent to current persons and circumstances, introduced a new voice in his hymns: he expressed the personal, using first-person pronouns, as in "Our God, our Help in Ages past," just noted. Horton Davies reflects on this change:

> Whereas the chief stress in Puritan worship was on the downward, revelational movement of God in sermon and Sacrament, now a new stress was given to the hymns and to the importance of the congregation. At times there was even a subjectivity in the worship, whereas objectivity had characterized the metrical psalmody of the previous century.[54]

The personal voice, articulated by Watts as hymn-writer, was meant to be expressed by each congregant and, in this way, become his or her personal voice as well. Pauline Parker identifies one of the "advances" of hymn-writing in the eighteenth-century to be "the discovery that the personal cry of one may also be the voice of many," and she notes that critics attribute this advance to Watts.[55] Thus, with Watts, new possibilities for religious expression and devotion were introduced into public worship, though the connection to previous modes of worship remains evident. Indeed, Watson locates Watts at the nexus of hymnody and psalmody, looking backward toward Scripture-based psalmody and forward toward the sometimes intense emotion that would appear in later eighteenth-century hymnody, such as in that of Charles Wesley.[56]

---

change that is reflected in most modern renderings of this hymn—was made by John Wesley when he included this hymn in *A Collection of Psalms and Hymns* (1737).

[52] Lovelace refers to Common Metre as "the workhorse of hymnody" as it is the metre most commonly used in early eighteenth-century hymnody and, before that, in psalmody. Lovelace, *The Anatomy of Hymnody*, 13, 35.

[53] Davie, *A Gathered Church*, 23.

[54] Davies, *Worship and Theology in England*, 99-100.

[55] Parker, "The Hymn as a Literary Form," 412.

[56] Watson, *The English Hymn*, 133, 152.

Charles Wesley

Charles Wesley (1707-1788) is perhaps most fully representative of the extraordinary successes of hymnody in the eighteenth century.[57] He wrote, according to some counts, an astonishing nine thousand hymns during his life, a significant number of which are still in use. Where Watts introduced the possibility of a personal, emotional voice in corporate worship, Wesley developed what Watts began. Wesley, a generation younger than Watts, began writing hymns in 1738, when Anne Steele was twenty-one, herself reaching adulthood and beginning to experiment with religious verse. Wesley's verse exhibits some significant differences from that of Watts. Whereas Watts's emotion was controlled, influenced by the intellectual nature of his Dissenting background, Wesley's emotion was more heightened; while Watts articulated a Calvinistic theology sometimes reflecting an anxiety concerning salvation, Wesley's hymns express the exuberance made possible by the idea of universal salvation as it was preached by the Wesleyan Methodists. The result is a confident enthusiasm that enlivens many of Wesley's hymns.

The form of Wesley's verse is, in Watson's words, "freer, more spontaneous, a natural development" to the versification of Sternhold and Hopkins, Tate and Brady, and, though he developed what came before him, Watts.[58] Gone is Watts's commitment to sinking the level of metaphors to the "Level of vulgar Capacities"; Davie comments that in Wesley's hymns "we encounter audacities, imaginative abstractings, that...ought to leave us gasping."[59] Wesley's language appears to be more spontaneously expressive and enthusiastically emotional than that of his predecessors, including Watts. See, for example, the way in which Wesley uses Watts's verse. Where Watts writes:

> Begin, my tongue, some heavenly theme,
>   Awake, my voice, and sing—

---

[57] Charles Wesley was a Church of England clergyman who is remembered chiefly for his remarkable contributions to the flourishing field of eighteenth-century hymnody. Guided by the motivating impulse of his brother, John Wesley (1703-1791), he played a significant role in the events of the Evangelical Revival, the aim of which was to revitalize the spiritual lives of those within the Established Church. Charles and John Wesley were founders of the new Methodist movement, famous for itinerant preaching, which Charles Wesley engaged in for nearly two decades before unstable health caused him to retire to more settled ministries in Bristol and later in London. Henry D. Rack, "Wesley, Charles (1707-1788)," *Oxford Dictionary of National Biography* (Oxford: Oxford University Press, 2004; online ed. October 2005 [http://www.oxforddnb.com/view/article/29067, accessed 17 April 2006]).

[58] Watson, *The English Hymn*, 231.

[59] Davie offers as example Wesley's lines on the Incarnation: "Being's source begins to be, / And God Himself is born!" Davie, "Enlightenment and Dissent," in *Dissentient Voice*, 21.

Wesley amplifies the sentiment of Watts:

> O for a thousand tongues to sing—

Watson describes this as "a development of Watts's restrained dignity."[60] Rather than restrained, Wesley's hymns are often energetic, fervent, even rhapsodic.

Where Watts's hymns are constrained by the various rules he established to guide his writing (for example, making metaphors accessible at a popular level rather than intended only for the educated élite, aiming for "Ease of Numbers and Smoothness of Sound"), Wesley's hymns introduce a greater freedom in matters of form. Donald Davie points out that Wesley loves oxymoron ("Impassive, He suffers; immortal, He dies"), and that a common feature of his hymnody is paradox ("Victim divine").[61] As well, throughout his hymns, Wesley makes liberal use of italics, capitals, and exclamation points in order to add emphasis and convey his spiritual assurance and enthusiasm.[62] Whereas Watts employed only a few hymn metres, Wesley's hymns appear in a vast assortment of metres; Bernard Manning suggests the need to "gasp with astonishment at the variety," and George Findlay notes that often "the very metre becomes vital to the message of the hymn."[63] Where Watts's stanzas are typically four lines in length, as dictated by the conventional metres he employed, Wesley's stanzas are generally longer.[64] His enthusiasm resulted in more naturally broken speech patterns making their way into his hymns; according to Frank Baker, the emotions inherent in the "longings, despairs, and raptures of the soul's contact with God," which form the subject of many of Wesley's hymns, effectively "burst the fetters of conventional verse, demanding expression in a rich and daring variety of lyrical forms."[65] In these ways, Wesley pushed the boundaries of the conventional hymn form.

As regards the content of Wesley's hymns, many are more thoroughly subjective than those of Watts. Wesley's hymns bear witness to the emotionalism associated with the Evangelical Revival, and an attempt should

---

[60] Watson, *The English Hymn*, 243-244.

[61] Davie, "The Classicism of Charles Wesley," in *Purity of Diction in English Verse*, 79.

[62] George H. Findlay, in *Christ's Standard Bearer* (London: Epworth Press, 1956), includes an entire chapter on Wesley's use of the exclamation point.

[63] Bernard L. Manning, *The Hymns of Wesley and Watts: Five Informal Papers* (London: Epworth Press, 1942), 50; Findlay, *Christ's Standard Bearer*, 21. Frank Baker refers to Wesley's "metrical versatility" as "genius." Frank Baker, *Charles Wesley's Verse: An Introduction* (London: Epworth Press, 1964), 68.

[64] The increased length of Wesley's verses reflect, in Frank Baker's words, his desire for "a stanza in which a theme could be announced, developed, and satisfactorily summarized, preferably with a foreshadowing of the theme for the following stanza." Ibid., 54.

[65] Ibid., 116.

be made to understand them with reference to the context for which they were written: that is, while Watts's hymns were written for the Dissenting church, Wesley wrote for a revival setting. In fact, his hymns were often sung outside of a church setting. The Methodism of John and Charles Wesley emphasized the necessity of the individual soul's heartfelt conviction of sin and acceptance of divine grace. This kind of conversion experience was often immediate and personal and therefore Wesley's hymns, in Watson's words, "have a kind of urgency which comes from a direct application of the self."[66] In fact, Wesley wrote his first hymn, "Where Shall My Wond'ring Soul Begin?" in response to his own experience of conversion. While Watts introduced a new subjective voice to the English hymn, Wesley more perfectly exhibits an awareness of his own ability to feel. Having thus experienced God's grace through conversion, Wesley wrote hymns in order to aid others in their efforts to articulate their own experiences of regeneration.

Both the style and substance of Wesley's hymns are significantly different from those of Watts. By means of example, let us consider the following hymn by Wesley:

> Lo! he comes with clouds descending,
>   Once for favour'd sinners slain!
> Thousand, thousand saints attending,
>   Swell the triumph of his train;
> Hallelujah! God appears on earth to reign.
>
> Ev'ry eye shall now behold him
>   Rob'd in dreadful majesty;
> Those who set at nought and sold him,
>   Pierc'd and nail'd him to the tree,
> Deeply wailing, Shall the true Messiah see.
>
> The dear tokens of his passion,
>   Still his dazzling body bears;
> Cause of endless exultation
>   To his ransom'd worshippers:
> With what rapture, Gaze we on those glorious scars!
>
> Yea! Amen! let all adore thee,
>   High on thy eternal throne!
> Saviour, take thy pow'r and glory,

---

[66] Watson, *The English Hymn*, 222.

> Claim the kingdom for thine own:
> Jah! Jehovah! Everlasting God, come down.[67]

The contrast between this and Watts's hymn, earlier recorded, is striking. To begin, this hymn has none of the formal restraint of Watts's hymn. The metre is aptly termed Peculiar Metre. More specifically, it has an 87.87.47. metre, and where Watts used an iambic line, Wesley uses a trochaic line, which starts with a strong beat. Austin Lovelace indicates that this form is used "when directness of thought and excitement are desirable" and "is an excellent pattern for texts requiring large scope yet calling for strength."[68] Notice also the prevalence of the exclamation point as a form of punctuation, and the way in which Wesley allows meaning to extend beyond a line into the next. While the form of this hymn shatters the restraint of Watts's earlier hymn, so too does the content. The robust formal features of this hymn are matched by the strength of Wesley's exuberance as he eagerly anticipates the return of Christ to earth.

While Wesley's hymns are replete with finely-wrought emotion, exemplifying a "steep rise in...emotional temperature" after Watts, at the same time they retain a didactic element, as was typical in eighteenth-century literature.[69] Marshall and Todd explain, "Wesley's purpose was not the expressive *venting* of feeling but rather the evangelical *directing* of feeling."[70] They refer to this characteristic of Wesley's hymns as "didactic subjectivity."[71] Donald Davie concurs, explaining that Wesley's verse is "throughout doctrinal, that is, didactic. His hymns are not, like most later hymns, so many geysers of

---

[67] Charles Wesley, "Hymn 64," *A Collection of Hymns, for the Use of the People Called Methodists*, a new edition (London: G. Whitfield, 1797), 68-69. This hymn is one of those added to later editions of the Wesleys' popular hymnbook, and may have originated with John Cennick (1718-1755). See John Cennick, "Hymn CXXVIII," *A Collection of Sacred Hymns*, 5th ed. (Dublin: S. Powell, 1752), 132. J.R. Watson judges Cennick's earlier imagery to be "clumsy and inappropriate," so that Wesley's adaptation of his hymn represents a significant improvement. Watson, *The English Hymn*, 270. Cennick was involved in the early days of the Evangelical Revival as one of the Methodists' first lay preachers. Increasing contact with Moravians, including Count Zinzendorf (1700-1760), led to his becoming a Moravian minister, and he spent much of his later life evangelizing Ireland. Peter J. Lineham, "Cennick, John (1718-1755)," *Oxford Dictionary of National Biography* (Oxford: Oxford University Press, 2004 [http://www.oxforddnb.com/view/article/4993, accessed 13 January 2007]).

[68] Lovelace, *An Anatomy of Hymnody*, 13, 73.

[69] Davie, *The Eighteenth-Century Hymn in England*, 57.

[70] Marshall and Todd continue, "while the *religion* of the Wesley brothers was highly emotional, the *hymn* was calculated and controlled, an evangelical tool, precisely used to encourage the people to express those emotions that led to, that testified to, conversion." Marshall and Todd, *English Congregational Hymns in the Eighteenth Century*, 79, 87 (italics in original).

[71] Ibid., 87.

warm 'feeling'. And yet, heaven knows, the 'feeling' is there."[72] Wesley hoped to effect a change in the hearts of those who sang his hymns, as they responded emotionally to the presence of God in their lives. Watson offers this comparison: "Watts's hymn points towards the grandeur of the divine: Wesley's towards human responsibility."[73] So Wesley's hymns, rather than enabling the expression of emotion in a kind of personal catharsis, direct singers in the expression of Christian doctrine. In this way, singers become practiced in the doctrine of the church.[74]

We have paid considerable attention to the hymnody of Isaac Watts and Charles Wesley, and have done so in an effort to locate major landmarks in the landscape of eighteenth-century hymnody. The hymn was a comparatively new genre when Anne Steele took it up, and its writers were experimenting with its possibilities even as they formulated theories regarding its use. Watts and Wesley represent two poles in eighteenth-century hymnody: with Nonconformist austerity and soberness on one side and Methodist enthusiasm and energy on the other. While this is a false continuum in many ways, since there are ample similarities between the work of Watts and Wesley, this distinction is helpful in providing a framework within which to position the work of other hymn-writers. In the following discussion, we will consider a number of hymn-writers whose work will reappear in subsequent chapters. It is hoped that by placing these additional markers in the field of eighteenth-century hymnody, we will be better able to understand the unique contribution of Anne Steele.

William Cowper

The hymns of William Cowper (1731-1800) introduce a dramatic shift in tone from that of Watts and Wesley, attributable, in part, to the purpose for which he wrote.[75] That is, while Watts and Wesley wrote hymns as ministers, Cowper

---

[72] Davie, "The Classicism of Charles Wesley," in *Purity of Diction in English Verse*, 79.
[73] Watson, *The English Hymn*, 245.
[74] Bernard Manning considers that in Wesley's hymns we encounter the "full-orbed and conscious orthodoxy of a scholar trained and humbled as he contemplates the holy, catholic, and evangelical faith in its historic glory and strength," adding, "The hymns are charged with dogma. They set forth, not the amiable generalizations of natural religion in which Wesley's contemporaries delighted, but the peculiar and pungent doctrines of uncompromising Christianity." Manning further indicates that "Wesley's confidence is rooted in the orthodox, catholic, evangelical faith. Nowhere have you a better body of sound doctrine. If you know Wesley's hymns, you receive (whether you wish it or not) a magnificent course of instruction in high dogmatic theology." Manning, *The Hymns of Wesley and Watts*, 27, 74.
[75] In the last decades of his life, William Cowper achieved considerable fame as a poet, precipitated by his long poem, "The Task." Earlier, however, he had been educated for the law, though he would not long practice this trade. Throughout Cowper's life he was

wrote as a layperson. Cowper's hymn-writing efforts were exercised alongside those of John Newton (1725-1807), then a Church of England clergyman at Olney, a fact which has often led to their comparison.[76] Donald Davie, for example, writes, "whereas Watts and Wesley and Cowper's Olney collaborator John Newton are uttering their hymns as it were from the pulpit, Cowper is one of those who sit at their feet, reporting faithfully how it seems to him, there, in the pew."[77] Perhaps because of this he was freer to explore his own religious experience in verse. Marshall and Todd attribute the "intrusion" of a "personal and idiosyncratic attitude" in Cowper's verse to his freedom from the "professional sense of responsibility of the clergyman."[78] Likewise, Watson fashions Cowper a "man in need, not a clergyman," and suggests that for this reason Cowper is able to be "more introspective, more probing into the uncertain moods of the self."[79] Watson concludes that Cowper's hymnody is distinctive because of this heightened degree of subjectivity and that Cowper was, in fact, motivated by emotion: "His most painful worry is 'to find I cannot feel.'"[80] His motivation is not primarily didactic in the same way as it is for

---

haunted by a conviction that he was eternally damned. He also suffered from a prolonged and profound depression and attempted suicide on several occasions. Later, he met John Newton, who welcomed him to the church he pastored at Olney and provided guidance to him as both spiritual director and friend. Cowper contributed 67 hymns to *Olney Hymns*, a collaborative effort between himself and Newton (Newton contributed 281, together with a preface). David Lyle Jeffrey, *English Spirituality in the Age of Wesley* (Grand Rapids, MI: Eerdmans, 1987; reprint, Vancouver, BC: Regent College Publishing, 2000), 454-457 (page citations are to the reprint edition).

[76] John Newton began his career as a sailor and slave trader, but later became a Church of England clergyman. His autobiography, *An Authentic Narrative* (1764), established a place for him among the leaders of the Evangelical Revival. He had a ministry at Olney for sixteen years, during which time he developed a close friendship with William Cowper and together they compiled the *Olney Hymns*, though Newton took a guiding role in the project. Bruce Hindmarsh notes, "The style and tone of these hymns fit somewhere between the sobriety of Old Dissent in Isaac Watts's *Hymns and Spiritual Songs* (1707) and the exuberance of Wesleyan Methodism in the standard *Collection of Hymns, for the Use of the People called Methodists* (1780)." D. Bruce Hindmarsh, "Newton, John (1725-1807)," *Oxford Dictionary of National Biography* (Oxford: Oxford University Press, 2004 [http://www.oxforddnb.com/view/article/20062, accessed 17 April 2006]). See also D. Bruce Hindmarsh, *John Newton and the English Evangelical Tradition: Between the Conversions of Wesley and Wilberforce* (Oxford: Oxford University Press, 1996; reprint, Grand Rapids, MI: Eerdmans, 2001).

[77] Davie, introduction to *The New Oxford Book of Christian Verse*, xxv.

[78] Marshall and Todd, *English Congregational Hymns in the Eighteenth Century*, 143.

[79] Watson, *The English Hymn*, 288.

[80] Ibid., quoting William Cowper, "The Contrite Heart," *Olney Hymns*, by John Newton and William Cowper (London: W. Oliver, 1779), 81. Many critics, in their attempts to define the hymn, specify that the hymn must be general, rather than personal; it must speak to the experience of each singer, rather than illuminate the individual experience

Watts or Newton. Rather, while Cowper's hymns do retain an element of didacticism, they have at their centre, in Donald Davie's words, "not doctrine, but *experience*."[81]

The mood so often revealed in Cowper's hymns is a self-conscious and self-doubting subjectivity in a way that has not yet been encountered. Wesley's sometimes overwhelming confidence is not to be found here. Watts's stately declarations of God's goodness are absent. Instead, Cowper doubts not only the assurance of his salvation, but the love of God which motivated many of Wesley's hymns. Consider the following lines by Cowper:

> The Lord will happiness divine
> On contrite hearts bestow:
> Then tell me, gracious God, is mine
> A contrite heart, or no?
>
> I hear, but seem to hear in vain,
> Insensible as steel;
> If ought is felt, 'tis only pain,
> To find I cannot feel.
>
> I sometimes think myself inclin'd
> To love thee, if I could;

---

of the hymn-writer. Pauline Parker, for example, defines a hymn as "of its nature congregational; ordinary men and women must feel that it speaks for them and to them. To do this it must echo common experience." Parker, "The Hymn as a Literary Form," 400. George Sampson, for his part, considers it "shocking" to sing in public hymns which are particularly private or personal. Sampson, "The Century of Divine Songs," 38. Cowper's hymns do reveal a high level of personal feeling. For this reason, Erik Routley judges him to be a poor hymn-writer. Routley notes "in the majority of [Cowper's hymns] an element of intimacy, in many an introversion, and in a few a positive hint of real mental corruption, which severely restrict their contribution to universal hymnody." Erik Routley, "The Hymns of Philip Doddridge," in *Philip Doddridge 1702-51: His Contribution to English Religion*, ed. Geoffrey F. Nuttall (London: Independent Press, 1951), 46-47. Cowper's biographer, Gilbert Thomas, likewise doubts the efficacy of Cowper's verse as hymns; he considers the feelings expressed in Cowper's hymns to be "too deep and individual" for congregational use, labeling them "*poems* of personal doubt and conflict rather than *songs* of faith and assurance." Gilbert Thomas, *William Cowper and the Eighteenth Century*, rev. ed. (London: George Allen and Unwin, 1948), 190 (italics in original).

[81] Davie suggests that the hymns of Watts and Wesley are "necessarily public utterance," whereas those of Cowper are more often "wistful private musing." Davie, "The Language of the Eighteenth-Century Hymn," in *Dissentient Voice*, 77 (italics in original).

> But often feel another mind,
>   Averse to all that's good.[82]

The content of this hymn is certainly different from that which we encountered in the works of Watts and Wesley. There is an element here of introspective questioning which results in a troubling doubt regarding Cowper's own ability to respond to God in faith and love. Cowper's hesitant "I sometimes think" and "if I could" appear in stark contrast to Watts's and Wesley's choice of language. Notice, however, that the form of this hymn corresponds to that seen earlier in the work of Watts: it appears in Common Metre, in language that is both simple and clear.[83]

Contra Watts, whom Marshall and Todd argue portrays his subject by painting a picture or "tableau," Cowper sometimes turns "from the vision to the viewer....The song itself is more useful as central theme."[84] His doubts about God are then reflected back onto his particular task, that of hymn-writing, so that both his subject and his method disclose a similar hesitation.[85] This

---

[82] Cowper, "The Contrite Heart," *Olney Hymns*, 81.

[83] The form of Cowper's hymn reflects the pattern stipulated by John Newton in the preface to *Olney Hymns*: "Perspicuity, simplicity and ease, should be chiefly attended to; and the imagery and coloring of poetry, if admitted at all, should be indulged very sparingly." Newton, preface to *Olney Hymns*, vii-viii.

[84] Marshall and Todd, *English Congregational Hymns in the Eighteenth Century*, 127. Watson notes that in the second half of the eighteenth century, "the movement of hymnody...was away from the general towards the individual and the particular situation, away from reason towards an authenticating personal experience. Watts's universals...gave way to...Cowper's rehearsal of particular anguish and hope." Watson, *The English Hymn*, 267.

[85] While some critics have focused their studies of Cowper on his recurring bouts of mental illness which tempted him to suicide on several occasions, and have linked these episodes with Cowper's evangelical influences, such as Newton, Watson is careful to explain that Cowper cannot be so easily categorized as "despairing." Watson writes, "Cowper's hymns are sometimes tentative and often uncertain, but they are not about despair. They are rather about hesitations, but also the joy and peace that comes 'sometimes' to the believer, about the providence of God, about the unlooked-for blessings, the occasional walk with God, the quiet sound of the divine voice." Ibid., 290-291, quoting Cowper, "Joy and Peace in Believing," *Olney Hymns*, 367. Donald Davie also notes the hesitancy in Cowper's hymn, "Joy and Peace in Believing," indicating that while it may be hoped that a light would surprise the singing worshipper more often than merely "sometimes," Cowper's words may, in fact, reflect a not uncommon experience in worship. Davie, introduction to *The New Oxford Book of Christian Verse*, xxv.

While for many years it was customary to lay the blame for Cowper's mental and spiritual anguish on the Calvinistic doctrine preached by his friend, Newton, more current scholarship shows that this is too simplistic an assessment. See, for example, Hindmarsh, *John Newton and the English Evangelical Tradition*, 2-4.

hesitancy and doubt in God and in his own abilities as a hymn-writer become prominent subjects in Cowper's hymns, and find echoes in the hymnody of Steele, as we will see. As well, Cowper's identification as a lay hymn-writer is instructive in a study of Steele's hymnody for she also wrote "from the pew," rather than for the edification of a particular congregation.

Elizabeth Singer Rowe and Anne Dutton

The proliferation of hymn-writing which occurred in the eighteenth century provided an important new means by which women were able to communicate their religious beliefs in public. Whereas long-established social and theological scruples obstructed women's access to public discourses, during the eighteenth century poetry and hymnody became increasingly seen as acceptable modes of public expression for women.[86] Karen Smith elaborates:

> Hymnody is an excellent example of the way women were able to cross over from the private to the public sphere without threatening the male patriarchy. Though often barred from the pulpit, it was considered gender appropriate for women to compose verse to be sung by members of the congregation. Hymnody was a means through which believers could give expression to the personal dimension of faith in public worship and it became a way for women to preach the Gospel.[87]

---

[86] Biblical imperatives against women speaking publicly (such as those based on texts in 1 Timothy and 2 Corinthians) were essentialized by many churches, including Steele's own Particular Baptist denomination. Michael Watts explains that, aside from being permitted to speak in a church meeting to make a public profession of faith, women were instructed to keep silent in accordance with "the inferiority of their sex." Watts, *The Dissenters*, 1: 320, citing the *Association Records of the Particular Baptists*, 1: 28. Karen Smith makes reference to the church covenant of the Lockerly Baptist Church, which includes, as a ninth item in their "Rules of Order to be observ'd at our Church-meetings": "No woman to be suffr'd to speak but to be in silence unless asked a question by way of evidence (1 Corin. 34:35; 1 Timothy 2:11-12)." Smith, "The Community and the Believer," 291-292.

[87] Karen E. Smith, "Beyond Public and Private Spheres: Another Look at Women in Baptist History and Historiography," *Baptist Quarterly* 34 (April 1991): 84. See also Margaret Maison, "'Thine, Only Thine!' Women Hymn Writers in Britain, 1760-1835," in *Religion in the Lives of English Women, 1760-1930*, ed. Gail Malmgreen (Bloomington, IN: Indiana University Press, 1986), 11-40. Because women were barred from most participation in public religious discourse, their contribution to Baptist life has been largely underrated. An attempt to compensate for this silence can be found in John Briggs, "She-Preachers, Widows and Other Women: The Feminine Dimension in Baptist Life Since 1600," *Baptist Quarterly* 31, no. 7 (July 1986): 337-352. See also Karen E. Smith, "Forgotten Sisters: The Contributions of Some Notable but Un-Noted British Baptist Women," in *Recycling the Past or Researching History? Studies in Baptist Historiography and Myths*, ed. Philip E. Thompson and Anthony R. Cross,

Margaret Maison correlates this increased opportunity for women with the Dissenting cause, noting, "It is refreshing to observe how many women of Nonconformist persuasion enjoyed an exceptional measure of liberty, equality and fraternity in religious activities throughout the eighteenth century."[88] Maison's comments are made in response to the disproportionate number of Dissenting women attempting expression in hymns, as compared to their sisters in the Established Church. This variance is likely due to the fact that, as Dissenters, these women were already operating beyond the bounds of propriety; that is, in accepting the Dissenting cause, they had already questioned established assumptions about what was correct moral and spiritual behaviour. It was in this context that Anne Steele composed and published her hymns. Though she would become the most successful, Steele was not the first eighteenth-century Dissenting woman to find a public hearing for her hymns.[89]

Steele was predated in her hymn-writing endeavours by Elizabeth Singer Rowe (1674-1737), who was a friend and correspondent of Isaac Watts.[90]

Studies in Baptist History and Thought, vol. 11 (Milton Keynes, UK: Paternoster, 2005), 163-183.

[88] Maison, "'Thine, Only Thine!' Women Hymn Writers in Britain, 1760-1835," in *Religion in the Lives of English Women*, 11.

[89] In fact, even before hymns began to swell in popularity during the eighteenth century, several women had begun to experiment within the genre. In 1654, the Baptist Anna Trapnel (*fl.* 1642-1660) published *The Cry of a Stone*, a series of "prayers and spiritual songs." Ernest A. Payne, "Baptists and Their Hymns," in *The Baptist Hymn Book Companion*, rev. ed., ed. R.W. Thomson (London: Psalms and Hymns Trust, 1967), 15. Trapnel was a self-styled prophetess who was given to visions and trances; she made various high profile predictions which led to her being accused of "witchcraft, madness, whoredom, vagrancy, and seditious intent." Trapnel defended herself, claiming that she was "God's seasoned chosen prophet," and that she was "a free single woman (and hence masterless), whose right to pray, publish, and travel were founded in common and divine law, backed by her rights as taxpayer." Stevie Davies, "Trapnel, Anna (*fl.* 1642-1660)," *Oxford Dictionary of National Biography* (Oxford: Oxford University Press, 2004 [http://www.oxforddnb.com/view/article/38075, accessed 17 December 2006]). See also Katharine Gillespie, *Domesticity and Dissent in the Seventeenth Century: English Women Writers and the Public Sphere* (Cambridge: Cambridge University Press, 2004), 92-106. In 1663, Katherine Sutton (*fl.* 1630-1663), another Baptist, would follow with *A Christian Woman's Experiences of the Glorious Working of God's Free Grace*. Sutton's verse, a kind of "primitive hymnody," was likely intended to be sung as solos in church, and therefore should be seen as a precursor to the eighteenth-century congregational hymn. Ian Mallard, "The Hymns of Katherine Sutton," *Baptist Quarterly* 20 (1963-1964): 24-25.

[90] Elizabeth Singer Rowe was a popular author of poetry, hymns, and other devotional writing, who published under the pseudonym, Philomela. She enjoyed friendships with various well-known contemporary writers, including Matthew Prior and Isaac Watts, and her work was admired by Alexander Pope and Samuel Johnson. Rowe married Thomas Rowe (1687-1715) in 1710, when she was thirty-five years old and he was

Rowe's hymns are compiled in several volumes, including *Divine Hymns and Poems on Several Occasions*, published in 1704 and revised in 1709 as *A Collection of Divine Hymns and Poems*. Her hymns are commonly scriptural, finding frequent inspiration in the Song of Songs, and often focus on her love for Christ and on his love for her. See, for example, the following:

> Immortal Fountain of my Life,
> My last, my noblest, End,
> Eternal Centre of my Soul,
>   Where all its Motions tend.

---

twenty-two. After just five years of marriage, he died of consumption in 1715. After Elizabeth Singer Rowe's death, Watts edited and arranged for the publication of her *Devout Exercises of the Heart in Meditations and Soliloquy, Prayer and Praise* (1737). Jonathan Pritchard, "Rowe, Elizabeth (1674-1737)," *Oxford Dictionary of National Biography* (Oxford: Oxford University Press, 2004 [http://www.oxforddnb.com/view/article/24198, accessed 17 April 2006]). In *Horae Lyricae*, Watts dedicated a poem to her, dated 19 July 1706, which shows another side to the usually sober Dissenting minister and hymn-writer:

> On the fair Banks of gentle Thames
>   I tun'd my Harp; nor did celestial Themes
>   Refuse to dance upon my Strings:
>   There beneath the Evening Sky
> I sung my Cares asleep, and rais'd my Wishes high
>   To everlasting Things.
>   Sudden from Albion's Western Coast
>   Harmonious Notes come gliding by,
> The neighbouring Shepherds knew the Silver Sound;
> "'Tis Philomela's Voice"....
> I was all Ear, and Philomela's Song
>   Was all divine Delight.

Watts, *Horae Lyricae*, 211.

Marjorie Reeves, in her book *Pursuing the Muses*, notes several similarities between Elizabeth Singer Rowe and Anne Steele: according to Reeves, both drew their intellectual stimulus from a largely male circle of friends, both had tendencies toward being recluses, and both became central figures in literary circles. Reeves, *Pursuing the Muses*, 25-26. See also Reeves, "Literary Women in Eighteenth-Century Nonconformist Circles," in *Culture and the Nonconformist Tradition*, 7-25. On the influence of supportive Nonconformist ministers and writers on Rowe's publishing success, see Sarah Prescott, "Provincial Networks, Dissenting Connections, and Noble Friends: Elizabeth Singer Rowe and Female Authorship in Early Eighteenth-Century England," *Eighteenth-Century Life* 25 (Winter 2001): 29-42. The Steele Collection at the Angus Library contains transcriptions, by various members of the Steele family, of some of Rowe's letters, a fact which led Reeves to conclude that Rowe may have "served as a role model" for Steele. Reeves, "Literary Women in Eighteenth-Century Nonconformist Circles," in *Culture and the Nonconformist Tradition*, 10. See STE 3/17/5.

> Thou Object of my dearest Love,
> My Heav'nly Paradice,
> The Spring of all my flowing Joys,
> My everlasting Bliss.[91]

Donald Davie characterizes Rowe as "a byword in her time for emotionalism," and the claim also could be made for a prevailing subjectivism.[92]

Rowe caused Watts some concern as a result of her tendency toward assuming a mystical tone, which was at odds with his Puritan convictions. Rowe writes frequently of her desire for union with God, aspiring for a more complete knowledge and experience of her Saviour, and she does this in language which is often decorative and highly wrought with emotion.[93] In his preface to *Devout Exercises of the Heart*, Watts conveys misgivings about her florid style, writing, "The Style, I confess, is raised above that of common Meditation or Soliloquy."[94] While admitting that in his youth he also, on occasion, "unwarily" expressed the "Fervours of devout Love to our Saviour in the Style of the Song of Solomon," he adds, "if I may be permitted to speak the Sense of maturer Age, I hardly think this the happiest Language in which Christians should generally discover their warm Sentiments of Religion, since the clearer and more spiritual Revelations of the New Testament."[95] As we have come to expect, Watts favoured a religious diction that was clear and plain, expressive of the life of devotion made possible after Christ. Rowe's style was quite different, and Henry Stecher attributes this difference to Rowe's exhibiting some of the characteristics of Pietism. Stecher elaborates regarding the significance of his claim:

> The pietistic writer often wrote in the first person in his attempt to depict his own personal experience. The hymn was a lyrical form well-suited for revealing the poet's inner state, and pietistic hymns are frequently a record of subjective experience, or psychic-emotional conditions. Such hymns differed greatly from

---

[91] [Elizabeth Singer Rowe], "Hymn," *Divine Hymns and Poems on Several Occasions, by Philomela* (London: R. Janeway, 1704), 118-119.
[92] Davie, *The Eighteenth-Century Hymn in England*, 57.
[93] Margaret Anne Doody writes, "Rowe longs for the final union with the divine which will make separations [such as that she experienced after the death of her husband] and distinctions unnecessary." Margaret Anne Doody, "Women Poets of the Eighteenth Century," in *Women and Literature in Britain, 1700-1800*, ed. Vivien Jones (Cambridge: Cambridge University Press, 2000), 223.
[94] Isaac Watts, preface to *Devout Exercises of the Heart in Meditation and Soliloquy, Prayer and Praise*, by Elizabeth Singer Rowe (London: R. Hett, 1738), xi.
[95] Ibid., xiii.

the typical orthodox, Protestant hymns which stressed faith, doctrine, or the congregational interest.[96]

Thus, while Rowe's hymns retain a conventional form, in the style of Watts, the substance of her hymns consistently inclines toward the sentimental and emotional.

But lest we think that the hymns of women tend only toward the strongly subjective, we have the hymnody of Anne Dutton (1692-1765).[97] Dutton, a

---

[96] Stecher defines Pietism as "a pejorative term for the enthusiastic nonconformity which developed within orthodox Lutheranism in the seventeenth century" and "was a mystically-orientated religious tendency, which ultimately influenced English Dissent and its aesthetic outlook." Henry F. Stecher, *Elizabeth Singer Rowe, the Poetess of Frome: A Study in Eighteenth-Century English Pietism* (Frankfurt: Herbert Lang Bern, 1973), 202, 200. Pietism was a religious movement in later seventeenth-century and eighteenth-century continental Europe, the aim of which was to revitalize Protestant church life. In this way, it can be understood as a sister movement to the Evangelical Revival in England. It was also, according to David Lotz, a "reaction against the arid intellectualism that characterized much of Lutheran and Reformed orthodoxy. Hence the pietists opposed 'pure life' to 'pure doctrine,' elevated 'doing' over 'knowing.'" Its leading figures include Philipp Jacob Spener (1635-1705) and August Hermann Francke (1663-1727). David W. Lotz, "Continental Pietism," in *The Study of Spirituality*, ed. Cheslyn Jones, Geoffrey Wainwright, and Edward Yarnold (New York: Oxford University Press, 1986), 449; Trond Enger, "Pietism," in *The SCM Dictionary of Christian Spirituality*, ed. Gordon S. Wakefield (London: SCM Press, 1983), 300-301.

[97] Anne Dutton was an ambitious and accomplished writer whose published volumes numbered more than fifty, with works representing the various genres of spiritual autobiography, hymns, theological tracts, and volumes of letters. Most of her work was published anonymously or under her initials, "A.D." She engaged in lengthy correspondences with many of the leaders of the Evangelical Revival, including John Wesley, George Whitefield, Howell Harris, and Philip Doddridge. She was, according to Karen O'Dell Bullock, "perhaps the most theologically capable and influential Baptist woman of her day." Karen O'Dell Bullock, "Dutton, Anne (1691x5-1765)," *Oxford Dictionary of National Biography* (Oxford: Oxford University Press, 2004 [http://www.oxforddnb.com/view/article/71063, accessed 9 February 2006]). See also Hindmarsh, *The Evangelical Conversion Narrative*, 294-301. Like Steele, Dutton was a member of the Particular Baptist denomination, and the theological convictions she held in relation to that association are evident throughout her writings. Of particular interest here is a possible connection between Steele and Dutton. The Angus Library at Regent's Park College, Oxford contains a Bible which has been inscribed by first Dutton and then Steele. See Broughton 10/1. Early twentieth-century efforts, archived in the Angus Library, to ascertain the nature of their relationship were inconclusive, though Reuben Heffer surmises that "probably they knew each other by correspondence." Reuben Heffer to Miss Parsons, 15 February 1919, Broughton 10/3. Also noteworthy is a letter appended to Dutton's autobiography, in which she offers an erudite argument for women's right to publish, taking into account the biblical imperative to keep silence in public. Dutton's argument hinges on the location associated with these prohibitions. She

prolific writer of theological literature, also published sixty-one hymns which appear appended to her lengthy poem, *A Narration of the Wonders of Grace* (1734). The hymns are decidedly doctrinal, as witnessed in the following excerpt from "The Mystery of the Trinity Reveal'd in Christ":

> The Glories of Jehovah shine
> In his own Son, who is Divine;
> Well he could tell the Father's Name,
> Because his Nature is the same.
>
> The Father, Son, and Spirit be
> One God most High, yet One in Three;
> The Godhead's Glory jointly share,
> Because that they Co-equal are.[98]

Dutton's fame was not won as a hymn-writer (unsurprisingly, given the example just cited). While the form of this hymn is strictly conventional, it has none of the grandeur or awe found in Watts. Her final line, "Because that they Co-equal are," is certainly an awkward way in which to end a stanza. While she has managed to incorporate the theologically-weighty word, "Co-equal," she has sacrificed elements of her art; theology has triumphed here, while the principles of literature have been adhered to only perfunctorily.

While Dutton's hymns do not reveal the full glory of the eighteenth-century hymn, they do foreground the significance of doctrine in the work of many eighteenth-century hymn-writers. Throughout this discussion, we have made a distinction between hymns that are more profoundly subjective and those that are more noticeably didactic, yet the greater part of eighteenth-century hymnody is doctrinal in nature, even as it is consistently subjective. Watts's hymnody is perhaps more clearly didactic than that of Wesley, yet we have seen that it was also subjective. Similarly, Wesley's hymnody reveals a more obvious subjectivity than that of Watts, but it is consistently seen to be didactic as well. And the examples of Cowper, Rowe, and Dutton have shown a greater range of possibilities with regard to style and substance. Subjectivity and

---

insists that while Scripture bans women from preaching in churches, it does not forbid them to teach in private, and books, she argues, are a form of private instruction. [Anne Dutton], "A Letter to Such of the Servants of Christ, who have any Scruple about the Lawfulness of Printing any Thing written by a Woman," in *A Brief Account of the Gracious Dealings of God, with a Poor, Sinful, Unworthy Creature* (London: J. Hart, 1750), the letter is unpaginated. Taking into account Dutton's sophisticated argument for a woman's right to express herself publicly, it is interesting to note a possible connection to Steele who, in publishing verse on sacred subjects, similarly challenged the boundaries of propriety.

[98] Anne Dutton, "The Mystery of the Trinity Reveal'd in Christ," *A Narration of the Wonders of Grace* (London: n.p., 1734), 73.

didacticism become a matter of degree which can be traced, in part, to theological convictions. To understand Steele's contribution to eighteenth-century hymnody, consideration must therefore be given to her particular denomination, the Baptists.

Baptist Hymnody

Steele may be, in Margaret Maison's assessment, "one of the brightest stars in the firmament of Baptist hymnody," but she certainly is not the only star shining in that sky.[99] The Particular Baptist minister, Benjamin Keach (1640-1704), is typically credited with introducing Baptist hymnody to congregational worship.[100] In fact, Hugh Martin claims that Keach was "the first to introduce the regular singing of hymns into the normal worship of an English congregation."[101] Keach's efforts to introduce hymn-singing met with sometimes fierce opposition: during the latter part of the seventeenth century, Keach was engaged in a bitter dispute with those who favoured metrical psalmody. He published a series of pamphlets advocating for the right to sing congregational hymns, the most important of which was *The Breach Repaired in God's Worship, or Singing of Psalms, Hymns and Spiritual Songs Proved to Be a Holy Ordinance of Jesus Christ* (1691). While the controversy raged, Keach and his congregation at Horselydown sang hymns in their worship services. Keach is mentioned here not on account of any direct influence he had on Steele, but because of his pioneering role within the field of Baptist

---

[99] Maison, "'Thine, Only Thine!' Women Hymn Writers in Britain, 1760-1835," in *Religion in the Lives of English Women*, 14.

[100] Paul Richardson points out that Keach was not the first Baptist to write hymns, citing, for example, the work of Anna Trapnel and Katherine Sutton, noted earlier. Richardson adds, however, that Trapnel and Sutton's verse was probably not sung corporately. Richardson, "Baptist Contributions to Hymnody and Hymnology," 60.

A Dissenting minister during the time of persecution, Keach's ministry was often attended by controversy and prosecution. He was one of the leading Baptist figures in seventeenth-century England, with close ties to William Kiffin (1616-1701) and Hanserd Knollys (1598-1691), whose influence inclined him towards Calvinism. Keach was engaged in several heated pamphlet wars, most notably arguing against paedobaptism and for congregational hymn-singing. Beth Lynch, "Keach, Benjamin (1640-1704)," *Oxford Dictionary of National Biography* (Oxford: Oxford University Press, 2004 [http://www.oxforddnb.com/view/article/15202, accessed 17 April 2006]). On Keach's contribution to hymnody, see Hugh Martin, "The Baptist Contribution to Early English Hymnody," *Baptist Quarterly* 19 (1961-1962): 195-208; Thomas R. McKibbens, Jr., "Our Baptist Heritage in Worship," *Review and Expositor* 80, no. 1 (Winter 1983): 53-69; Richardson, "Baptist Contributions to Hymnody and Hymnology," 59-74; W.T. Whitley, "The First Hymnbook in Use," *Baptist Quarterly* 10 (1941): 369-375; Robert H. Young, *The History of Baptist Hymnody in England from 1612 to 1800* (PhD diss., University of Southern California, 1959), 55-59.

[101] Martin, "The Baptist Contribution to Early English Hymnody," 199.

hymnody. His efforts to introduce hymn-singing to congregational worship transpired a generation prior to Watts, yet Horton Davies points out that "what the Baptists did first, others did better."[102] Nevertheless, the efforts of early Baptists such as Keach did yield a rich tradition of Baptist hymnody.

A significant proportion of early Baptist hymnody resulted from the efforts of ministers to summarize their sermons in verse.[103] Horton Davies styles the Baptist minister, Benjamin Beddome (1717-1795), "the indefatigable sermon summarizer in verse"; Beddome was one of those ministers who wrote a hymn each week to serve as a sort of musical précis of his sermon.[104] Davies ascribes

---

[102] Davies, *Worship and Theology in England*, 136. Hugh Martin writes, "As a prose writer Keach is far from negligible, but his hymns and other verses are just terrible." Martin, "The Baptist Contribution to Early English Hymnody," 200. Another early Baptist contributor to hymn-writing was the Baptist minister Joseph Stennett (1663-1713) who, along with Keach, engaged in a pamphlet war defending the right to sing hymns. Stennett was friends with Nahum Tate of Tate and Brady fame. Louis Benson notes that Isaac Watts incorporated several lines from Stennett's hymnody in his own compositions. Benson, *The English Hymn*, 101. Stennett's son, Samuel Stennett (1728-1795), would also become a hymn-writing Baptist minister.

[103] Louis Benson relates Watts's influence on the Baptists to their distinctly "homiletical hymnody." Ibid., 142-147.

[104] Beddome was a Particular Baptist minister, who studied under Bernard Foskett at Bristol Academy, where he became close friends with Caleb Evans and John Ash. When Beddome was ordained in 1743, Joseph Stennett preached the sermon and Foskett gave the charge. Beddome was the pastor of the Baptist church at Bourton-on-the-Water for fifty-five years. W.B. Lowther, "Beddome, Benjamin (1717-1795)," rev. Karen E. Smith, *Oxford Dictionary of National Biography* (Oxford: Oxford University Press, 2004 [http://www.oxforddnb.com/view/article/1921, accessed 17 April 2006]). See also Michael A.G. Haykin, "Benjamin Beddome (1717-1795)," in *The British Particular Baptists, 1638-1910*, 1: 166-183.

Philip Doddridge (1702-1751) was one such minister who, according to Hay Colligan, "wrote hymns to the texts or topic of his sermons, and gave them out, couplet by couplet, to be sung after Sermon." J. Hay Colligan, *Eighteenth Century Nonconformity* (New York: Longmans, Green, and Co., 1915), 95. Doddridge was an Independent minister, and a contemporary and friend of Isaac Watts, who actually planned Doddridge's most popular and influential work, *The Rise and Progress of Religion in the Soul* (1745). Doddridge's hymns were published posthumously as *Hymns Founded on Various Texts in the Holy Scriptures*, by his friend, Job Orton (1717-1783). Orton's preface to the 1755 collection explains Doddridge's motivation in composing his hymns:

> These Hymns being composed to be sung, after the Author had been preaching on the Texts prefixed to them, it was his Design, that they should bring over again the leading Thoughts in the Sermon, and naturally express and warmly enforce those devout Sentiments; which he hoped were then rising in the Minds of his Hearers, and help to fix them on the Memory and Heart.

Beddome's efforts to a "very pedagogical understanding of the function of a hymn, as almost a jingle by which to sum up the message of the sermon."[105] However, J.R. Watson cautions against considering Beddome merely "predictable, homiletic, and boring"; Watson notes that while at times this judgement is just, at other times Beddome employs a "clarity of line and simplicity of image" that earns for him a significant place "in the transition of eighteenth-century hymnody from the grandeur of Watts to the sensitivity of Cowper."[106] Consider, for example:

> My Times of Sorrow and of Joy,
> Great God, are in thy Hand;
> My choicest Comforts come from thee,
> And go at thy Command.[107]

Louis Benson refers to the activity of Steele, alongside various Baptist ministers, as "the golden age of Baptist Hymnody."[108] This "golden age" would

---

Job Orton, preface to *Hymns Founded on Various Texts in the Holy Scriptures* by Philip Doddridge, 3rd ed. (London: J. Buckland, et al., 1766), iv. Similarly, John Fawcett (1740-1817), a Particular Baptist minister, explains his purpose in writing hymns:
> When I have digested my thoughts on some portion of God's word, I have frequently attempted to sum up the leading ideas, in a few plain verses, to be sung after the sermon; that so they might be more impressed on my own heart, and on the hearts of my hearers.

John Fawcett, preface to *Hymns: Adapted to the Circumstances of Public Worship, and Private Devotion* (Leeds: G. Wright and Son, 1782), iii.

[105] Davies, *Worship and Theology in England*, 136. In the eighteenth century, many of Beddome's hymns were published in collections of hymns, such as John Rippon's *Selection of Hymns from the Best Authors* (1787), which will be discussed later in this chapter. In 1818, the Baptist minister Robert Hall (1764-1831) collected and published 830 of Beddome's hymns as *Hymns Adapted to Public Worship, or Family Devotion*.

[106] Watson, *The English Hymn*, 202.

[107] Benjamin Beddome, "Resignation; or, God Our Portion," *A Selection of Hymns from the Best Authors, Intended to be an Appendix to Dr. Watts's Psalms and Hymns*, by John Rippon (London: Thomas Wilkins, 1787), hymn 276.

[108] Benson, *The English Hymn*, 215. W.R. Stevenson, in Julian's *Dictionary of Hymnology*, similarly refers to the "palmy days of Baptist hymnody." W.R. Stevenson, "English Baptist Hymnody," in *Dictionary of Hymnology*, ed. John Julian, 1: 112. A comprehensive list of hymn-writing Baptist ministers would be lengthy indeed, but notable names include Robert Robinson (1735-1790), Samuel Medley (1738-1799), John Fawcett (1740-1817), and Daniel Turner (1710-1798). Fawcett, who was converted after hearing George Whitefield preach and who is likely best known today as the author of "Blest Be the Tie That Binds," was a Particular Baptist minister who published *Hymns Adapted to the Circumstances of Public Worship and Private Devotion* in 1782. In 1785, Medley, also a Particular Baptist minister, "gathered into several volumes…his hymns that had appeared in leaflets and periodicals." Benson, *The English Hymn*, 215.

gather the chief of its successes in a series of influential hymnbooks—including those by John Ash and Caleb Evans and, later, John Rippon, all Baptist ministers—which did much to disseminate Steele's work beyond the borders of Broughton and into a wide network of Baptist churches. In this way, the Baptists exerted another kind of influence on the flourishing hymn genre: in addition to producing a series of successful hymn-writers, the chief of whom is Steele, they acted to perpetuate the work of those writers by publishing their efforts collectively. Steele's work had a prominent place in these anthologies. Robert Young's thesis on Baptist hymnody in the seventeenth and eighteenth centuries demonstrates the extent of Steele's representation in these hymnbooks; her work appears only less often than that of Isaac Watts and Philip Doddridge.[109]

In 1769, John Ash and Caleb Evans published *A Collection of Hymns Adapted to Public Worship*, which would become more commonly known as the "Bristol Collection" (see Figure 4). Prior to this, most hymnbooks comprised the compositions of a single hymn-writer; according to Paul Richardson, Ash and Evans's hymnbook is "considered by many to be the first hymnal in the modern sense—that is, an anthology," allowing congregations to sing the works of a variety of authors.[110] Ash and Evans, introduced in the

---

Turner published numerous hymns, including "Beyond the Glittering Starry Skies," which he wrote with his brother-in-law, James Fanch (1704-1767), himself a Baptist minister and correspondent of Steele's. Robinson, whose "Come, Thou Fount of Every Blessing" continues to be popular today, was also particularly influenced by the preaching of Whitefield. Whitefield had a significant influence on eighteenth-century Baptists, stemming from their shared Calvinistic theology. Morgan Patterson notes that, unlike John Wesley, "Whitefield was admired and loved, and he was looked upon as a friend of Baptists. He was always welcomed in Baptist pulpits and by Baptist auditors." W. Morgan Patterson, "The Evangelical Revival and the Baptists," in *Pilgrim Pathways: Essays in Baptist History in Honour of B.R. White*, 254. Steele's father, himself a Particular Baptist minister, heard Whitefield preach on various occasions. In 1832, Joseph Ivimey, the early Baptist historian, judged John Wesley to be "very far inferior" in regards to "the correctness of his religious sentiments" than Whitefield. Joseph Ivimey, *A History of the English Baptists: Including an Investigation of the History of Baptism in England from the Earliest Period to Which It Can Be Traced to the Close of the Seventeenth Century, to Which Are Prefixed Testimonies of Ancient Writers in Favor of Adult Baptism, Extracted from Dr. Gill's Piece Entitled, The Divine Right of Infant-Baptism Examined and Disproved* (London: n.p., 1811-1830), 3: 290. See also W.T. Whitley, "The Influence of Whitefield on Baptists," *Baptist Quarterly* 5 (1930-1931): 30-36.

[109] Young, *The History of Baptist Hymnody in England from 1612 to 1800*, 122-124. Charles Wesley's absence here is attributable to a matter of theological fidelity, for the Baptists were Calvinistic, as was Watts, while Wesley's theology was more characteristically Arminian.

[110] Richardson, "Baptist Contributions to Hymnody and Hymnology," 62. Part of Ash and Evans's impetus for publishing their collection was a desire to enable "singing

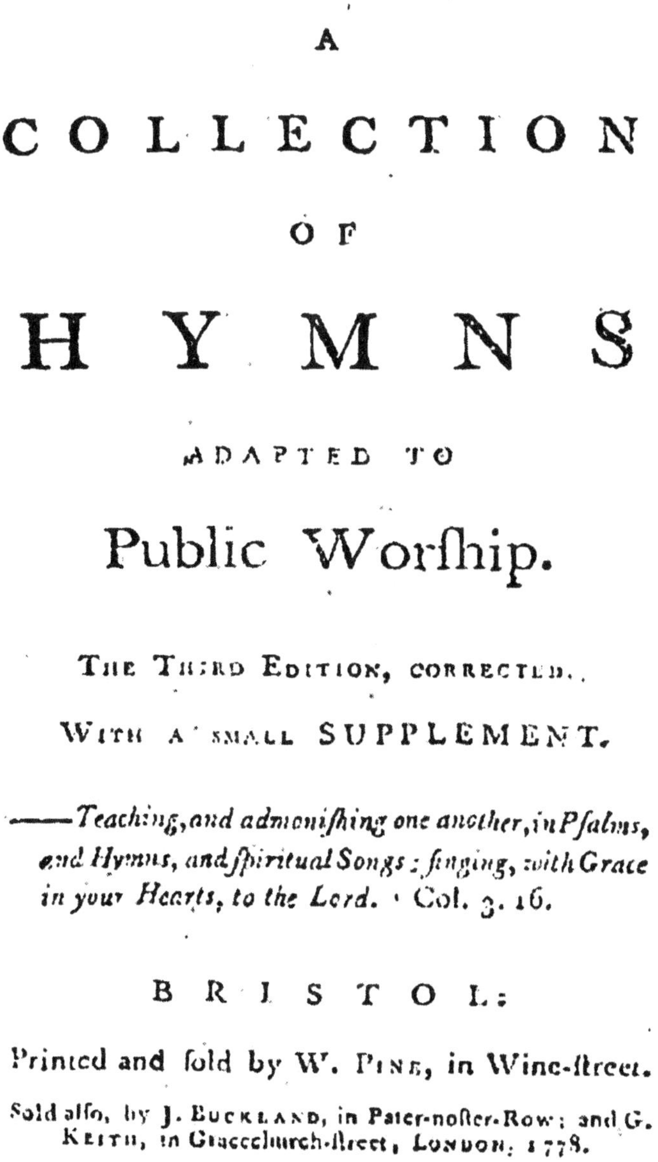

A COLLECTION OF HYMNS ADAPTED TO Public Worſhip.

THE THIRD EDITION, CORRECTED,

WITH A SMALL SUPPLEMENT.

——*Teaching, and admoniſhing one another, in Pſalms, and Hymns, and ſpiritual Songs: ſinging, with Grace in your Hearts, to the Lord.* Col. 3. 16.

BRISTOL:

Printed and ſold by W. PINE, in Wine-ſtreet.

Sold alſo, by J. BUCKLAND, in Pater-noſter-Row; and G. KEITH, in Gracechurch-ſtreet, LONDON: 1778.

Figure 4: Title Page of Ash and Evans's "Bristol Collection"

without reading Line by Line." By supplying an inexpensive collection of hymns from a variety of hymn-writers, they hoped that as many people as possible would "bring Books with them, and look on the Words while they sing, so far as to make the Sense compleat." Ash and Evans, preface to *A Collection of Hymns Adapted to Public Worship*, 3rd ed. (Bristol: W. Pine, 1778), iii.

previous chapter as influential friends of Steele's, were part of a group of verse-writing friends which gathered around her.[111] In the publication of their hymnbook they considered themselves indebted to Steele who not only revised some hymns for its publication, but "likewise favored the Editors with several valuable Originals."[112] The "Bristol Collection" provided a popular debut for

---

[111] Evans (1737-1791) was a Particular Baptist minister and friend of Anne Steele; he played an important role in the posthumous publication of the 1780 edition of her hymns and poems. He was the son of Hugh Evans, the minister of Bristol's Broadmead church and principal of the Bristol Baptist Academy, at that time the primary training centre for Particular Baptist ministers. Evans assisted two prominent Baptist ministers, Samuel Stennett and Philip Furneaux, before returning to Bristol to assist his father at the church and academy. In 1770, Evans created the Bristol Education Society, associated with the academy; this organization was concerned for "the education of 'pious candidates for the ministry...[and] the encouragement of missionaries to preach the Gospel'" and was supported by the proceeds from the publication of Steele's hymns. Roger Hayden, "Evans, Caleb (1737-1791)," *Oxford Dictionary of National Biography* (Oxford: Oxford University Press, 2004 [http://www.oxforddnb.com/view/article/40192, accessed 17 April 2006]), quoting Caleb Evans, *The Kingdom of God: A Sermon Preached in Broadmead, Bristol, before the Bristol Education Society* (Bristol: W. Pine, et al., 1775), 24. The Bristol Baptist Academy educated many prominent eighteenth-century Baptist ministers who participated in the new wave of hymn-writing and who maintained connections throughout their lives. See Eric Sharpe, "Bristol Baptist College and the Church's Hymnody," *Baptist Quarterly* 28 (1979): 7-16. After his father's death in 1781, Evans became principal of the academy as well as minister of the Broadmead church. Evans was part of a writing circle that included Anne Steele. He had a great personal affection for Steele and, after her death, wrote a series of consoling letters (three of which are extant) to her niece, Mary Steele Dunscombe. He characterizes Steele as a "humble, resign'd, steady, patient, cheerful Xian" and notes that since her death he has been unable to read her verse "without a moisten'd eye, & a heavnig [sic] heart." Caleb Evans to Mary Steele Dunscombe, 23 February 1779, STE 5/16 (iv). See also Kirk Wellum, "Caleb Evans (1737-1791)," in *The British Particular Baptists, 1638-1910*, 1: 213-233; Norman S. Moon, "Caleb Evans, Founder of the Bristol Education Society," *Baptist Quarterly* 24 (1971-1972): 175-190.

John Ash (1724-1779) studied for the ministry at the Bristol Baptist Academy and was pastor of the Pershore Baptist Church. He was, along with Evans, a member of a group of verse-writing friends and family members who gathered around Steele. Along with his work on the "Bristol Collection" of hymns, Ash is remembered as the author of *A New and Complete Dictionary of the English Language* (1775). See Geoffrey F. Nuttall, "John Ash and the Pershore Church: Additional Notes," *Baptist Quarterly* 22 (1967-1968): 271-276; G.H. Taylor, "The Reverend John Ash, LL.D., 1724-1779," *Baptist Quarterly* 20 (1963-1964): 4-22.

[112] Ash and Evans, preface to *A Collection of Hymns Adapted to Public Worship*, iv. Steele's work similarly formed the core of other hymn anthologies, including, in 1795, that of Jeremy Belknap. Belknap, a Congregational minister in America, published a popular anthology of hymns entitled *Sacred Poetry, Consisting of Psalms and Hymns, Adapted to Christian Devotion, in Public and Private*. In his preface, Belknap notes that

Steele's hymns, as with its publication her hymns were more widely disseminated than they had been previously.[113] Sixty-two of her hymns are included in Ash and Evans's hymnbook (which had a total of 412 hymns).

John Rippon's collection, *A Selection of Hymns from the Best Authors, Intended as an Appendix to Dr. Watts's Psalms and Hymns*, was published in 1787 and would prove to be even more popular than Ash and Evans's anthology.[114] While Rippon was also a Baptist, his collection included the works of those from other denominations. Rippon displays his ecumenical spirit in his preface:

---

he is "largely indebted" to Steele for her hymns, which played an important role in his compilation. He then dedicates a full two-thirds of his preface to a recitation of the various merits of Steele's life and hymnody. Of the 300 hymns in Belknap's compilation, those of Isaac Watts number a third, while Philip Doddridge and Steele equally make up another third; the remaining third are the work of an additional thirty hymn-writers. Jeremy Belknap, *Sacred Poetry, Consisting of Psalms and Hymns, Adapted to Christian Devotion, in Public and Private*, 2nd ed. (Boston: Thomas and Andrews, 1797). John Julian indicates that Belknap's hymnbook was one of American hymnody's "most notable collections," further adding that psalmody had dominated over hymnody in America prior to 1800, thereby confirming the importance of Steele's presence in the early stages of American hymnody. Julian, *Dictionary of Hymnology*, 1: 59, 57. Similarly, Steele's hymns featured prominently in a hymnbook produced in 1808 by Trinity Church, an Episcopal church in Boston. So impressed with Steele's hymns were the compilers of this hymnbook, that of the 152 hymns collected in it, 59 were by Steele. In a preface, the compilers explain that they "extracted more copiously from…Steele, than from any other writer," and that in doing so they did "no more, than what [they] thought due to her poetical superiority." Preface to *Hymns, Selected from the Most Approved Authors, for the Use of Trinity Church, Boston* (Boston: Munroe, Francis and Parker, 1808). The count of 59 is that of Louis Benson in *The English Hymn*; according to the indexing of The Dictionary of American Hymnology, 48 of the hymns in this compilation are by Steele. Benson, *The English Hymn*, 214; The Dictionary of American Hymnology, Oberlin College, Ohio.

[113] The "Bristol Collection" also introduced the hymns of Benjamin Beddome. Young, *The History of Baptist Hymnody in England from 1612 to 1800*, 121.

[114] John Rippon (1751-1836) was a popular Particular Baptist minister, who preached in London from 1773, succeeding the theologian John Gill (1697-1771). From 1790 to 1802, Rippon edited the *Baptist Annual Register*, which, according to Ken Manley, "reflected and stimulated the new evangelical vitality in the churches of both England and America." He also was a leading figure in the creation of the Baptist Union in England in 1812 and, again according to Manley, "did more than any other to promote a sense of denominational identity and unity among Particular Baptists." His greatest influence was felt through his contribution to eighteenth-century hymnody. Ken R. Manley, "Rippon, John (1751-1836)," *Oxford Dictionary of National Biography* (Oxford: Oxford University Press, 2004 [http://www.oxforddnb.com/view/article/23666, accessed 17 April 2006]). See also Manley, "'Sing Side by Side': John Rippon and Baptist Hymnody," in *Pilgrim Pathways: Essays in Baptist History in Honour of B.R.*

It has given me no small Pleasure, to unite, as far as I could, different Denominations of Ministers, and Christians on Earth, in the same noble Work....It has not been my Enquiry, *whose* Hymns shall I choose, but *what* Hymns; and hence it will be seen, that Churchmen and Dissenters, Watts and Tate, Wesley and Toplady, England and America sing Side by Side.[115]

The impressive popularity of Rippon's *Selection* not only generated greater exposure for the hymns of Baptist writers but, according to Paul Richardson, resulted in "their inclusion in subsequent collections across denominational lines."[116] Rippon's hymnbook was extremely popular in England and gained widespread acceptance in America as well; it was revised twenty-seven times during his lifetime, and the forty-fourth edition, called the "Comprehensive Rippon," was published in 1844.[117] Fifty-three of Steele's hymns were included in the first edition of Rippon's *Selection* (from a total of 588 hymns).[118] Well into the last half of the nineteenth century, Rippon's *Selection* "enjoyed a virtual monopoly—with Watts—of Baptist praise," in addition to finding popular usage among non-Baptists.[119]

Rippon's *Selection* and, to a lesser degree, Ash and Evans's "Bristol Collection" worked to replace "the more literary or devotional writings of individuals," such as Steele's *Poems on Subjects Chiefly Devotional*.[120] These anthologies thereby also served to distribute Steele's hymns far beyond the Broughton church where they were first rehearsed and made to express the devotion of their singers; as Ken Manley argues, Rippon's *Selection* was "without doubt the single greatest factor in the extensive circulation of the best of Baptist hymnody created in one of their most productive periods."[121] Further,

---

White, 127-163; Sharon James, "John Rippon (1751-1836)," in *The British Particular Baptists, 1638-1910*, 2: 57-75.

[115] Rippon, preface to *A Selection of Hymns from the Best Authors*, the preface is unpaginated (italics in original).

[116] Richardson, "Baptist Contributions to Hymnody and Hymnology," 62.

[117] In 1791, Rippon published an accompanying tune book, which "pioneered the linking of hymns with particular tunes." Ken R. Manley, "Rippon, John (1751-1836)," *Oxford Dictionary of National Biography* (Oxford: Oxford University Press, 2003 [http://www.oxforddnb.com/view/article/23666, accessed 17 April 2006]).

[118] Rippon also included 101 hymns by Doddridge, 39 by Watts (from sources other than his *Hymns and Psalms*, since Rippon's *Selection* was intended as an appendix to that work), 34 from the *Gospel Magazine*, and 32 from *Olney Hymns*. The Baptist writers most represented are Steele, Beddome, and Samuel Stennett. See Ken R. Manley, "'Sing Side by Side': John Rippon and Baptist Hymnody," in *Pilgrim Pathways: Essays in Baptist History in Honour of B.R. White*, 132-133.

[119] Ibid., 153-154.

[120] Ibid., 162.

[121] Ibid. Manley explains Rippon's significance: "As M. Frost observed, the Independents had Watts as the basis of their hymnody, and the Methodists had the Wesleys' or Whitefield's collections; but…only with Rippon's *Selection* did the Baptists

Manley suggests that Rippon's hymnbook is an accurate indicator of "the devotional content of Baptist worship during his lifetime and is a valuable pointer to Baptist spirituality for the period."[122]

In this chapter, the eighteenth-century hymn has been introduced as a work of both theology and literature, and in the process, we have considered various representative hymn-writers and their compositions. We have seen how the eighteenth-century hymn was used to teach and transmit doctrine while simultaneously allowing for the heartfelt expression of Christian devotion in corporate worship, and we have observed various hymn-writers labouring to apply their poetic skills to serve their religious beliefs. In the following chapters, we will turn more specifically to the hymnody of Anne Steele and observe the points of convergence and divergence between her hymnody and the hymnody of those hymn-writers considered in this chapter. The following chapters will therefore clarify Steele's theology as well as illuminate her individual literary style. In the process, we will see how Steele's hymnody can be used as a "valuable pointer" toward her particular spirituality.

---

have a 'commanding nucleus round which to group their hymnody.'" Ibid., quoting M. Frost, ed., *Historical Companion to Hymns Ancient and Modern* (1962), 110.

[122] Manley, "'Sing Side by Side': John Rippon and Baptist Hymnody," in *Pilgrim Pathways: Essays in Baptist History in Honour of B.R. White*, 129.

CHAPTER 3

"How Shall These Poor Languid Powers... Display the Grace My Soul Adores?": Anne Steele and the Problem of Language

Anne Steele occupies an important place in the field of eighteenth-century hymnody, on account of both her impressive popularity and her unique contribution to the expression of Christian devotion. Her hymns sound a new note in eighteenth-century hymnody, largely because through them she introduces a self-conscious reflection on the ability of language to offer meaningful praise to God. She expresses considerable doubt regarding her personal ability to articulate praise while at the same time doubting the capacity of language itself to convey meaning when God is the subject. While this concern with the powers and limitations of language in relation to devotional expression is by no means new in literature and theology, Richard Arnold observes that Steele's preoccupation with it is "unprecedented in English hymnody."[1] And, since the genre of the hymn is necessarily verbal, Steele's lack of faith in language itself presents a notable problem for her as a hymn-writer.

Steele's struggle to communicate her understanding of God and the devotional life is central to a discussion of her hymnody. In one sense, her effort reveals a very personal battle with self-doubt and inarticulacy, while in another, larger sense, it conveys particular theological notions regarding the fundamental inability of language to express truth about God; in both senses, Steele aligns herself with other writers who express similar concerns with inexpressibility and ineffability.[2] Before exploring how Steele's reflection on

---

[1] Arnold, "A 'Veil of Interposing Night': The Hymns of Anne Steele," 376. While we saw in the previous chapter that William Cowper's hymns are also characterized by self-doubt, a distinction can be made here between a self-conscious subjectivity and hesitancy, which Cowper and Steele share, and a more fundamental questioning of the capacity of language, which is unique to Steele.

[2] An example of this ongoing concern with inexpressibility and ineffability can be found in the poem, "Salve caput cruentatum," originally written in Latin and attributed to Bernard of Clairvaux (1153). In the seventeenth century, this poem was translated into German by Paul Gernhardt (1656), and in the nineteenth century, it was translated into English by James Waddel Alexander (1830). The English translation is entitled "O

the problem of language found expression in her hymns specifically, it will be helpful to position Steele within a larger discussion of ineffability and to consider the theme broadly with reference to her life and writings. We will begin this chapter, then, by surveying Steele's thoughts on writing and language as they are recorded in her letters and verse.[3]

Anne Steele on Writing and Language

An analysis of the theme of ineffability in Steele's hymns first requires some understanding of her thoughts on the act of writing as well as on the power and limitations of language itself. Steele was a consistently self-conscious writer, a trait that can be traced through her letters, poems, and hymns. In both prose and verse she reflects on the role she, as writer, plays in the transference of meaning. She recognizes the unique talent she has as a writer, referring repeatedly to her "powers," and she associates those "powers" with her vocation to write works of praise to God. She writes:

> What is the business and the joy above,
> But this, to know, to worship, and to love?
> For this, my powers were given; this great employ
> Should be my ardent wish, my constant joy.[4]

We see that Steele had a strong sense of vocation as a writer. She considers that "the arduous, yet delightful employment for which this soul of mine was made" should be the primary focus of her personal energy, in order to fulfill the purpose for which her "powers" were given.[5] In a letter to her cousin, Marianna Attwater, Steele specifies that she understands her writing abilities, again referred to as her "powers," to be a "tallent intrusted" to her from God, for

---

Sacred Head, Now Wounded." The challenge of using imperfect human language to address a perfect God can be discerned in the following verse:
> What language shall I borrow to thank Thee, dearest friend,
> For this Thy dying sorrow, Thy pity without end?
> O make me Thine forever, and should I fainting be,
> Lord, let me never, never outlive my love to Thee.

"O Sacred Head, Now Wounded," The Cyber Hymnal (http://cyberhymnal.org/htm/o/s/osacredh.htm, accessed 13 January 2007).

[3] While Steele unfortunately did not leave a journal, her poems and hymns, along with nearly fifty extant letters, give us access to her recorded thoughts on various subjects and, therefore, while Steele's hymnody forms the primary focus of this book, her poems and correspondence will be used to develop a clearer picture of her character and spirituality.

[4] Steele, "Retirement and Meditation," *Poems on Subjects Chiefly Devotional*, II, 77.

[5] Steele, "Human Frailty," *Poems on Subjects Chiefly Devotional*, III, 159.

which she "must be accountable to our Great Maker."⁶

While Steele consciously and gratefully accepts the responsibility of her capacity to write, noting that her writing abilities belong to God and that God's mercies are her "chief" and "darling theme," she also expresses grief that her "powers" often fail her.⁷ She lacks confidence in her personal abilities. Even as she prepares her verse for publication, her "Mind with dark Ideas fill'd" as she judges her poetry to be "spiritless" ("How low the Line how dull the Page").⁸ This hesitancy and self-doubt regarding her writing abilities is illustrated in a series of letters written between Steele and her sister, Mary Steele Wakeford, in which we begin to form a picture of Steele as a writer and to perceive her thoughts on the powers and limitations of language. The correspondence begins shortly after Steele's sister marries Joseph Wakeford and leaves Broughton to reside in Andover, a distance of less than ten miles, but far enough to prevent the daily interaction previously enjoyed by the two sisters.⁹ As is common in the correspondence and verse written by and about Steele and her family and friends—and in keeping with the fashion of the day—the sisters use pseudonyms: Steele is Silviana while Wakeford is Amira.

In their correspondence, Steele and Wakeford specifically and self-consciously consider the act of writing. Immediately evident is the personal effort it takes each of them to write. Wakeford refers to letter-writing as a "forc'd scribble" and adds, "I believe it has cost me more labour then Youngs Night Tho'ts did him."¹⁰ Steele, for her part, considers her devotional writing "a

---

⁶ Steele to Marianna Attwater, undated, STE 3/12 (iii). In verse, Steele prays:
  O may I employ
  The fleeting remnant of my precious time
  In that important work for which 'tis given.
Steele, "The Complaint and Relief," *Poems on Subjects Chiefly Devotional*, II, 114.
⁷ Steele, "On Recovery from Sickness," *Poems on Subjects Chiefly Devotional*, III, 84.
⁸ Steele, "Reviewing My Verses for Publication," STE 3/3/1, p. 1.
⁹ Joseph Wakeford attended the Independent Church in Andover, and was friends with the Independent minister, Philip Furneaux (1726-1783). Wakeford likely introduced Steele to Furneaux, thereby initiating a relationship that would have significant consequences for Steele as a writer, since Furneaux helped Steele to publish *Poems on Subjects Chiefly Devotional* in 1760. Furneaux was a popular preacher and would rank, by the mid-1770s, "among the most highly regarded figures within English nonconformity," and be seen as "the leading ministerial champion of their rights." Alan Ruston, "Furneaux, Philip (1726-1783)," *Oxford Dictionary of National Biography* (Oxford: Oxford University Press, 2004 [http://www.oxforddnb.com/view/article/10249, accessed 20 April 2006]).
¹⁰ Mary Steele Wakeford to Steele, 4 July 1757, STE 3/10 (x). Edward Young (*bap.* 1683-1765) was a popular poet and playwright, and much admired in the Steele family circle. He is best known as the author of *The Complaint, or, Night-Thoughts on Life, Death, and Immortality* (1742-1746), a poem of nine "Nights," comprised of nearly 10,000 lines of blank verse. In the first of these nights, the "nocturnal speaker" of Young's poem laments "the loss of child, spouse, and friend," losses similarly endured

work of serious importance," but adds, "since it must be done, I wish it were finish'd."[11] Her weary tone reveals something of the effort it often took her to write and the effect that effort had on her personally; she writes, "I want to have my Mind calm and even."[12] Her manner also reflects the determination with which she approaches this task which she understands to have been given her by God.

A common theme in this letter sequence is the sisters' mutual feelings of diffidence. In a series of letters in which Steele and Wakeford refer to Steele's writing as her "Flowers," which are cultivated by God and watered with the "Dews of Heaven," Steele remarks that if her writing is found to be "pleasurable to my fellow Travellers, and acceptable to the Great Donour" she will be happy "in the reflection of having communicated what I have received."[13] But this deferential acceptance is lost by the next line of her letter

---

by Young in the years prior to the publication of *Night-Thoughts*. James E. May, "Young, Edward (*bap.* 1683, *d.* 1765)," *Oxford Dictionary of National Biography* (Oxford: Oxford University Press, 2004 [http://www.oxforddnb.com/view/article/30260, accessed 10 July 2006]). Young's *Night-Thoughts* is often referenced in the writing of the various Steele family members. Steele wrote an unpublished poem entitled "On Dr. Youngs Night Thoughts," in which she lauds Young's poetic genius. STE 3/3/2, p. 25.

[11] Steele to Mary Steele Wakeford, undated, STE 3/10 (iii).

[12] Ibid.

[13] Ibid. Also in this letter, Steele responds to her sister's encouragement to consider the recent marriage proposal of "a gentle Swain"; Steele refuses, saying that she is happy alone and that her view of life married to this unnamed gentleman appears devoid of "flowers" and complicated by "a great many thorns, and I suppose there are more hid under the leaves." While Steele acknowledges that this "gentle Swain" is a "Good and worthy Man," in composing her letter something compels her to cross out the words "I rank him among my Friends." Steele to Mary Steele Wakeford, undated, STE 3/10 (ii). Steele prefers to pursue her "quiet way alone" in the "Ever-verdant Groves" where her art is stimulated by "the Muse...and Contemplation." Steele to Mary Steele Wakeford, undated, STE 3/10 (iii). Wakeford responds, again urging Steele to reconsider marriage ("why pray shouldn't you conform to custom as well as otherfolk?"), yet she concedes that if Steele will not marry, Wakeford wishes Steele well in her writing—in her "frequent journeys to those evergreen Groves." Mary Steele Wakeford to Steele, 10 November 1757, STE 3/10 (xiii). It is significant that in this letter exchange both sisters seem to understand that if Steele were to choose marriage she would choose also to relinquish at least some of her writing which, as we have seen, she understood to be a God-given task.

For further evidence of Steele and Wakeford's conflicting notions regarding marriage and singleness, see Steele's unpublished poem, "A Dialogue," which takes the form of a conversation between Steele as Silviana and Wakeford as Amira. In it, Amira argues that marriage is a preferable state, for "single folks" are burdened by cares in the form of "Some lurking disquietude racking their breasts / Some love in a corner oft breaking their rest," commenting further on the "terrour from wrinkles" that single women must certainly experience. Silviana, for her part, counters that singleness is a

when she complains that a "Cloud of diffidence" prevents her from hoping for anything more than the obliging ears of her friends.[14] Wakeford responds, assuring Steele that her "printing is to be sure a thing of serious importance" and that she has "no reason to be at all uneasy about it."[15] Wakeford, for her part, complains that she cannot write because she cannot "think any thing into words, & might as well atempt to fetch music out of a post"; Steele expresses a similar frustration, distressed that "every lively thought" is "lost in a stupid inattention."[16] Steele is troubled that, while at certain times she has been able to engage fruitfully in her "necessary and indispensable work," of late she has lost her ability to engage in that work; she cannot write as she wishes she could.[17] In another letter, when Steele plays the encourager to a self-doubting Wakeford, Steele hopes that when her current "writing fit" passes, as she is certain it will, Wakeford will encourage her similarly: "if I talk of unworthiness, call it compliment, and if I plead incapacity tell me 'tis only diffidence." She adds, "I have much reason to be disatisfy'd with my self, much cause of complaint as well as you," but hopes that she and Wakeford can serve and encourage each other by "endeavouring to enliven each other."[18]

This series of letters between Steele and her sister effectively reveals the self-doubt and hesitancy that Steele regularly experienced with regard to her writing. She was revisited with doubts about her abilities, and while she enjoyed success from time to time, she worried that each time would be the last—that her "powers" would ultimately fail her. Steele consistently used the classical language of the muse to describe her inspiration to write, so her failure

---

preferable state, referring to the "chains" and "fetters" of marriage which are willingly assumed only when women bid "friend Reason adieu." While Amira argues for "the pleasure of love & obey," Silviana declares that when women marry they "give up their freedom in one fatal day." Steele, "A Dialogue," STE 3/3/1, pp. 38-44. The dialogue was a fashionable form of poetry in the eighteenth century.

[14] Steele to Mary Steele Wakeford, undated, STE 3/10 (iii).

[15] Mary Steele Wakeford to Steele, 10 November 1757, STE 3/10 (xiii).

[16] Mary Steele Wakeford to Steele, 23 July 1757, STE 3/10 (xii); Steele to Mary Steele Wakeford, undated, STE 3/10 (ix). Wakeford was herself something of a poet; the Steele Collection in the Angus Library contains a manuscript notebook of her poetry. See STE 10/2.

[17] Steele to Mary Steele Wakeford, undated, STE 3/10 (ix).

[18] Steele to Mary Steele Wakeford, undated, STE 3/10 (xiv). The sisters began their correspondence in an effort to express their "serious tho'ts" to each other and thereby reflect on and improve their devotional experiences. Mary Steele Wakeford to Steele, 23 September 1749, STE 3/10 (i). Steele asserts that "Religious Conversation," such as that in which she and her sister proposed to engage, is a means by which believers can "provoke one another to love & to good works." Steele to Mary Steele Wakeford, undated, STE 3/10 (ii). Similarly, Steele asks, "Why my dear Sister do we not endeavour more to quicken and animate each other?" Steele to Mary Steele Wakeford, undated, STE 3/10 (iii).

in writing was attributed to her abandonment by the muse.[19] She writes, for example:

> To tune my Lyre I sought in vain
> With pensive thought and akeing head
> I try'd the jarring strings again
> And wonder'd where the Muse was fled.[20]

Her abandonment by the muse is similarly lamented in this unpublished poem:

> No more the Muses haunt the flow'ry scenes
> Nor bind your temples with immortal greens
> No more in joyous strains your notes prolong
> The listening Groves no more approve the song[21]

Steele locates her poetic inspiration in the "Ever-verdant Groves" where she is sometimes favoured by the company of the muse.[22] This preferred sylvan setting may be related to her choice of a familial pseudonym: Silviana.

---

[19] It was fashionable in the eighteenth century for poets to ascribe their literary inspiration to the muse. Steele's verse is replete with this classical reference. In various poems, she also refers to specific muses who were recognized to inspire particular arts. Melpomene, it was said, inspired tragedy. See Steele, untitled, STE 3/3/6, no. 26. Urania, for her part, was the muse of astrology and was associated with love and the Holy Spirit. See, for example, Steele, "The Absent Muse," *Poems on Subjects Chiefly Devotional*, I, 233; Steele, "Eusebia and Urania, or Devotion and the Muse," *Poems on Subjects Chiefly Devotional*, II, 102; Steele, untitled, STE 3/3/1, pp. 20-24.

[20] Steele, "Silviana," STE 3/3/1, p. 54. A further example of Steele's reflection on her disappointing inability to write, and her attributing this fact to the muse's absence, is found in this more light-hearted poem:
> Ah when are now those happy times
> When I cou'd laugh & scribble rhymes
> Then fancy tho't the muses nigh
> Alas for my poor stupid head
> The Muses & the rhymes are fled

Steele, untitled, STE 3/3/6, no. 31.

[21] Steele, "A Pastoral Elegy," STE 3/3/6, no. 36.

[22] Steele to Mary Steele Wakeford, undated, STE 3/10 (iii). John Sheppard, in his 1863 memoir of Steele, refers to her composing her verse in the garden at "The Grandfathers." Sheppard's comment is partly conjectural, but he does suggest that "family tradition" supports his claim. Sheppard, "Memoir," in *Hymns, Psalms, and Poems, by Anne Steele*, vii-viii. See also Steele's unpublished poem, "On the Walks of Bath May 1751," where she remarks on her difficulties in composing verse when she is surrounded by the "laughing Crowd" and "gay Parades" on the walks of Bath. She longs instead for the "Sylvan Muse" who visits her when she is at home among her "Dear Native rural Scenes." Steele, "On the Walks of Bath May 1751," STE 3/3/6, no. 21.

The influence of the classical style on Steele can be perceived in the frontispieces appearing in the three volumes of her *Poems on Subjects Chiefly Devotional*. The frontispiece of volume I (see Figure 5) shows two women dressed in classical flowing robes. The woman on the left, with a Bible open in her hand and a cross on her breast, raises her right arm toward heaven and in the distance are seen the ruins of a classical temple.[23] While the woman on the left points upward, the woman on the right looks down demurely; behind her is a wooded glade which is, perhaps, Steele's "Ever-verdant Grove." The scene suggests that the standing woman is instructing the seated woman in matters of religion, drawing her attention beyond earthly realities toward God. Traditional iconography used an open book to symbolize knowledge, so that here, the open Bible is used to represent revealed knowledge, a vital element of Steele's faith as a Particular Baptist.[24]

Steele's verse often combines the classical and religious in this way. She introduces her second volume of *Poems on Subjects Chiefly Devotional* with a poem entitled "The Invocation." In it, she appeals to the muse to inspire her imagination and enable her song. Yet she combines this classical invocation with a further appeal to "heaven-born Faith, fair seraph," exclaiming, "How weak the muse's power without thy aid!"[25] This baptizing of the muse is illustrated further in Steele's poem, "Eusebia and Urania, or Devotion and the Muse," where Eusebia represents Christian devotion and Urania is one of the nine classical muses. The poem begins with a standard appeal to the muse:

---

[23] In the figure of the standing woman are found allusions to three central themes in Steele's hymnody and spirituality: Scripture, Christ, and heaven. We will consider these themes in detail later in this book.

[24] For an eighteenth-century lexicon of icons, see George Richardson, *Iconology; or, a Collection of Emblematical Figures; Containing Four Hundred and Twenty-Four Remarkable Subjects, Moral and Instructive; in which are Displayed the Beauty of Virtue and Deformity of Vice. The Figures are Engraved by the Most Capital Artists, from Original Designs; with Explanations from Classical Authorities* (London: G. Scott, 1779). Richardson's popular book is an English edition of Cesare Ripa's *Iconologia* (1593), which provided explanations for classical iconic figures. Richardson (1737/8-c. 1813) was an architect much influenced by a trip to Rome in which he grew to love the classical buildings there. His influential *Iconology* was subscribed to by "most of the principal architects, painters, sculptors, designers, craftsmen, manufacturers, patrons, and connoisseurs." Iain Gordon Brown, "Richardson, George (1737/8-c. 1813)," *Oxford Dictionary of National Biography* (Oxford: Oxford University Press, 2004 [http://www.oxforddnb.com/view/article/23553, accessed 23 November 2006]). Steele's use of emblematic illustrations as frontispieces highlights the eighteenth-century aesthetic ideal, discussed in the previous chapter, which supported a model of art as both instructive and pleasing. This ideal is observed in icons generally, and in Steele's frontispieces more specifically.

[25] Steele, "The Invocation," *Poems on Subjects Chiefly Devotional*, II, 3.

Figure 5: Frontispiece of the first volume of *Poems on Subjects Chiefly Devotional*

> Say, dear Urania, silent why so long
> I languish for thy sweet reviving song.
> Wilt thou unkind, neglect a Sister's moan,
> And leave me wretched to complain alone?

But very quickly Christian devotion is introduced into this conventional scene, for it is the "active life" of Eusebia, or devotion enabled by God's grace, that must "wake the silent strings."[26] Showing how nature and grace together inspire her song, Steele succinctly states, "when Eusebia breathes, Urania sings."[27]

The picture of Steele as writer is defined further by her comments regarding the quality of her verse and her opinion regarding whether it should be published. In an unpublished poem, Steele is self-deprecating with regard to her art. She writes, "I sometimes have a Rhyming fit," further claiming that she makes "no great pretence / To poetry."[28] She concludes the poem with these self-conscious words:

> If your Goodnature ask no farther
>   My worthless Rhymes to see
> I wish you merry but had rather
>   You would not laugh at me[29]

She feels that her "worthless Rhymes" are not worthy of being published. When her niece, Mary Steele Dunscombe, urges her to submit some of her verse to the *Gentleman's Magazine* for publication, Steele protests that her "triffling stuff" does not "charm the ear or touch the heart."[30] While friends and family have obliged her, she doubts that her "untaught airs" will please amid the "politer scenes" that have been used to the verse of her literary heroes: John Milton, James Hervey, and Edward Young.[31] Indeed, while she reminds herself,

---

[26] Steele, "Eusebia and Urania, or Devotion and the Muse," *Poems on Subjects Chiefly Devotional*, II, 102.
[27] Ibid.
[28] Steele, untitled, STE 3/3/1, p. 104.
[29] Ibid.
[30] Steele, "On Being Desired to Send Some Verses to the Gentlemans Magazine," STE 3/3/1, p. 56.
[31] Steele, "To Lysander," *Poems on Subjects Chiefly Devotional*, I, 190. Lysander was a pseudonym assumed within the Steele family circle by John Lavington (*c.* 1690-1759), a Presbyterian minister with a congregation in Exeter from 1715. He played a prominent role in the Exeter Trinitarian controversy of the early eighteenth century, taking an orthodox view while others held Arian beliefs. David L. Wykes, "Lavington, John (*c.* 1690-1759)," *Oxford Dictionary of National Biography* (Oxford: Oxford University Press, 2004 [http://www.oxforddnb.com/view/article/16137, accessed 20 April 2006]). Lavington belonged to the writing circle which gathered around Steele and he is known to have visited Broughton in May 1751, along with Philip Furneaux. Anne Cator Steele

"I must believe that I once *cou'd* write to please my Friends," her diffidence does not allow her to hope for more than that.³²

Steele compares her "worthless Rhymes" to the verse of other, more famous writers and finds her own wanting. Young's words, for example, rise on "soaring pinions," while hers "faintly fluttering try / To raise their feeble wings" but in the end disappointingly "sink to Earth."³³ Elsewhere, she exclaims, "O could I write like Watts," but again she laments her inabilities.³⁴ She longs to be blessed with

>   the animating fire
> That tun'd harmonious Watt's lyre,
>   To sweet seraphic strains!³⁵

Young and Watts, of course, were admirable writers, and Steele may have been correct in finding her own verse inferior to theirs in quality. Yet much of her verse is fine poetry, an assessment which she heard regularly from encouraging

---

diary, 15 May 1751, STE 2/1/2. Steele was absent from Broughton in 1751 when Lavington and Furneaux visited, ill health having drawn her to Bath with her sister-in-law, Mary Bullock Steele. Steele gives an account of their visit in an unpublished poem, "By Mr. Lavington on Visiting Broughton with Dr. Furneaux," STE 3/3/1, pp. 89-91.

James Hervey (1714-1758) was a favourite in the Steele family circle. He was the author of *Meditations and Contemplations* (1746-1747) and *Theron and Aspasio* (1755), both of which were lauded by Steele in verse; see, for example, Steele, "To Mr. Hervey on His Theron and Aspasio," *Poems on Subjects Chiefly Devotional*, II, 69; Steele, "On Reading Mr. Hervey's Meditations," *Poems on Subjects Chiefly Devotional*, I, 211. Steele also wrote a poem of mourning on the death of Hervey: Steele, "On the Death of Mr. Hervey," *Poems on Subjects Chiefly Devotional*, II, 71. Hervey was an extremely popular author with an affected, classically polite style. While he was educated at Lincoln College, Oxford, where he came under the influence of John Wesley, his *Theron and Aspasio* introduced a great controversy over the doctrine of imputed righteousness, and drew sharp criticism from Wesley. Isabel Rivers, "Hervey, James (1714-1758)," *Oxford Dictionary of National Biography* (Oxford: Oxford University Press, 2004 [http://www.oxforddnb.com/view/article/13113, accessed 6 July 2006]).

[32] Steele to Mary Steele Wakeford, undated, STE 3/10 (ix). Elsewhere she writes, "I hardly dare hope for more than obliging my Friends." Steele to Mary Steele Wakeford, undated, STE 3/10 (iii). Recall also that Caleb Evans, in his prefatory "Advertisement" to volume III of the 1780 edition of *Poems on Subjects Chiefly Devotional*, records that "it was not without extreme reluctance she was prevailed on to submit [her verse] to the public eye." Evans, "Advertisement," in *Poems on Subjects Chiefly Devotional*, III, vii.

[33] Steele, "On Dr. Youngs Night Thoughts," STE 3/3/2, p. 25. Similarly, Steele cautions herself against aspiring to the literary heights of Milton and Young: "But aim not, my ambitious song, / To rise with Milton, or with Young." Steele, "Ode on a Rural Prospect in June," *Poems on Subjects Chiefly Devotional*, III, 43.

[34] Steele, "On Being Desired to Write on the Death of Dr. Watts," STE 3/3/2, pp. 13-14.

[35] Steele, "Christ the Christian's Life," *Poems on Subjects Chiefly Devotional*, II, 109.

family and friends.[36] One wonders if Steele's protestations reveal nothing more than a careful modesty.

One might question, as well, if Steele's self-effacing remarks reveal something about her experience as a woman writing in the eighteenth century. We have noted that as a woman writing about sacred subjects, Steele challenged the boundaries of what was considered socially and theologically acceptable behaviour. Convention encouraged women's demure silence, particularly in matters of religion. In addition, Steele's culture elevated modesty as a particularly feminine virtue. The anonymous author of the popular *The Whole Duty of a Woman* (1737), for example, writes, "As a Man without Courage is said to be no Man, so a Woman without Modesty is as much out of Nature and Kind."[37] So, while the eighteenth century did introduce increased

---

[36] An unpublished poem by Steele is suggestive of the kind of encouragement she received from her brother-in-law, Joseph Wakeford, who assumed the familial pseudonym, Portius. The poem also offers an interesting commentary on Steele's religious milieu, which was suspicious of both Catholicism and "enthusiasm":

> By Portius hand the works I've done
> How exquisitely painted
> If he was Pope and I a Nun
> I surely shou'd be sainted
> Each fragment, then, which scaped the flame
> A relique would be counted
> And now and then on wings of fame
> A miracle be mounted
>
> But since we're Protestants you know
> And no not aim at flying
> Enthusiastic flights forgoe
> With common sense complying

Steele, untitled, STE 3/3/1, p. 88. The Steele Collection also contains a letter from Richard Pearsall to Joseph Wakeford, which Pearsall asked Wakeford to forward to Steele. In his letter, Pearsall generously praises Steele's published hymns and poems: "When Grace is joined to such Gifts, lively Imagination to such purity of Soul, Devout Affections to so fine a Fancy; and when Humility lays the Soul low as a Sinner before the Cross and Throne, while the Mind soars in speculation; how charming the conjunction!" According to Pearsall, Steele's pseudonym, Theodosia, which means gift of God, was "a proper name indeed." Richard Pearsall to Joseph Wakeford, undated, STE 3/6/4. Richard Pearsall (1698-1762) was an Independent minister at Warminster in Wiltshire from 1731 until he moved to Taunton in 1747. He corresponded with, among others, Philip Doddridge, George Whitefield, and James Hervey, and published several poems, devotional meditations, tracts, sermons, and letters. W.A. Shaw, "Pearsall, Richard (1698-1762)," rev. Karen E. Smith, *Oxford Dictionary of National Biography* (Oxford: Oxford University Press, 2004 [http://www.oxforddnb.com/view/article/21701, accessed 22 November 2006]).

[37] *The Whole Duty of a Woman: Or, an Infallible Guide to the Fair Sex* (London: T. Read, 1737), 4.

opportunities for women to appear in print, there remained an expectation that women who published should, in Katharine Rogers's words, "respect convention and disclaim ambition."[38] In fact, in publishing her hymns under a pseudonym, "Theodosia," Steele distinguished herself from her many male counterparts. Marilyn Williamson identifies a group of eighteenth-century women writers who "seldom write for money" and who "hesitate to publish or call attention to themselves," further noting that this group of writers often used pseudonyms.[39] Significantly, Elizabeth Singer Rowe and Anne Dutton, other early women hymn-writers, also used pseudonyms or published anonymously.

Eighteenth-century assumptions about femininity likely did contribute to Steele's reflections on the act of writing, as her language suggests a conventional feminine reticence, yet the situation is surely more complex than this. Steele protests that her skill as a poet often falters and that she cannot compose verse as she would wish; she insists that where better poets can communicate meaningfully, she cannot find the words; and her demurring attitude to her own writing is in keeping with eighteenth-century feminine ideals. However, when Steele's thoughts on language itself are considered, it becomes evident that the failure of speech as she experiences and conveys it is not merely "a matter of individual character and aesthetics" or a matter of gender but, rather, that in articulating her failures she discloses something fundamental about her ideas regarding the nature and limitations of language itself.[40]

Steele's inability to express herself adequately cannot be explained as primarily a personal failure; in a larger sense, she saw her failure as a participation in the common experience of being encumbered by flawed human language. That is, language itself prevents Steele from being able to say what she means; the tools with which she was equipped to exercise her "powers" were themselves flawed, causing her words to fall short of her meaning on any given subject. She doubts the power of language to express adequately even her good wishes on the marriage of a friend:

> Here my ideas here my soaring wishes
> Are lost eer faint slow words can follow them.[41]

---

[38] Katharine M. Rogers, *Feminism in Eighteenth-Century England* (Urbana, IL: University of Illinois Press, 1982), 23.

[39] Marilyn Williamson, *Raising Their Voices: British Women Writers, 1650-1750* (Detroit: Wayne State University Press, 1990), 21-22, 108.

[40] Heather McClave, "Tongued with Fire: The Primitive Terror and The Word in T.S. Eliot," in *Ineffability: Naming the Unnamable from Dante to Beckett*, ed. Peter S. Hawkins and Anne Howland Schotter, AMS ARS Poetica, no. 2 (New York: AMS Press, 1984), 163.

[41] Steele, "To a Friend on His Marriage Oct. 6 1743," STE 3/3/2, p. 34.

This claim to inarticulacy could be understood as a topos, such as is commonly invoked in statements such as, "I cannot tell you how much I love you," or its eighteenth-century equivalent, "Words cannot describe the ardency of my flame."[42] While her language sometimes does find echoes in conventional expressions of inarticulacy, the notion of inexpressibility has a greater meaning in Steele's verse, revealing something essential about her spirituality.

Most often, language fails Steele when she attempts to articulate meaning about God and the devotional life. According to Steele, God's grace and mercy are so far beyond human understanding that human language cannot express it:

> How shall my heart receive the vast idea,
> Or feeble words express it? Scanty power
> Of human thought—the force of language fails[43]

Similarly:

> But O, in vain our humble songs
> Attempt the honours of thy Name,
> Too weak our words too low our tongues
> Thy countless favours to proclaim.[44]

Steele accepts her God-given vocation—the task of writing hymns and poetry about God and the religious life—but she also acknowledges her requisite failure, hindered as she is by the limitations of human language.

Steele's hesitancy with regard to her capacity to use words and her failure to express her understanding of God is, of course, not unique. In communicating this lack of faith in language where God is the subject of her searching for words, Steele articulates the classic spiritual theme of the ineffability of God. Even as Steele herself experienced the frequent frustration of inarticulacy, she recognized in God the related quality of ineffability. Ineffability refers to the failure of language to be able to put something into words; it signifies that which is too great for words, transcending expression. It is often used in reference to God. The theme of ineffability has a long history in literature and theology.

---

[42] Eliza Fowler Haywood, *The History of Miss Betsy Thoughtless*, 2nd ed. (London: T. Gardner, 1751), 3: 6.

[43] Steele, "Hope Reviving in the Contemplation of Divine Mercy," *Poems on Subjects Chiefly Devotional*, II, 97.

[44] Steele, "On the Same," STE 3/1/4, no. 9 (the previous poem was entitled "On Nov. 29th a Day of Thanksgiving for National Blessings").

Ineffability in Literature and Theology

For centuries, poets and theologians alike have laboured to express the ineffable. In religion, ineffability refers to the experience of being unable to find adequate words to articulate truth about God. Since God is in an essential sense mysterious and unknowable, human words are incapable of communicating truth about him. This idea has been reiterated by centuries of Christians, dating back to the early Church Fathers. Augustine (354-430), for example, writes of his desire, and subsequent failure, to speak about God:

> Have I spoken something, have I uttered something, worthy of God? No, I feel that all I have done is wish to speak; if I did say something, it is not what I wanted to say.[45]

Augustine's desire fuels his attempt to convey meaningful praise to God, but his desire cannot compensate for the fact that God is profoundly "unspeakable."[46] Also in the fourth century, Gregory of Nyssa (c. 330-379) expresses his own failure with words and his own understanding of God, noting that God is "incapable of being grasped by any term, or any idea, or any other device of our apprehension, remaining...above all expression in words."[47] Pseudo-Dionysius, in the fifth century, wonders how frail humanity can attempt to speak about "the Transcendent" if it

> surpasses all discourse and all knowledge, if it abides beyond the reach of mind and of being, if it encompasses and circumscribes, embraces and anticipates all things whilst itself eluding their grasp and escaping from any perception, imagination, opinion, name, discourse, apprehension, or understanding? How can we enter upon this undertaking if the Godhead is superior to being and is unspeakable and unnameable?[48]

Pseudo-Dionysius's experience of ineffability is absolute; he believed that when we encounter God, we "find ourselves not simply running short of words but actually speechless and unknowing."[49]

---

[45] Augustine, *On Christian Doctrine*, ed. and trans. R.P.H. Green (Oxford: Clarendon Press, 1995), 17.
[46] Ibid.
[47] Gregory of Nyssa, *Against Eunomius*, trans. William Moore and Henry Austin Wilson, The Nicene and Post-Nicene Fathers, series II, vol. 5 (Grand Rapids, MI: Eerdmans, 1957), 99, quoted in John Hick, "Ineffability," *Religious Studies* 36, no. 1 (March 2000): 37.
[48] Pseudo-Dionysius, *The Divine Names*, in *The Complete Works of Pseudo-Dionysius*, trans. Colm Luibheid, Classics of Western Spirituality (New York: Paulist Press, 1987), 53.
[49] Pseudo-Dionysius, *The Mystical Theology*, in *The Complete Works of Pseudo-Dionysius*, 139.

Pseudo-Dionysius's views regarding the inadequacy of language to describe God were influential in forming the views of classic mystical writers such as Meister Eckhart, Julian of Norwich, and the author of *The Cloud of Unknowing*. They affirmed that, where God is the subject, all words and their meaning break down. Meister Eckhart (1260-1327) states it simply and rather starkly: "All words fail...nothing true can be spoken of God...no one can express what he actually is."[50] The mystics, in fact, believed that the closer one draws to God, the source of all knowledge and language, the less one is able to articulate anything meaningful about God and the religious experience.[51] In their view, the closer one is drawn to God, the greater the darkness that veils God's presence; the closer one comes to God, the more one comes to know God in a way that cannot be verbalized. Julian of Norwich (*c.* 1342-1420), writing in the fourteenth century, uses simple images to hint at meaning where she feels that more complex language would fail. According to Belden Lane, "The only way [Julian] knew how to convey what she had experienced was to offer tiny images that reduced language to a bare minimum"; she uses, for example, the image of a hazelnut to reflect on the enormity of God's goodness and love.[52] The anonymous fourteenth-century author of *The Cloud of Unknowing* seems about to attempt to speak about "the ineffable secrets of [God's] divine wisdom" but stops himself:

> I am at a loss to say more, for the experience is beyond words. Even if I were able to say more I would not now. For I dare not try to describe God's grace with my crude and awkward tongue. In a word, even if I dared I would not.[53]

The mystics maintain that when the soul approaches union with God, all human language fails because the experience of God transcends the power of words to convey.

---

[50] Meister Eckhart, *The Works of Meister Eckhart*, trans. C. de B. Evans (New York: Lucis Publishing Co., 1924), 82, quoted in Winston L. King, "Negation as a Religious Category," *The Journal of Religion* 37, no. 2 (April 1957): 107.

[51] Pseudo-Dionysius stated that the closer we get to God, "the more language falters." Pseudo-Dionysius, *The Mystical Theology*, in *The Complete Works of Pseudo-Dionysius*, 139. Mark McIntosh explains Pseudo-Dionysius's negative theology: "the crucial point is that the final stage of this journey [to God] is not the silence which is utterly null and void of meaning but the silence of embrace, unity with God who unspeakably comes forth from divine life in order to draw what is not divine into divinity." Mark A. McIntosh, *Mystical Theology: The Integrity of Spirituality and Theology*, Challenges in Contemporary Theology (Oxford: Blackwell Publishing, 1998), 55.

[52] Belden C. Lane, *The Solace of Fierce Landscapes: Exploring Desert and Mountain Spirituality* (New York: Oxford University Press, 1998), 68; Julian of Norwich, *Revelation of Love*, ed. and trans. John Skinner (New York: Image Books, 1996), 9-11.

[53] *The Cloud of Unknowing*, ed. and intro. by William Johnston (New York: Image Books, 1973), 84.

In language that is reminiscent of the medieval mystics, George Steiner extends the discussion of the theme of ineffability to poets: "As the poet draws near the Divine presence, the heart of the rose of fire, the labour of translation into speech grows ever more exacting. Words grow less and less adequate to the task of translating immediate revelation."[54] Poets have long struggled with this "labour of translation," accepting the burden of using language that is certain to fail. Religious poets experience this failure on two sides: as we have already seen in Steele, they experience the personal frustration of not being able to find the words to convey what they want to express; furthermore, they experience the related defeat associated with the inability of language to translate adequately the experience of God into words. They cannot press language to "contract the *Logos* into the word."[55] Faced with failure, the task of the poet remains to toil with words.

A great many Christian poets have wrestled with the problem of communicating their religious understanding and experience of divine mysteries. This list includes such noted poets as Dante Alighieri and T.S. Eliot, for both of whom the themes of inexpressibility and ineffability were of pivotal importance in their verse. Stuart Peterfreund ranks Dante (1265-1321) as "perhaps the greatest poet of the ineffable."[56] In the *Paradiso*, Dante has a vision of the Trinity, "conceives its significance, and then attempts to imitate both vision and conception in language which proves unequal to its task."[57] Language cannot contain the vision he was given by God. Dante believed that "the poet is a prophet and teacher" and thereby that he had vital meaning to convey to his readers, meaning that had been revealed by God. Yet the inadequacy of language thwarted his divinely-given task and so he was able only to gesture, inarticulately, toward God.[58]

---

[54] George Steiner, *Language and Silence: Essays 1958-1966* (London: Faber and Faber, 1967), 60.

[55] Ibid.

[56] Peterfreund adds, "In the *Paradiso* the poet speaks haltingly, in language which is full of self-negation and deprecation, of the inability of his language to assume its expressive burden." Stuart Peterfreund, "The Two Languages and the Ineffable in Shelley's Major Poetry," in *Ineffability*, 124.

[57] Ibid., 125. For Dante, the problem of language is also experienced in his attempt to write about his love for Beatrice. In her study of Dante's poetic theory, Marcia Colish notes Dante's comments on the limits of poetry when "he says that he must hold his peace until he is able to write a poem truly worthy of Beatrice, a task which he regards his art as now inadequate to perform." Marcia L. Colish, *The Mirror of Language: A Study in the Medieval Theory of Knowledge* (New Haven: Yale University Press, 1968), 249. Colish references Dante, *Vita nuova*, XLII, 1-2.

[58] Colish, *The Mirror of Language*, 225. In his study of the theme of ineffability in Dante, Peter Hawkins writes, "A straightforward declaration [of] what the poet is about to tell us cannot, in fact, be put into words. Given this basic limit of language, the most he can do is bear witness with this, his mute essemplo, thereby pointing the reader to

Moving ahead to the twentieth century, T.S. Eliot (1888-1965) expresses the task of the poet using the evocative phrase, "a raid on the inarticulate."[59] In Eliot's mind, great and possibly reckless courage was needed in the attempt to use human language to articulate one's understanding of a God who is beyond human language. His experience of the world as a place of suffering, and his attempts to articulate meaning in that world, caused him to despair of the possibilities of language:

> So here I am, in the middle way, having had twenty years—
> Twenty years largely wasted, the years of *l'entre deux guerres*
> Trying to learn to use words, and every attempt
> Is a wholly new start, and a different kind of failure[60]

For Eliot, the possibilities and limits of language mingle as the writer is compelled to approach the "frontiers of consciousness beyond which words fail, though meanings still exist."[61] Language was woefully "shabby equipment" and, where meaning had "once or twice, or several times" been articulated, it had been the work of "men whom one cannot hope / To emulate."[62] Yet still Eliot was obligated to try—"For us, there is only the trying"—to make once more his "raid on the inarticulate" in order to attempt to convey his experience of God's presence, and seeming absence, in the world.[63] The duty of the religious poet is, in Steiner's words, to bring back "one single spark" from "that literally unspeakable light and glory."[64]

Ineffability and Anne Steele

So we return to Anne Steele, having demonstrated that the problem of language in her verse has been similarly addressed by ample and noteworthy predecessors and successors. While Steele's struggle with language can be understood, in part, by aligning her with others who express similar themes in their writing, the notion of ineffability in her verse will be realized further by considering her particular religious convictions. Here, we will probe further the idea of ineffability in Steele's writing, in an attempt to understand the foundations and meaning of this theme in her verse. Along the way, we will ask

---

that beatitude which he can himself neither remember nor describe." Peter Hawkins, "Dante's *Paradiso* and the Dialectic of Ineffability," in *Ineffability*, 8.

[59] T.S. Eliot, "East Coker," in *Four Quartets* (San Diego: Harcourt, 1943), 31.

[60] Ibid., 30-31.

[61] T.S. Eliot, *On Poetry and Poets* (London: Faber and Faber, 1957), 30.

[62] Eliot, "East Coker," in *Four Quartets*, 31. Compare Eliot's unfavourable comparison of his work to that of "men whom one cannot hope / To emulate" with Steele's comparison of her own verse to that of Watts and Young, considered earlier.

[63] Ibid.

[64] Steiner, *Language and Silence*, 60.

particular questions about the significance of ineffability in hymns as a genre.

Steele's frustration with her own inabilities to articulate her experience of God was related to the views she held regarding sin. For, as she understood her writing to be a divinely-ordained task, she attributed her failure to accomplish that task to be a result of her straying from God. Just when she determined to dedicate her "powers" to God, her "weak inconstant mind" was tempted away by "Trifles, as empty as the wind."[65] She complains:

> In vain I charge my thoughts to stay,
> And chide each vanity away,
> In vain, alas! resolve to bind
> This rebel heart, this wandering mind.[66]

In her verse and letters, Steele repeatedly admonishes herself for her proclivity to sinfulness; she is bothered by her "stupid inattention," her "languid" tendencies; she considers her failure to complete God's work to be a result of her "inexcusable…guilty lethargy."[67] She challenges herself, pointedly, "how can I open my polluted lips in the presence of infinite purity?"[68]

Steele expresses a significant measure of self-doubt with regard to her abilities to articulate praise to God, and she attributes her failure to her own personal sinfulness. Yet we have seen that Steele also expresses a lack of confidence in the powers of language more generally, and this has to do with her perception of language as fallen, even as the world is fallen.[69] In a poem

---

[65] Steele, "Resigning the Heart to God," *Poems on Subjects Chiefly Devotional*, I, 117-118.

[66] Steele, "The Inconstant Heart," *Poems on Subjects Chiefly Devotional*, I, 119.

[67] Steele to Mary Steele Wakeford, undated, STE 3/10 (ix). As early as 1736, when Steele was just nineteen years of age, she complains in a letter to her brother, William Steele, "Alas my mind is cover'd with a senseless stupidity." While the occasion of Steele's complaint was a visit to Trowbridge, a far busier and noisier town than her native Broughton ("the continual din of a noisey town, seems to dull my sences, and turn my tho'ts all into confusion"), Steele is careful to attribute the blame for her "stupidity" to her own "carelessness which sinks me into such a dead inactive frame; and dulls the nobler faculties of my soul." Steele to William Steele, 27 June 1736, STE 3/8 (i). In verse, Steele again berates herself for the lethargy which prevents her from writing effectively:
> What death-like lethargy detains
> My captive powers with fatal art,
> And spreads its unrelenting chains
> Heavy and cold, around my heart!
Steele, "Cold Affections," *Poems on Subjects Chiefly Devotional*, I, 121.

[68] Steele, "God's Omnipresence," *Poems on Subjects Chiefly Devotional*, III, 194-195.

[69] Steele's belief that fallen language is a hopeless tool with which to craft meaning is similarly expressed by the poet George Herbert (1593-1633). Robert Shaw notes that, according to Herbert, "the divine gift by which Adam named the beasts in Paradise has

that refers to people as "wretched Sinners," Steele wonders how we can use "imperfect" language to address a perfect God.[70] She enlarges on the theme in her poem, "Desiring to Praise God for the Experience of His Goodness":

> Ah how shall these poor languid powers
> With frail mortality opprest,
> Display the grace my soul adores?
> How speak the transports of the blest?[71]

Her "powers" and, indeed, language itself are burdened by sinfulness so that she is unable to articulate praise worthy of the grace she has received.

As with other eighteenth-century Calvinistic Baptists, Steele had a large view of her own sinfulness. She considers herself a "wretched, wand'ring, vile, ungrateful rebel" who shows ingratitude and a lack of repentance to God.[72] Her

---

become a tainted and a fractured idiom, duplicitous as the serpent's forking tongue." Robert B. Shaw, "George Herbert: The Word of God and the Words of Man," in *Ineffability*, 83. Herbert indicates his own understanding of the inadequacy of language to offer meaningful praise to God in poems such as the following:
> My God, Man cannot praise thy name:
> Thou art all brightness, perfect purity;
> The sun holds down his head for shame,
> Dead with eclipses, when we speak of thee:
> How shall infection
> Presume on thy perfection?

George Herbert, "Misery," *The Complete English Poems*, ed. John Tobin (London: Penguin Books, 1991), 93. Robert Shaw points out that several of Herbert's poems, including this one, "employ the trope which rhetoricians of his time would have called 'adynaton'....this figure is an admission on the part of the speaker that what he has to say is beyond the power of words to convey." Shaw, "George Herbert: The Word of God and the Words of Man," in *Ineffability*, 82.

[70] Steele, "On a Day of Prayer for Success in War," *Poems on Subjects Chiefly Devotional*, III, 123.

[71] Steele, "Desiring to Praise God for the Experience of His Goodness," *Poems on Subjects Chiefly Devotional*, III, 79. According to Steele, words fail to express both the depths of human sin and the glories of God. Compare "Our sins, our aggravated faults, / Too num'rous for our words or thoughts" and "But how can our faint praises reach / The Glories of Redeeming Love?" Steele, "On the 17th February a Day Appointed for General Prayer &c," STE 3/1/1, no. 17; Steele, "The Nativity of Christ," STE 3/1/1, no. 16.

[72] Steele, "Hope Reviving in the Contemplation of Divine Mercy," STE 3/3/2, p. 105. A version of this poem was later published in *Poems on Subjects Chiefly Devotional*, II, 97, but the quotations included here are from the unpublished portion of Steele's poem. Similarly, in a letter to Philip Furneaux, Steele writes that people are "such worthless worms such ungrateful creatures" who are fit only for God's "just indignation," yet she adds that God, in his mercy, "instead of crushing us to nothing in a moment he preserves

imperfect contrition she describes as "half penitential"; mere "faint wishes" rise to God. Steele conceives of the world, "this dying globe," as a "nest of worms" within which she is "a little particle of breathing dust."[73] And, having experienced God's grace, she agonizes over her inability to love God adequately:

> But ah! how weak, how languishing and low
> My strongest gratitude, my highest love.
> How cold, the warmest ardors of my soul,
> For blessings so divine! how poor a gift
> This vile this wretched heart! and yet 'tis all
> A worthless worm can offer, mean return![74]

As she reflects on her enduring sinfulness, she concludes that her literary efforts are undone by her very nature: her own frail humanity. In her prose meditation, "Of the Knowledge of Ourselves," she thoughtfully considers her "native misery" and then, soberly, concludes, "The more we know of ourselves, the less room we find for vanity and self-applause."[75]

Steele's conception of sin reflects her Particular Baptist roots. She summarizes this doctrine of sin in a letter to her brother: "Our hearts are depraved with sin, and we have lost the original purity of our first creation, and are utterly incapable of our selves, of doing any thing acceptable in the sight of God."[76] The 1644 Baptist Confession declares more formally this doctrine, as Steele would have been taught it in the Particular Baptist church in Broughton. It states:

> All since the Fall are conceived in sinne, and brought forth in iniquitie, and so by nature children of wrath, and servants of sinne, subjects of death, and all other calamities due to sinne in this world and for ever.[77]

---

us in the hollow of his hand from all the dangers that our frailty continually expose us." Steele to Philip Furneaux, undated, STE 3/13 (ii).

[73] Steele, "The Complaint and Relief," *Poems on Subjects Chiefly Devotional*, II, 115.

[74] Steele, "Friendship," *Poems on Subjects Chiefly Devotional*, III, 179. Similarly, she writes, "When I consider my own heart, even in its best desires and firmest resolves, conscious of my extreme weakness, I cannot but renounce every thought of dependence on myself, and acknowledge that I am wretched, vile, and utterly unworthy!" Steele, "Comfort Under the Painful Sense of Frailty, in the Unchangeable Goodness of God," *Poems on Subjects Chiefly Devotional*, III, 203.

[75] Steele, "Of the Knowledge of Ourselves," *Poems on Subjects Chiefly Devotional*, III, 161.

[76] Steele to William Steele, 27 June 1736, STE 3/8 (i).

[77] "The Confession of Faith, Of those Churches which are commonly (though falsly) called Anabaptists," in William L. Lumpkin, *Baptist Confessions of Faith* (Valley Forge,

For eighteenth-century Particular Baptists, sin so thoroughly penetrated the world that human will and effort and, in fact, language itself, as a human creation, was "brought forth in iniquitie" and stained by the effects of the fall.

The imagery most often used by Steele to illustrate the vast distance between imperfect people and a perfect God is that of light and darkness.[78] Throughout her writings, Steele distinguishes all that is divine and heavenly as that which brings light, from all that is human and earthly as that which sinks her into darkness. She contrasts "heaven-born hope" which is "serenely bright" with "this mortal night."[79] Significantly, darkness hides God from her—"A veil of

---

PA: Judson Press, 1959), 157. The 1644 Confession marked the cohesion of Calvinistic Baptists as a "self-conscious group," as this confession was the first formal articulation of their beliefs. Smith, "The Community and the Believer," 18. The 1644 Confession, popularly known as the First London Confession, was signed by representatives from seven London churches in an effort to formulate their beliefs and contradict damaging accusations regarding their faith and practices. The 1644 Confession was Calvinistic in theology and distinguished the Particular from the General Baptists. Particular Baptists were Calvinistic, believing that Christ died for the elect, or for particular people; General Baptists, on the other hand, were Arminian, believing that Christ's death was for all men and women. William H. Brackney, *A Genetic History of Baptist Thought: With Special Reference to Baptists in Britain and North America*, Baptists: History, Literature, Theology, Hymns (Macon, GA: Mercer University Press, 2004), 27-32. In the 1644 Confession, we find evidence of the Dissenters' desire to set themselves apart as a "gathered church," or voluntary assembly of believers: "which Church, as it is visible to us, is a company of visible Saints, called & separated from the world, by the word and Spirit of God, to the visible profession of the faith of the Gospel, being baptized into that faith, and joyned to the Lord, and each other, by mutuall agreement." Lumpkin, *Baptist Confessions of Faith*, 165. Or, as Isaac Watts put it in verse: "We are a Garden wall'd around, / Chosen and made peculiar Ground." Watts, "The Church the Garden of Christ," *Hymns and Spiritual Songs*, 71.

[78] Linda Ching Sledge indicates that this imagery was used by other poets, including Henry Vaughan (1624-1695), in whose verse, as in Steele's, "The deity is seen through the 'veils' of night and day, clouds and stars. These images derive from sources as diverse as medieval and hermetic mystical texts and the Book of Revelation." Linda Ching Sledge, "Typology and the Ineffable: Henry Vaughan and the 'Word in Characters,'" in *Ineffability*, 103. While many mystics, including those discussed previously, experienced the onset of darkness the closer they came to God, for Steele and others (including Origen of Alexandria [c. 185-254] before her), "darkness remained a sign of all that separates the soul from the light of God." Mark McIntosh, "Lover Without a Name: Spirituality and Constructive Christology Today," in *Minding the Spirit: The Study of Christian Spirituality*, ed. Elizabeth A. Dreyer and Mark S. Burrows (Baltimore: Johns Hopkins University Press, 2005), 217.

[79] Steele, "God the Soul's Only Portion," *Poems on Subjects Chiefly Devotional*, I, 69. Revealing something of her thoughts on the Catholic religion and Britain's colonial interests, Steele even contrasts Britain, a country that "enjoys the sweets of sight" because they are lit with "the Gospels heav'nly ray" with, on the other hand, those lands that are darkened by "Papal pow'r, or Pagan Night." Steele, "On Oct. 19th 1760. A Day

interposing night / His radiant face conceals"—but her salvation is won by "Christ my star," who saves her from the smothering dark:

> The storms and tempests now recede,
>   And guilts dark glooms decay;
> The rising sun from Nights deep shade
>   Thus brings th'Auspicious Day.[80]

Steele often contrasts the Bible, which "shall give me light," with the sight she currently lacks due to her being "Wrapt in the mournful shades of night."[81] She refers, in various poems, to the Bible as a "glass" which brings light. See, for example, "To Florio," where Steele writes:

> But upward point this glass of truth, and see
> A fairer guest descending from the sky,
> Celestial hope![82]

The frontispiece of volume II of *Poems on Subjects Chiefly Devotional* (see Figure 6) shows a woman with a tongue of flame above her head, holding a telescope or "glass." She gestures toward another woman who gazes to heaven while leaning on an anchor, emblematic of the Christian hope of the cross. According to George Richardson, in *Iconology* (1779), the tongue of flame indicates "an ardent love to God," while the woman with uplifted countenance denotes reverence.[83] The rays of light from above signify "the infusion of intellectual light, and the enjoyment of divine blessings."[84] Central to this frontispiece is the presence of light—flame, rays, and "glass"—which bring intellectual and spiritual enlightenment as they focus the mind and heart on God.

---

of Thanksgiving for National Successes," STE 3/1/4, no. 12. Similarly, in a letter to her cousin, Marianna Attwater, we read of a recent visit from an "American Minister" and of Steele's desire that the Gospel be preached "among the poor unenlightened savages." She continues, "O may the consideration of the advantages we enjoy in this Land of Light exite [sic] our pity for the multitudes of our fellow creatures who are surrounded with the gloom of pagan darkness or popish errors." Steele to Marianna Attwater, undated, STE 3/12 (iii).

[80] Steele, "Christ the Supreme Beauty," *Poems on Subjects Chiefly Devotional*, I, 156; Steele, untitled, STE 3/1/1, no. 57.

[81] Steele, "The Blind Man's Petition," STE 3/1/4, no. 10.

[82] Steele, "To Florio," *Poems on Subjects Chiefly Devotional*, II, 6. Florio was the pseudonym of Steele's cousin, Gay Thomas Attwater.

[83] Richardson, *Iconology; or, a Collection of Emblematical Figures*, 2: 110.

[84] Ibid., 2: 112.

Figure 6: Frontispiece of the second volume of *Poems on Subjects Chiefly Devotional*

Steele relates this distinction between the perfect light of heaven and the darkness of earth, representing human sinfulness, with her inability to compose adequate words of devotion. This is compellingly depicted in her unpublished poem, "On Being Desired to Write on the Death of Dr. Watts." The poem is an expression of Steele's desire to articulate praise to God, along with her frustration at not being able to compose verse as she would wish; she compares herself to Isaac Watts and notes the unfortunate dissimilarities. Watts's verse is able to "waken joy amid the shades of woe"; his songs, though once "in this dark World confin'd," are now, after his death, "enlarg'd and bright…in Worlds of perfect Light."[85] The dim light of earth results in a dim understanding of God and therefore leads to imperfect praise; now in heaven, Steele argues that Watts's understanding of God has been clarified and that therefore his praise, always good, is now transformed into unclouded greatness. On the other hand, Steele is still confined, along with her verse, to the darkness of earth. She laments:

> In vain my thoughts attempt the dazling height
> And with the Glories of Etherial Light
> They sink, and mingle with surrounding shades
> And the faint dawning ray expiring fades
> O lost to Earth![86]

Steele's light imagery—"Etherial Light" is typical of her vocabulary—illustrates how she exhibits some distinguishing features of the classical style, of which we have similarly seen evidence in her references to the muse and in the frontispieces published in *Poems on Subjects Chiefly Devotional*. In literature, this classicism, neoclassicism, or, indeed, Augustanism (for our purposes, the terms are interchangeable), is exemplified by "serenity," "clear expression," and "refined 'eloquence.'"[87] The Augustan style is typically polite and didactic in nature, and often expressed in the rhymed couplet, a clear mark of Steele's verse. John Hoyles identifies Isaac Watts as a representative of the

---

[85] Steele, "On Being Desired to Write on the Death of Dr. Watts," STE 3/3/2, pp. 13-14. T.S. Eliot expresses a similar sentiment regarding the transformation and perfection of human language following death:
> And what the dead had no speech for, when living,
> They can tell you, being dead: the communication
> Of the dead is tongued with fire beyond the language of the living.

Eliot, "Little Gidding," in *Four Quartets*, 51.

[86] Steele, "On Being Desired to Write on the Death of Dr. Watts," STE 3/3/2, pp. 13-14.

[87] John Hoyles, *The Edges of Augustanism: The Aesthetics of Spirituality in Thomas Ken, John Byrom and William Law* (The Hague: Martinus Nijhoff, 1972), 33. For a more comprehensive cataloguing of the characteristics of Augustan poetry, see Ralph Cohen, "The Augustan Mode in English Poetry," *Eighteenth-Century Studies* 1, no. 1 (Autumn 1967): 3-32.

Augustan style and then provides evidence of Watts's influence on Steele's verse.[88] Nevertheless, while Steele exhibits the clarity of expression, didacticism, and formal, refined qualities characteristic of Augustanism—characteristics which might logically be associated with confidence of expression—she consistently doubts her powers of articulation and the capabilities of language itself.

As we have noted, the consequences of Steele's failures with language are significant in that her particular genre, the hymn, is necessarily verbal. Not only is language required by the hymn-writer to articulate meaning on paper, but language then is used by congregants to express that meaning orally. To employ words to say that language is inadequate to express meaning introduces a compelling paradox—a paradox which itself can either convey meaning or deny it. Ann Chalmers Watts points out that good poets do not introduce this paradox lightly; she writes, "They often dare [inexpressibility's] profundity and let its paradox trespass on the medium of their art...making inexpressibility introduce, provide the excuse for, more words."[89] This paradox, once introduced, can either point toward a simple and certain failure of language or can elicit further possibilities for meaningful expression.

The ability to convey clear meaning is of especial importance to the hymn-writer, as congregations are meant to sing and understand what they are singing without the benefit of time to reflect at length on the hymn-writer's words. Meaning, therefore, cannot be bolstered by sophisticated turns of phrases or complex, extended metaphors. Simplicity is the key. In formulating his hymn theory, Isaac Watts reflects specifically on these necessary and self-imposed limitations:

> In many of these Composures I have just permitted my Verse to rise above a Flat and indolent Style; yet I hope it is every where supported above the just Contempt of the Criticks; tho' I am sensible that I have often subdu'd it below their Esteem; because I would neither indulge any bold Metaphors, nor admit of hard Words, nor tempt an ignorant Worshipper to sing without his Understanding.[90]

---

[88] Citing Hoxie Neale Fairchild, Hoyles argues that Steele, following Watts, imitated the poet, Mathias Casimir Sarbiewski (1595-1649), sometimes called the "Horace of Poland." John Hoyles, *The Waning of the Renaissance*, 205. Fairchild contends that Steele's poem, "The Elevation" is a "kind of serious evangelical parody of Casimir's much-imitated ode, *E rebus humanis excessus*." Hoxie Neale Fairchild, *Religious Trends in English Poetry*, vol. 2, *Religious Sentimentalism in the Age of Johnson* (New York: Columbia University Press, 1942), 112.

[89] Ann Chalmers Watts, "*Pearl*, Inexpressibility, and Poems of Human Loss," *Publications of the Modern Language Association* 99, no. 1 (January 1984): 27.

[90] Watts, preface to *The Psalms of David Imitated in the Language of the New Testament*, xxvi.

We have seen that in the same way that hymn-writers are restrained in matters of diction, they function under certain constraints of metre. While Charles Wesley distinguished himself by experimenting with a wide variety of hymn metres, the vast majority of hymn-writers, including Isaac Watts and, indeed, Steele, wrote most of their hymns using only a few metres. Of the 105 hymns in *Poems on Subjects Chiefly Devotional*, Steele used Common Metre 51 times, Long Metre 48 times, and Short Metre 5 times.[91]

These restrictions of language and metre raise questions regarding how the form of a hymn affects the meaning a hymn-writer labours to communicate. For if the form and content of a hymn are fundamentally correlated, how something is articulated affects the message that is conveyed. Steele expresses hesitancy with regard to the ability of language to express meaning about God while confining her verbal attempts to the very structured hymn form, limited as it is by demands on its diction and metre. It is interesting to observe that Steele raises questions about inarticulacy within the classic hymn form, rather than a form less strictly bound by formal conventions. Is it possible that the boundaries of the hymn form actually alleviated the difficulties she routinely encountered in her literary efforts?

T.S. Eliot, in *Four Quartets*, confronts the problem of ineffability, indicating that words often ineffectually "reach into the silence."[92] He elaborates, clarifying his frustration with the ability of words to communicate profound truth:

> Words strain,
> Crack and sometimes break, under the burden,
> Under the tension, slip, slide, perish,
> Decay with imprecision, will not stay in place,
> Will not stay still.[93]

Faced with the failure of language, Eliot turns to form and states, simply:

> Only by the form, the pattern,
> Can words or music reach
> The stillness[94]

---

[91] Steele's only remaining hymn in *Poems on Subjects Chiefly Devotional*, "A Rural Hymn," uses the metre of the 148th Psalm in Sternhold and Hopkins's *The Whole Booke of Psalmes* (1562), a metre which, according to J.R. Watson, "begins with 6.6.6.6., rhyming ABAB, and then moves into 4.4.4.4., delightfully rhyming CDDC. The verse form is exploited to provide one long, complicated, joyous, energetic sentence." Watson, *The English Hymn*, 32-33, 35.
[92] Eliot, "Burnt Norton," in *Four Quartets*, 19.
[93] Ibid.
[94] Ibid.

Eliot recognizes that when language will not hold under the demands pressed on it, artistic form can relieve the burden of meaning—and how much more so when the subject demanding expression is as potentially difficult as the nature of God, or the reflection on great personal loss. In these instances, formal structure can bolster meaning and devotional reflection where language fails.

In the fashion of most eighteenth-century hymn-writers, and Particular Baptist hymn-writers in particular, Steele's compositions are thoroughly scriptural. In fact, many of her published hymns appear prefaced by a verse of Scripture. This scriptural element becomes part of the formal nature of her hymnody, so that a great deal of her meaning is directed by her consistently biblical approach. Where human language is unable to articulate divine meaning, Steele thus relies on revealed truth to guide her verse. In this way also, the form of the hymn is made to bear the burden of what human language cannot express.

Throughout her hymnody, Steele asserts her belief that the nature of God transcends human expression, and in so doing she uses the classic formal qualities of the eighteenth-century hymn—including its plain, simple language—to convey a profound truth. Ironically, she does this perhaps more effectively than if she were to employ the full potential of language in an effort to articulate more comprehensively God's greatness. Steele approaches her subject, knowing that her literary efforts cannot fully reach her goal. The paradox is that Steele's reflection on the incapacity of language ends with her using language to do just what she claims it cannot do: she praises God. Effectively, she conveys meaning in language by reflecting on the inadequacies of language, and she specifically does this within the constraints of the hymn form. Having traced the contours of the theme of ineffability in Steele's thought and writings, let us now turn to a more thorough exposition of several of her hymns in which the theme is addressed directly.

Tracing the Theme of Ineffability in Anne Steele's Hymns

In writing hymns in praise of God, Anne Steele engages in a paradoxical act, as do many others who attempt to give expression to matters of faith. She applies her literary efforts to a subject which centuries of Christians have deemed inexpressible. Robert Shaw states it this way: "The heavenly glory that compels man's praise is one which at the same time bafflingly transcends it."[95] Steele feels this paradox keenly. Her hesitancy with regard to her own ability to fulfill the task of the hymn-writer and her doubts regarding the ability of language to sustain true and meaningful statements about God would appear to cripple her endeavour before she can even begin. Yet instead of accepting defeat, Steele chooses to introduce her 1760 collection of hymns by confronting the problem directly.

---

[95] Shaw, "George Herbert: The Word of God and the Words of Man," in *Ineffability*, 81.

Steele begins the first volume of *Poems on Subjects Chiefly Devotional* with a series of hymns that directly address the possibility of writing hymns of praise, and by thus foregrounding the subject of inexpressibility, she emphasizes the theme and intensifies the paradox. In these hymns, Steele self-consciously reflects on her identity as hymn-writer. Her first published hymn, "Desiring to Praise God," begins in this way:

> Almighty author of my frame,
> To thee my vital powers belong;
> Thy praise, (delightful, glorious theme!)
> Demands my heart, my life, my tongue.
>
> My heart, my life, my tongue are thine:
> Oh be thy praise their blest employ!
> But may my song with Angels join?
> Nor sacred awe forbid the joy?
>
> Thy glories, the seraphic lyre
> On all its strings attempts in vain;
> Then how shall mortals dare aspire
> In thought, to try th' unequal strain?[96]

The hymn begins in the first-person singular, as Steele acknowledges that her role as author is sustained by the first author. Assuming a stance of humility, she acknowledges that her "vital powers" belong to God—indeed, that she is powerless to begin the act of writing without the involvement of God. According to Richard Arnold, the nature of Steele's self-conscious identification of herself as a writer had not previously been encountered in English hymnody; he writes, "She prays that God will simply give her the ability to write, an ability that earlier hymn-writers never questioned in themselves."[97] Throughout her hymns, Steele repeats, as a kind of refrain, that the praise of God requires "my heart, my life, my tongue"—that is, all of her, including the part of her that is uniquely a writer.[98]

Having dedicated her "powers" to God, and prayed that "thy praise" would be the "blest employ" of her heart, life, and tongue, by the second verse Steele begins to question whether there is hope of her accomplishing the task she has been given. She asks, still self-consciously identifying herself as hymn-writer, "may my song with Angels join?" She judges the song of angels to be superior to hers, and yet even their song "attempts in vain" to attain the heights of God's glory. In Steele's estimation, her mortal thought is incapable of comprehending

---

[96] Steele, "Desiring to Praise God," *Poems on Subjects Chiefly Devotional*, I, 1-2.
[97] Arnold, "A 'Veil of Interposing Night': The Hymns of Anne Steele," 376.
[98] Steele, "Desiring to Praise God," *Poems on Subjects Chiefly Devotional*, I, 1.

the nature of God and, therefore, since she understands language to originate from thought, there is no hope for her to be able to articulate meaningful praise to God—for if she cannot understand God, how can she express anything about God?[99] Elsewhere, she reflects on the blessings she has received from God, and exclaims, "But O how shall my narrow thoughts and narrower words recount them!"[100]

Yet Steele must try, trusting that God, who "bends a gracious ear," will not despise her "mean tribute." The hymn continues:

> Yet the great Sovereign of the skies
> To mortals bends a gracious ear;
> Nor the mean tribute will despise,
> If offer'd with a heart sincere.
>
> Great God, accept the humble praise,
> And guide my heart, and guide my tongue,
> While to thy name I trembling raise
> The grateful, though unworthy song.[101]

Steele's published hymns begin with this posture of humility and uncertainty. She is hesitant yet determined; she does not doubt that her praise will fail to express properly what she wishes, but she has a strong sense of her vocation, believing that God has granted her unique "powers"—"powers" which she will use, "trembling" and, even as she begins, certain that her song will be "unworthy."

Steele's second published hymn, "Imploring Divine Influence," begins in this way:

---

[99] It was common in the eighteenth century to understand language as a "dress of thought," an idea that was propagated by, among others, Samuel Johnson and Alexander Pope. P.W.K. Stone identifies the "doctrine" that language is a "dress of thought" as "the fundamental principle of the Neo-Classic theory of style." See Stone's chapter, "Language as the Dress of Thought," in *The Art of Poetry, 1750-1820: Theories of Poetic Composition and Style in the Late Neo-Classic and Early Romantic Periods* (London: Routledge and Kegan Paul, 1967), 47. We will return to this idea in the next chapter.

[100] Steele, "Thoughts in Sickness, and on Recovery," *Poems on Subjects Chiefly Devotional*, III, 221.

[101] Steele, "Desiring to Praise God," *Poems on Subjects Chiefly Devotional*, I, 2. In the fourth century, Gregory of Nazianzus similarly refers to the trembling fear that comes with speaking about God: "I shall continue to say the same thing about the same thing, with that tremor in my voice, in the spirit and in thought, which I feel whenever I talk of God." Gregory of Nazianzus, *Discourse* 39, quoted in Henri de Lubac, *The Discovery of God*, trans. Alexander Dru, footnotes trans. Mark Sebanc and Cassian Fulsom (Grand Rapids, MI: Eerdmans, 1996), 138.

> My God, whene'er my longing heart
> Thy praiseful tribute would impart,
> In vain my tongue with feeble aim,
> Attempts the glories of thy name.
>
> In vain my boldest thoughts arise,
> I sink to earth and lose the skies;
> Yet I may still thy grace implore,
> And low in dust thy name adore.[102]

Here, Steele again reflects on her "feeble" inabilities. While she longs to raise a "praiseful tribute" to God, her song falters, incapable of surmounting the frailty of her human nature. Steele contrasts her flawed mortal praise with that immortal praise which is so much closer to the source of its inspiration:

> Thy name inspires the harps above
> With harmony, and praise, and love;
> That grace which tunes th' immortal strings,
> Looks kindly down on mortal things.
>
> O let thy grace guide every song,
> And fill my heart and tune my tongue;
> Then shall the strain harmonious flow,
> And heaven's sweet work begin below.[103]

While mortal praise falters, the praise of heaven achieves some measure of success because God's grace "tunes th' immortal strings." Still, despite her necessary failure, Steele again determines that she must and will continue to attempt this praise. Her thoughts and her expression of those thoughts are raised in vain, and her frail praise is lifted only hesitatingly from the "dust," but she resolves to continue the attempt to praise. For this, she must rely on God's grace to "guide every song"; she prays that God will inspire both her devotion and her ability to express that devotion: "fill my heart and tune my tongue." For apart from the grace of God, "each languid weak desire" which she experiences is destined to falter and dissipate without being translated into words.[104]

---

[102] Steele, "Imploring Divine Influence," *Poems on Subjects Chiefly Devotional*, I, 2-3. Steele's location of herself "low in dust" reflects her Calvinistic Baptist theology, as seen earlier in this chapter.

[103] Ibid., 3.

[104] Ibid. While these initial hymns have been used to demonstrate Steele's lack of faith in her own abilities and, indeed, in mortal language to express meaningful praise to God, the theme is repeated throughout her verse. She writes, for example, "My highest praise, alas, how poor / How cold my warmest love!" and "But frail mortality in vain / Attempts

Steele's hymn, "The Exalted Saviour," offers an example of the influence of Isaac Watts on her hymnody. In a verse reminiscent of Watts's "Were the whole Realm of Nature mine, / That were a Present far too small," Steele writes:

> Were universal nature ours,
> And art with all her boasted store,
> Nature and art with all their powers,
> Would still confess the offerer poor![105]

The influence of Watts is obvious, but Steele adds her own self-conscious reflection on the art of hymn-writing. Not only is nature an inadequate gift to God, but the human act of creation and its outcome—art itself—are incapable of creating an offering worthy of God's acceptance.

These hymns demonstrate Steele's self-conscious feelings of hesitancy with regard to her own ability to use language to articulate praise to God. In other hymns, Steele more directly explores the theme of ineffability as she strives to translate into language her experience and understanding of divine mystery; that is, in other hymns she shifts her attention from her own inarticulacy to the ineffable nature of God. She begins to explore this theme in her hymn, "Humble Worship," which begins with these words:

> Great King of kings, eternal God,
> Shall mortal creatures dare to raise
> Their songs to thy supreme abode,
> And join with angels in thy praise?
>
> The brightest Seraph veils his face;
> And low before thy dazling throne,
> With prostrate homage all confess
> Thou art the infinite unknown.

---

the blissful song." Steele, "Praise to God for the Blessings of Providence and Grace," *Poems on Subjects Chiefly Devotional*, I, 52. Elsewhere she exclaims, "But ah! the song, how cold it flows!" Steele, "Intreating the Presence of Christ in His Churches," *Poems on Subjects Chiefly Devotional*, I, 77. In a poem entitled "An Evening Walk," Steele writes:
> Praise, a tribute ah how poor!
> Language, what is all thy store,
> My boundless obligations to display?

Steele, "An Evening Walk," *Poems on Subjects Chiefly Devotional*, II, 13.

[105] Watts, "Crucifixion to the World, by the Cross of Christ," *Hymns and Spiritual Songs*, 189; Steele, "The Exalted Saviour," *Poems on Subjects Chiefly Devotional*, I, 174.

> Man, ah how far remov'd below,
> Wrapt in the shades of gloomy night:
> His brightest day can only show
> A few faint streaks of distant light.[106]

Here, Steele indicates that the "brightest Seraph veils his face" in front of God's "dazling throne," and she wonders how she can "dare to raise" her song, if even the inhabitants of heaven hesitate to address God.[107] Mortal worshippers, Steele included, are "far remov'd below / Wrapt in the shades of gloomy night"; their distance prevents them from being able to see God and properly find the words to raise to God in worship. Steele summarizes the problem: "Thou art the infinite unknown."[108]

Steele elaborates on the theme of the ineffability of God in her hymn, "The Condescension of God." In this hymn, Steele develops her reflection on the distance between God and humanity, and the ensuing lack of clarity which prevents human language from being able to formulate meaningful statements about God. She begins:

> Eternal power, almighty God,
> > Who can approach thy throne?
> Accessless light is thy abode,
> > To angel-eyes unknown.
>
> Before the radiance of thine eye
> > The heavens no longer shine,
> And all the glories of the sky
> > Are but the shade of thine.[109]

God is enrapt in light, compared to the darkness in which mortals dwell, and this light is "accessless" to not only mortals, but "angel-eyes" as well. Steele enlarges on God's unknowability:

> How strange! how awful is thy love!
> > With trembling we adore:
> Not all the exalted minds above
> > Its wonders can explore.[110]

She prays that God will accept the inadequate praise which results from her

---

[106] Steele, "Humble Worship," *Poems on Subjects Chiefly Devotional*, I, 37.
[107] Ibid.
[108] Ibid.
[109] Steele, "The Condescension of God," *Poems on Subjects Chiefly Devotional*, I, 65.
[110] Ibid., 66.

inability to understand God and his ways. She concludes, again comparing her song to that of heaven:

> While golden harps, and angel tongues
> Resound immortal lays,
> Great God, permit our humble songs
> To rise and mean thy praise.[111]

Nowhere is the theme of ineffability stated more directly than in one of Steele's unpublished hymns, which ends:

> Almighty Three, Eternal One,
> Ineffable, mysterious Name!
> The awful Glories of thy Throne
> Nor men, nor Angels can proclaim.[112]

Christ's name, she concludes, is "beyond expression sweet!"[113] In fact, in her hymn, "Redeeming Love," Steele indicates that she is utterly incapable of speaking God's name without his help:

---

[111] Ibid. Again, while I have engaged Steele's treatment of the ineffability of God via a close reading of several of her hymns, the theme is repeated throughout her verse. For example, her hymn, "The Mysteries of Providence," begins with the lines:
> Lord, how mysterious are thy ways!
> How blind we are! how mean our praise!
> Thy steps can mortal eyes explore?
> 'Tis ours, to wonder and adore.

Steele, "The Mysteries of Providence," *Poems on Subjects Chiefly Devotional*, I, 131.

[112] Steele, "A Hymn of Praise to God the Father, Son, and Spirit Praise to the Sacred Trinity," STE 3/1/4, no. 6. Augustine also struggled to explain the trinity in words. He writes, "But the formula three persons has been coined, not in order to give a complete explanation by means of it, but in order that we might not be obliged to remain silent." Augustine, *The Trinity*, trans. Stephen McKenna, The Fathers of the Church, vol. 45 (Washington, DC: Catholic University of American Press, 1963), 188.

[113] Steele, "Rest and Comfort in Christ Alone," *Poems on Subjects Chiefly Devotional*, III, 119. This verse, published in the third volume of the 1780 edition under the heading, "Miscellaneous Poems," demonstrates the difficulty in distinguishing between hymns and poems within Steele's corpus. While Caleb Evans classifies this verse as a poem, adding that the verse in the third volume was, "in the form and order in which they...appear, put into the hands of the editor for publication, by the ingenious authoress herself, some months before her decease"—thereby suggesting that Steele herself may have classified this verse as a poem—it seems clear that it could be used as a hymn. Caleb Evans, "Advertisement," in *Poems on Subjects Chiefly Devotional*, III, v-vi. It is written in Long Metre, as are a great many of Steele's hymns, and, in fact, was published in 1863 as "Hymn CXXIX" in *Hymns, Psalms, and Poems, by Anne Steele*, 142.

> And teach my heart, and teach my tongue
> The Saviour's lovely name.[114]

This deference to profound mystery and this hesitancy regarding the possibilities of language caused Steele to consider silence as a possible response to God.

The Inexpressible and Silence

In light of the preceding discussion of ineffability and the exposition of the theme in Steele's hymns, one might not be surprised to find evidence of language breaking down in her hymnody. Indeed, Steele refers often to inarticulate breathings and silence in her verse. When she cannot craft words and sentences into praise that is meaningful, she asks that God instead accept her hollow, meaningless "breathings," and recognize her "wish to praise."[115] She identifies moments of extreme distress and doubt as those moments when she is least likely to be able to express herself. She writes:

> When sins and fears prevailing rise,
> And fainting hope almost expires;
> Jesus, to thee I lift my eyes,
> To thee I breathe my soul's desires.[116]

When "sins and fears" threaten to overwhelm her and she is incapable of addressing God using speech, she continues to approach him in silence and is able to "breathe" her sorrows at his side.

Steele further reveals her ideas about silence in one of her poems, "An Evening Meditation," in which she casts a scene of nature praising God "in their different language."[117] In this poem, Steele refers to "Poor Philomel" singing her "melancholy airs." Philomel has become a poetic or literary name

---

[114] Steele, "Redeeming Love," *Poems on Subjects Chiefly Devotional*, I, 7-9.

[115] Steele, "An Evening Walk," *Poems on Subjects Chiefly Devotional*, II, 13.

[116] Steele, "Christ the Life of the Soul," *Poems on Subjects Chiefly Devotional*, I, 138. Similarly, to her question, "And can the ear of sovereign grace / Be deaf when I complain?" Steele answers:
> No, still the ear of sovereign grace
>   Attends the mourner's prayer;
> O may I ever find access,
>   To breathe my sorrows there.

Steele, "God the Only Refuge of the Troubled Mind," *Poems on Subjects Chiefly Devotional*, I, 145-146.

[117] Steele, "An Evening Meditation," *Poems on Subjects Chiefly Devotional*, I, 192.

for the nightingale, whose voice is heard at night and is a cry of lament.[118] As such, it is a meaningful reference for Steele to use as she reflects on the effort required to speak when "sins and fears" threaten to silence her. The nightingale's inarticulate song of lament might seem the only expression possible. Yet Steele was well versed in classical mythology and may well have known the story behind the name "Philomel"; her reference to Philomel may hint at something more.

The reference to Philomel, in keeping with many classical references in Steele's verse and in other verse of the time, suggests something essential about Steele's thoughts regarding the inexpressible and silence. Philomel was, in Greek mythology, the sister of Procne, and Procne was married to King Tereus. As the story goes, Tereus abducts Philomel and rapes her and, to prevent her from revealing his crime, cuts out her tongue. Philomel, determined to communicate Tereus's offence to Procne, contrives to weave her story into a rug and has the rug delivered to Procne, who understands at once the evil that has occurred. Procne and Philomel's revenge is brutal—they trick Tereus into eating his and Procne's son, Itys—and the story ends with Tereus pursuing the sisters. In the pursuit, all three are metamorphosed into birds and fly away: Procne is changed into a swallow, Tereus into a hawk, and Philomel into a nightingale.[119]

The image of Philomel, deprived of her tongue yet finding a way to express herself despite this handicap, is a poignant picture of the artist determined to convey meaning despite the limitations of her medium.[120] As such, the image has become meaningful for various writers, including Steele's near contemporary, Elizabeth Singer Rowe, who assumed the pseudonym, Philomela. A poem in the *Poetical Register* (1719-1720) refers to Rowe and her poetical gifts:

---

[118] The *Oxford English Dictionary* indicates that usages of "Philomel" roughly contemporary with Steele refer to expressions of lament, as in Schopperus (1706), who writes, "And Philomel at Night bewails her Wrong," and Thomson (1748), who writes, "And now and then sweet Philomel would wail." On lament and the nightingale, see R.J. Dingley, "The Misfortunes of Philomel," *Parergon* 4 (1986): 78. For an in-depth treatment of the image of the nightingale in literature, see the introductory essay by J.L. Baird in J.L. Baird and John R. Kane, *Rossignol: An Edition and Translation* (Kent, OH: Kent State University Press, 1978).

[119] William Smith, ed., *A Dictionary of Greek and Roman Biography and Mythology* (London: Walton and Maberly, John Murray, 1862), 3: 305, 1002; Edith Hamilton, *Mythology: Timeless Tales of Gods and Heroes* (New York: Warner Books, 1942), 283-285; Ovid, *Metamorphoses* VI, 565.

[120] In fact, the story of Philomel has been appropriated by artists and feminists alike—and in particular women writers—who see Philomel as a voiceless woman who finds a way to express herself, despite violent attempts to maintain her silence. For a historical and literary survey of Philomel's story in women's literature, see Vicki Mistacco, "The Metamorphoses of Philomel," *Women in French Studies*, special issue (2005): 205-218.

> The charming Philomela sings no more,
> Her lover's lost, and seeks a foreign shore.
> She was the glory of the groves and plains,
> Pride of her sex, and joy of all the Swains.
> But now she's mute. The rest with tuneless throats,
> Like screech-owls, hoot their harsh unpleasing notes.[121]

Much later, T.S. Eliot takes up the image and includes it in *The Waste Land*:

> The change of Philomel, by the barbarous king
> So rudely forced; yet there the nightingale
> Filled all the desert with inviolable voice
> And still she cried[122]

Steele's "Poor Philomel" cries her "melancholy airs," even as Eliot's nightingale continues to cry, filling the desert with "inviolable voice." So Steele, despite her own inadequacies and the limitations of language itself, does not surrender to silence, but instead continues to struggle to express her devotional experience, for in the end she continues to consider it her particular duty, her divinely-appointed vocation, to attempt to write hymns of praise to God. And this is the problem and the challenge of ineffability: the "irrepressible 'obligation to express'" is "an obligation foreordained to failure."[123]

As we saw earlier in this chapter, Augustine addressed the problem of language as it pertains to expressing religious meaning. He doubted that he could speak about God "in any worthy way." Yet he asks himself, "Having found that you cannot express what you perceive, will you be silent, will you not praise God?"[124] Steele challenges herself similarly. Impeded by the frailty of human language, recognizing the languidness of her praise, awed by inexpressible matters of divine mystery, Steele concludes, with Augustine, that she cannot remain silent. She must make her own "raid on the inarticulate." She is compelled to praise God. Steele had to attempt expression, despite not understanding the suffering she witnessed and experienced on earth—which further inhibited her attempts to praise God—as we shall see in the following chapter.

---

[121] Quoted in Stecher, *Elizabeth Singer Rowe, the Poetess of Frome*, 222.

[122] T.S. Eliot, *The Waste Land and Other Poems* (San Diego: Harcourt, Brace and Company, 1930), 33.

[123] Peter S. Hawkins and Anne Howland Schotter, *Ineffability: Naming the Unnamable from Dante to Beckett*, 1, quoting Samuel Beckett, *Transition*, no. 5.

[124] Augustine, *Enarratio in Psalmum* XCIX, 6, *CC*, *39*, 1396-1397, quoted in Colish, *The Mirror of Language*, 34. Augustine remarks, more urgently, "And what have I now said, my God, my life, my holy joy? Or what does any man say when he speaks of You? Yet woe to him who does not speak." Augustine, *The Confessions of Saint Augustine* (New Kensington, PA: Whitaker House, 1996), 14.

CHAPTER 4

"Depress'd by Pain and Sickness, All My Powers / Are Dull and Languid": Anne Steele and the Problem of Suffering

The previous chapter introduced the problem of language in Anne Steele's hymnody, and related this problem to her personal feelings of inarticulacy and her doubt in the ability of language itself to express meaningful praise to God. In this chapter, we will explore the theme further, more specifically considering the relationship between language and understanding. Gerard Ebeling addresses this relationship when he writes, "Wrestling for verbal expression is always…a wrestling to understand the substance of the matter which it is intended to utter."[1] More succinctly, he states, "where understanding fails, language is silent."[2] It would seem, then, that in her attempts to articulate praise to God in her hymns, Steele's capacity to comprehend the nature and ways of God will be significant in either causing or preventing her silence.

In this chapter, we will explore Steele's efforts to understand God by attending to her experiences of loss and suffering, and by considering her subsequent efforts to articulate her experience of the seeming silence or absence of God. As in the previous chapter, before turning to Steele's hymns specifically, it will be helpful to consider the problem of suffering more broadly, setting her reflections in their various contexts—historical, theological, and literary. Within these contexts, we will be better able to understand Steele's thoughts regarding the incomprehensibility of God. We begin, however, by turning to Steele's own experiences of pain and suffering.

---

[1] Gerard Ebeling, *Introduction to a Theological Theory of Language*, trans. R.A. Wilson (London: William Collins Sons, 1973), 119. Bernard McGinn distinguishes "between unknowability, which relates to the mind, and inexpressibility, which relates to the mind's ability to communicate what it knows," adding that "most authors will assert that the latter implies the former." Bernard McGinn, *The Foundations of Mysticism*, vol. 1, *The Presence of God: A History of Western Christian Mysticism* (New York: Crossroads, 1991), 31. Similarly, Robert Funk writes, "Language and understanding give birth to each other; they also hold each other captive." Robert Funk, *Language, Hermeneutic, and Word of God: The Problem of Language in the New Testament and Contemporary Theology* (New York: Harper and Row, 1966), 4.
[2] Ebeling, *Introduction to a Theological Theory of Language*, 106.

Anne Steele on Suffering and the Silence of God

Steele's status as a prominent and popular eighteenth-century hymn-writer has warranted her inclusion in numerous volumes wherein hymns and their writers are discussed—very often, anecdotally. Almost without exception, Steele's entries in these volumes rely heavily on various experiences of great personal loss. These experiences include the early loss of her mother, her fall from a horse as a teenager which left her an invalid, and, most dramatically, the loss of her fiancé by drowning just hours before their intended wedding.[3] These episodes combine to form a poignant picture of an injured, reclusive, introspective poet—an image that appeals to a love for the dramatic and romantic. Perhaps the image also appealed to Joseph Ivimey, the nineteenth-century Baptist historian, as the story of Steele's doomed romance can be traced back to him, but no further.[4] At any rate, it has become customary to consider Steele's hymns as directly resulting from her inability to recover from the shock of such great loss early in life.

As noted in the Introduction, above, a more accurate picture of Steele is, of course, more finely nuanced. Her mother, Anne Froude Steele, did indeed die in 1720, when Steele was just three years of age.[5] In 1723, her father married Anne Cator, who had a daughter, Mary, in 1724. While some have cast Steele as the neglected child of a previous marriage, by all accounts she and her

---

[3] For writers whose treatments of Steele prominently feature these dramatic scenes of loss see, for example, Bailey, *The Gospel in Hymns*, 70-71; David R. Breed, *The History and Use of Hymns and Hymn-Tunes* (Chicago: Fleming H. Revell, 1903), 119-122, 251; Theron Brown and Hezekiah Butterworth, *The Story of the Hymns and Tunes* (New York: George H. Doran, 1906), 196-198; Burrage, *Baptist Hymn Writers and Their Hymns*, 46-49; Hatfield, *The Poets of the Church*, 570-573; Pitman, *Lady Hymn Writers*, 66-72.

[4] Ivimey, *A History of the English Baptists*, 4: 312. Ivimey (1773-1834) was a Particular Baptist minister and historian, who began his career as an itinerant preacher before being recognized as a minister and settling at Wallingford. He was concerned about missions and served on the committee of the Baptist Missionary Society, but he is best known for his *History of the English Baptists*, a four volume work published between 1811 and 1830. Alexander Gordon notes that this work "contains a great deal of information which should...be used only with caution." Alexander Gordon, "Ivimey, Joseph (1773-1834)," rev. L.E. Lauer, *Oxford Dictionary of National Biography* (Oxford: Oxford University Press, 2004 [http://www.oxforddnb.com/view/article/14503, accessed 21 August 2006]). It should be noted, however, that Ivimey was born and raised in Ringwood, the town where James Elcomb, Steele's assumed fiancé, lived and later drowned. Ivimey notes that he recollects a "tradition" that at the time Elcomb was struggling for his life in the river "below the town," his "shrieks were heard in the town." Ivimey, *A History of the English Baptists*, 4: 312. See also J.C. Doggett, "Joseph Ivimey (1773-1834)," in *The British Particular Baptists (1638-1910)*, 3: 113-131.

[5] It is likely that Steele's mother died in childbirth. She was buried on 7 May 1720 and Steele's infant brother, Thomas Steele, was buried on 1 July 1720.

stepmother had a good relationship and Steele flourished in the warmth of her family home.[6] The thirteen extant letters written by Steele to Anne Cator Steele may lack some of the intimacy found in others of her letters, but they do reflect a fair degree of affection and solicitousness. For her part, Anne Cator Steele, in the diary she faithfully and meticulously kept, reveals an effort to treat her daughter and stepdaughter equally and fairly, as well as a persistent concern for Steele's physical and spiritual health.

The event of James Elcomb's death, to whom Steele may have been engaged, plays a central role in most discussions of her life and hymnody. The pathos of the event has created a kind of myth which eclipses what is in all likelihood a less shocking reality. For in actuality, there is no evidence to substantiate this event that has seized the imaginations of so many chroniclers of Steele's life and hymnody. A man named James Elcomb did die in 1737, and Steele appears to have known him, though the nature of their relationship is not certain.[7] A letter, dated 25 May 1737, survives in which Steele's father, William Steele, is appraised by James Manfield of Elcomb's death:

> I heartily wish the Subsequent part of my Letter may not be an Unseasonable Surprize to any of your Family and therefore 'tis with very great Concern I acquaint you that this Evening our dear friend Mr. Elcombe was unfortunately drown'd in the River....
>
> I submit to your Prudence to Communicate this Unhappy Accident to the rest of your family in a Suitable manner & not knowing how far he may have prevail'd in the Affections of Miss Steele I send my Man on Purpose to prevent any Shock that may attend her hearing It in too Sudden a manner.[8]

Manfield was well known to the Steeles, having married a cousin some years earlier, and Steele herself spent many days at Ringwood with the Manfields. It

---

[6] On Steele's alleged ill-treatment by her stepmother, see, for example, Margaret Maison, who writes, "Her mother died when she was three, and a stepmother and stepsister brought conflicts and tensions into the household." Maison, "'Thine, Only Thine!' Women Hymn Writers in Britain, 1760-1835," in *Religion in the Lives of English Women*, 14.

[7] Ivimey records the inscription on Elcomb's tombstone:
Here lieth the body of
JAMES ELCOMB
Who departed this life
May 23, 1737,
Aged 21 years.
"Stand still and see how frail are we,
Who walk with life and vigour here.
He with one breath suck't in his death,
Though danger seem'd not to be near."
Ivimey, *A History of the English Baptists*, 4: 312.

[8] James Manfield to William Steele, 25 May 1737, STE 1/5.

seems unlikely that Steele and Elcomb might have been engaged without James Manfield knowing, and it certainly would be peculiar for him to write in such a way if the wedding were imminent.[9] Whatever the nature of their relationship, it is surely too simplistic to attribute the nature of Steele's entire corpus to this one event suffered when she was twenty years old.

The question of Steele's health is more difficult to answer. Some accounts of her life note that she fell from a horse as a teenager and that the effects of that injury were carried throughout the remainder of her life. Alluding to this incident, Albert Bailey, for example, notes that as a child, "the poet had an accident that made her an invalid through life."[10] The conclusion drawn here is certainly faulty. Anne Cator Steele records in her diary on 6 August 1735 that "Nany return'd tho' the hors she rid throw her & hurt her hip."[11] But in the days that follow there are no further comments regarding Steele's injuries, and certainly she was not an invalid as she was able to ride, and fall off, her horse again. On 11 July 1752, Anne Cator Steele writes, "Nany's hors Fright'd and throw'd her yet thro the mercy of God she was not much hurt but extremely surpriz'd & was weak and bad after she came home; cause of thankfullness that it was no wors."[12] Steele's letters and verse, along with her stepmother's diary, make it clear that Steele was no long-term invalid but for many years lived a moderately active life.

Having dispelled the fogs of myth that obscure Steele's life, let us consider what archived letters and journals reveal about her health and experience of

---

[9] John Sheppard, in his memoir of Steele published in 1863, refers to his frequent visits to Broughton where he talked about Steele with her niece, Anne Steele Tomkins. Tomkins was born in the same year, 1769, that Steele went to live with her and her parents, William and Martha Steele. Tomkins did not relate the story of Steele's lost fiancé to Sheppard, and while Sheppard notes "a prospect of marriage," he adds that he learned this from "another source" rather than "in any writing or communication of [Steele's] own which has been preserved." That other source may indeed have been Ivimey's *History of the English Baptists.* Sheppard, "Memoir," in *Hymns, Psalms, and Poems, by Anne Steele*, viii-ix. Hugh Steele-Smith, a descendent of Steele's brother, William Steele, carefully researched the history of his family, and he records the conclusions of other descendents of the Steele family with regard to Steele's drowned fiancé: "My great-aunt makes no mention of the matter in her reminiscences of the Steeles; The Reverend Edward Langdon, a descendent of the Steeles who lived in Broughton for many years before his death in 1970, and who knew as much about Anne Steele as anyone, thought the story apocryphal." Hugh Steele-Smith, "The Steeles of Broughton: Some Notes on a Hampshire Family," unpublished manuscript, Angus Library, Oxford, 1986. See also Michael F. Dixon and Hugh F. Steele-Smith, "Anne Steele's Health: A Modern Diagnosis," *Baptist Quarterly* 32 (July 1988): 351-356.
[10] Bailey, *The Gospel in Hymns*, 70. Dixon and Steele-Smith argue that Bailey was the first to introduce the story of Steele's crippling fall from her horse. Dixon and Steele-Smith, "Anne Steele's Health: A Modern Diagnosis," 351.
[11] Anne Cator Steele diary, 6 August 1735, STE 2/1/1.
[12] Anne Cator Steele diary, 11 July 1752, STE 2/1/2.

suffering. Certainly, Steele did not enjoy robust health. In her diary, Steele's stepmother recites a litany of Steele's various ailments—ailments, we should remember, which were suffered at a time when the state of medicine in Britain was primitive, often increasing the patient's suffering rather than alleviating it.[13] Beginning when she was a teenager, Steele suffered repeated bouts of "the ague" and a tendency "to go into the consumption."[14] Steele's stepmother frets that Steele is "in a sort of declining state" and took her, on at least one occasion, to the Stockbridge doctor who "prescrib'd means."[15] Throughout her life, Steele suffered from a "bad pain in her head" and was often "indispos'd in her stomack."[16] These complaints recur in letters by and about her, in which we

---

[13] Bruce Hindmarsh uses the formula, "pre-analgesic, pre-antiseptic, pre-anesthetic," to illuminate the severe circumstances under which the ill suffered during the eighteenth century. For further information about eighteenth-century health conditions, see Roy Porter and Dorothy Porter, *In Sickness and In Health: The British Experience 1650-1850* (London: Fourth Estate, 1988), 97-165.

[14] Anne Cator Steele diary, 3 November 1731, STE 2/1/1. Anne Cator Steele's references to Steele's ill health are pervasive throughout her diary. See, for example, entries for 19 May 1731, 17 November 1731, 22 January 1732, 20 March 1733, 10 June 1734, and 5 April 1736. A collaborative effort of Michael Dixon, a lecturer and consultant in pathology, and Hugh Steele-Smith attempts to diagnosis Steele on the basis of Anne Cator Steele's diary and references to Steele's health in various family letters. Dixon and Steele-Smith conclude that Steele "suffered from malaria for most of her life," likely precipitated and encouraged by the location of Broughton near a low-lying, marshy area. Chronic malaria, they note, "would have had a progressively debilitating effect...the major consequences of which would have been anaemia, weakness, lassitude, and susceptibility to other infections." They add, "Consumption (pulmonary tuberculosis) was a common disease and probably complicated malaria fairly frequently. The complication must have been greatly feared as it was almost invariably fatal." Dixon and Steele-Smith, "Anne Steele's Health: A Modern Diagnosis," 353-354.

[15] Anne Cator Steele diary, 10 June 1734, STE 2/1/1. Also characteristic of Anne Cator Steele's piety and concern for Steele's health is the comment, "Nany Steele have not been very well for some time past but she is wors and she do look very pale & bad, this rais'd my compassion and I was enabled to cry to the Lord very earnestly on her account." Anne Cator Steele diary, 19 September 1732, STE 2/1/1.

[16] Anne Cator Steele diary, 3 August 1733, 11 August 1735, STE 2/1/1. These twin complaints are common; on 30 December 1745, Steele writes, from Ringwood where she is staying with the Manfields, to her stepmother, indicating a "frequent pain in my head and...disorder in my stomach...yesterday I believe I took Cold and last night was very much out of order." Steele to Anne Cator Steele, 30 December 1745, STE 3/7 (ix). References to Steele's poor health increase in the later volumes of Anne Cator Steele's diary; she writes, for example, that Steele's "converse is delightfully sweet tho it seems too much for her poor weak body to support" and later that she is "in a very weak way...being frequently carried abroad for the benefit of the air." Anne Cator Steele diary, 15 July 1754, 16 July 1758, STE 2/1/3. Visits to the doctor also increase, as do questionable methods prescribed in order to encourage her recovery; on 3 April 1757, for example, she is "bleeded," and on 3 September 1776, William Steele records "Dr.

read of her "usual complaint of the Head ake" and her "long-continued pain & weakness."[17] This chronic state of general ill health deteriorated in the last decade of her life so that she appears to have spent much of her time at home and in bed; indeed, Caleb Evans notes that she was "confined to her chamber some years before her death."[18] By this time she was living with her brother, William Steele, and his family, and a series of letters from William Steele to his daughter, Mary Steele Dunscombe, written between 1770 and 1777, catalogues Steele's various maladies, including "fits," "pain at her Heart," "fever," and "ague"; also in this letter sequence we begin to read about Steele's need for a "Watcher" at night.[19] In the last year of her life, her brother records, sadly, that Steele also suffered from deafness and that "her lucid intervals are very short."[20]

In addition to her physical suffering, Steele endured various emotional traumas through the deaths of those whom she loved. There was, of course, the early death of her mother, though it is difficult to say how this loss subsequently affected her, as Steele offers no comment on her death. Later losses she is able to feel and reflect on in verse and letter. The death of her stepmother, Anne Cator Steele, in 1760, issued in a "tempest of the mind" and

---

B's Advice" to make "issues." Anne Cator Steele diary, 3 April 1757, STE 2/1/3; William Steele to Mary Steele Dunscombe, 3 September 1776, STE 4/5. Roy Porter and Dorothy Porter explain that issues are "deliberately inflicted minor wounds, artificially kept open." Porter and Porter, *In Sickness and In Health*, 106.

[17] Steele to Mary Bullock Steele, 24 October 1751, STE 3/9 (ii); Steele to William Steele, 4 March 1762, STE 3/8 (x). See also Steele to William Steele, 5 January 1763, STE 3/8 (xi), where Steele writes, "I am yet in a very poor state of Health & see no probability at present of being better." As well, "My profuse Night sweats are very weakening to my emaciated Nature." Steele to Marianna Attwater, undated, STE 3/12 (ii). In 1763 (Steele was 46 and would live to be 61), Caleb Ashworth writes, "The state of your health affects me. I sympathize tenderly with you in your sufferings." Caleb Ashworth to Steele, 31 August 1763, STE 3/13 (x). Caleb Ashworth (d. 1775) was a Dissenting minister and the successor to Philip Doddridge as the tutor at the academy at Northhampton and later at Daventry. He was also a supporter of Steele's poetic efforts and is known to have visited her at Broughton. See James Hardeman, "Caleb Ashworth of Cloughfield and Daventry," *Baptist Quarterly* (1936-1937): 200-206.

[18] Evans, "Advertisement," in *Poems on Subjects Chiefly Devotional*, III, ix.

[19] William Steele to Mary Steele Dunscombe, 12 September 1772, 28 June 1771, 24 February 1773, 26 November 1773, STE 4/5. A watcher was someone called in "to keep attendance in the sick-room, especially overnight, particularly if death were feared." Porter and Porter, *In Sickness and In Health*, 194-195. Nearly every letter in this correspondence references Steele's health; often letters begin with a sentence such as, "the dear Circle at home all well except your Aunt who is worse." William Steele to Mary Steele Dunscombe, 20 August 1774, STE 4/5.

[20] William Steele to Mary Steele Dunscombe, 24 December 1777, 1 September 1777, STE 4/5.

threatened her with a "cloud of woe."[21] This death was followed by that of her sister-in-law, Mary Bullock Steele, in 1762, her nephew, Samuel Wakeford, in 1767, and her sister, Mary Steele Wakeford, in 1772, in addition to various aunts, uncles, and cousins throughout the years.[22] However, the death which she mourns most personally and poignantly is that of her father, William Steele, in 1769. Of this death Steele writes of her "heart oppressing grief":

> Still bleeds the deep, deep wound!—Where is the friend
> To pour with tender, kind indulgent hand,
> The lenient balm of comfort on my heart?
> Alas, that friend is gone!...
> ...what am I?
> A helpless, solitary worm, that creeps
> Complaining on the earth!...
> Ah! now one tender, one endearing tie

---

[21] Steele, "To Amira on the Sudden Death of Her Mother," *Poems on Subjects Chiefly Devotional*, III, 39.

[22] The deaths of various family members, several from smallpox, were noted in the introductory chapter. The threat of smallpox appears to have loomed large on the eighteenth-century consciousness; the Steele family letters make frequent reference to communities being devastated by the disease. A letter from Steele to her brother, for example, notes, "The small-pox encreasing at Salisbury...makes your presence at home necessary." Steele to William Steele, 29 November 1736, STE 3/8 (iv). Steele also wrote a poem, "Support in Trouble," which in its manuscript form contains a note, in her hand, "the smallpox in the neighbourhood 1759." The poem begins:
> Though terrors late alarm'd my breast,
> And rais'd a threatening tempest there,
> Yet, Lord, my passions own thy hand,
> The storm subsides at thy command.

Steele, "Support in Trouble," *Poems on Subjects Chiefly Devotional*, III, 34; Steele, "Support in Trouble," STE 3/3/5, sheet 14. Roy Porter notes the endemic nature of certain diseases, such as smallpox, in eighteenth-century England. He writes, "Microorganisms still tyrannized over English bodies. Medicine was not yet winning the battle against disease and death." People had little recourse against infectious diseases, and therefore feared them mightily. Roy Porter, *English Society in the Eighteenth Century*, rev. ed. (London: Penguin Books, 1991), 13. Elsewhere, Porter quantifies the awful conditions: "In the generation after 1720, the population of England and Wales actually *declined*, primarily because of the ravages of epidemic disease." Porter and Porter, *In Sickness and In Health*, 2 (italics in original). Death was certainly a reality and a very present threat for Steele, as evidenced by her anxious appeals, in letters, for safety for her family when they are apart. Porter and Porter explain that "English people during the 'long eighteenth century' were over-shadowed by the facts and fears of sickness and by death itself." Ibid., 5.

> That held me down to earth, death has torn off,
> And with it rent my heart strings—[23]

Certainly, Steele's sorrow was deeply-felt, and these repeated losses likely wore on a body already weak with chronic illness.

It would be difficult to posit and problematic to substantiate conclusions drawn from the effect of these occasions of sickness and death on Steele's hymnody. But we can observe what Steele herself writes about personal suffering and about the nature of God's response to that suffering, and from this we might discern how the problem of suffering may have influenced her ability to make affirmations about God in her hymnody. Steele often writes of life as a journey—a journey on which she suffered many disappointing delays and painful detours. She travels this journey "in a frail, shatter'd bark," language which brings to mind the fragile body in which she moved through life.[24] Life, for Steele, is a "toilsome journey"; more than this, it is a "disastrous journey" marked by "pain and grief."[25] Elsewhere, Steele judges life to be "a mazy Wild" in which "We pant, and toil, and wish in vain for rest"; but rest is not found in "this dark Wilderness, this vale of tears."[26]

Steele's gloomy perspective of life's pains is likely related to her own experiences of chronic illness. In a letter to her sister-in-law, Mary Bullock Steele—who was herself chronically ill and would die later that year—Steele notes that "long-protracted pain and weakness" is often attended by "faintness and dejection of spirit."[27] In a prose meditation entitled "Thoughts in Sickness, and on Recovery," she elaborates:

> Of what a feeble texture is this mortal tabernacle! and how much is the tenant mind (though of an immortal nature) pained and depressed by its weakness, and hurt by the storms which shake the tottering frame! The first attacks of a fever

---

[23] Steele, quoted by Caleb Evans, "Advertisement," in *Poems on Subjects Chiefly Devotional*, III, vii-viii.

[24] Steele, "Refuge in Distress," *Poems on Subjects Chiefly Devotional*, II, 95.

[25] Steele, untitled, STE 3/1/4, no. 21. For an extended meditation on this motif, see Steele's prose piece, "The Journey of Life," in which she notes, "Difficulties attended my journey, cold piercing blasts and chilling showers, pained and oppressed my shivering frame." Steele, "The Journey of Life," *Poems on Subjects Chiefly Devotional*, III, 153.

[26] Steele, "A Prospect of Life," STE 3/3/2, p. 26. Elsewhere, Steele remarks on the "difficulties and dangers of our painful Pilgrimage." Steele to Mary Bullock Steele, 16 March 1762, STE 3/9 (v). And again, "In this dark wilderness of pain and woe / I wander mournful." Steele, "The Pilgrim," *Poems on Subjects Chiefly Devotional*, II, 57.

[27] Steele to Mary Bullock Steele, 16 March 1762, STE 3/9 (v). Earlier, in a discussion with her stepmother on the subject of sickness, Steele comments on the "inquietudes and gloomy apprehensions" that attend illness. Steele to Anne Cator Steele, 18 May 1751, STE 3/7 (xi).

have so weakened my nerves and spirits, that every sprightly faculty, and almost every cheerful thought is sunk in a stupid languor, a listless inattention even to common things overspreads me, conversation is tasteless, and reading and thinking almost impracticable—but alas, this is not the worst! the bounties of providence, and the blessings of grace hardly excite a grateful thought, or quicken a warm desire—wretched state! And can I know it, and yet not be affected with it? Am I enough awake to feel my chains, and yet not wish for liberty? Let me try to rouze myself from this lethargy of the mind, and if I cannot look forward through the gloom which hangs so heavy on my intellectual sight, let me look back and try to recover some little remembrance of past scenes.[28]

She reflects specifically on illness, and her emotional response to it, in a poem entitled "Wrote in an Ill State of Health in the Spring." The setting of this poem is early spring, when all nature extravagantly is restored to life, when "All nature smiles!"; yet Steele laments, "I, alas, am sad!"[29] She writes:

> A gloom of sadness hangs upon my spirits,
> And prompts the frequent sigh, and silent tear.
> Depress'd by pain and sickness, all my powers
> Are dull and languid, every joy is tasteless;
> All nature fades, and pleasure is no more![30]

We see that Steele's ability to write, to use her "powers," is compromised by this overwhelming malaise. She remarks on the changing nature of her inspiration:

> Thus melancholy tun'd the mourning lay:
> The cheerful muse withdrawn, the gloomy power,
> Usurp'd her lyre, and chang'd its soothing notes
> For sounds of woe; dark clouds oppressive hung
> Around her seat, and spread their deepening shade
> Till every pleasing object sunk in night.[31]

---

[28] Steele, "Thoughts in Sickness, and on Recovery," *Poems on Subjects Chiefly Devotional*, III, 217-218.

[29] Steele, "Wrote in an Ill State of Health in the Spring," *Poems on Subjects Chiefly Devotional*, II, 60.

[30] Ibid. Similarly, Steele writes:
> How weak, how languid is the immortal mind!
> Prison'd in clay! ah, how unlike her birth!
> These noble powers for active life design'd,
> Depress'd with pain and grief, sink down to earth.

Steele, "A Thought in Sickness," *Poems on Subjects Chiefly Devotional*, II, 118.

[31] Steele, "Wrote in an Ill State of Health in the Spring," *Poems on Subjects Chiefly Devotional*, II, 61.

Steele suffers in a "mental night" which prevents her from being able to "raise the mind / Which sinks dejected."[32] She has lost her capacity to write, to compose praise to God; instead her "poor state of health...together with the severity of the season" has rendered her "unfit for anything but to hover over the fire."[33]

Steele's reflections on death serve to clarify further her thoughts on earthly suffering and begin to suggest how her ability to write was affected by the losses she experienced. In her letters and verse, she repeatedly deals with the topic of death—both the endured deaths of those she loved and the thought of her own impending death. Death was a very near threat which claimed those nearest and dearest to her. In a poem which personifies death, Steele writes:

> —Death is abroad;
> Close at my side he twangs his deadly blow.
> Unerring flies the shaft, Sarissa falls.[34]

The death of those she loved wore on her heavily. In a letter to her cousin, Anna Attwater, on the death of Attwater's sister (Steele's cousin), Steele writes of the "dismal gloom of uneasiness and slavish fears which so often oppresses my spirit."[35] About her own death, she writes:

> A few sad hours, a few more painful steps,
> And life's fatiguing pilgrimage is o'er.
> Soon will my weary eyelids close in death,
> And these poor feeble limbs sink down to rest,
> In the cold bosom of the silent grave.[36]

---

[32] Ibid.

[33] Steele to Marianna Attwater, undated, STE 3/12 (iii).

[34] Steele, "A Reflection, Occasioned by the Death of a Neighbour," *Poems on Subjects Chiefly Devotional*, II, 48. Sarissa is a pseudonym for Sarah Froude, possibly a relative of Steele's mother, Anne Froude Steele.

[35] Steele to Anna Attwater, 24 November 1741, STE 3/12 (i).

[36] Steele, "The Pilgrim," *Poems on Subjects Chiefly Devotional*, II, 58. Again personifying death, Steele writes:
> —Death onward comes
> With hasty step, though unperceiv'd and silent.
> Perhaps (alarming thought!) perhaps he aims
> E'en now the fatal blow that ends my life....
> Behold the gaping tomb! it seems to speak,
> With silent horror, to my shivering heart;
> Bids me survey my swift approaching doom,
> And view the dark retreat which waits my coming.

Steele, "A Meditation on Death," *Poems on Subjects Chiefly Devotional*, I, 217-218.

Certainly the spectre of death figured prominently in her imagination and may be expected to have influenced her perception of the spiritual life as she attempted to give voice to it in verse. In fact, language fails her as she considers the death of those she loved; she asks, "Who can describe the unutterable woe" that fills the heart at the thought of losing those who are dearest and best loved?[37]

Steele's life, as we have seen, was stained with sorrow of various kinds, and these griefs profoundly influenced her experience of life. She writes:

> Ah, what is life! what glimpse of real joy,
> Has ever smil'd to bless the gloomy scene!
> Anxieties, and fears, and pains, and sorrows,
> Thick interwoven, rise in every part,
> Through all the dreary wild...
>   So withers all my bloom of life away!
> So pain and sickness waste this sinking frame!
> The lingering hours roll heavily along,
> All dark and sad[38]

Steele's character might not be summed up so easily as a triptych of loss—mother, mobility, and marriage—but her life was marked by recurring suffering, and the losses she endured surely would come to bear on her hymnody, even as they shaped her mind and spirit.

Steele's writings also reveal her persisting sensitivity to God's response to the suffering she witnessed and experienced in the world. In many cases she experienced that response as one of absence and silence, negations that would complicate her attempts to make affirmations about God and the spiritual life in her hymnody. Her struggle to make sense of the seeming absence of God is compellingly depicted in an untitled and unpublished poem which forms part of the Steele Collection. The poem—or hymn, as its presentation is in Common Metre—takes the form of a series of questions, posed first to herself and then to God. The initial questions probe her own suffering and the emotional desert in which she feels abandoned, as in:

> Why is my heart so oft distrest
>   For seeking comfort here
> Why do my thoughts unstable prove
>   And seldom calm appear[39]

She wonders why her soul is vexed and grieved "With weariness and pain /

---

[37] Ibid., 219.
[38] Steele, "The Complaint and Relief," *Poems on Subjects Chiefly Devotional*, II, 112.
[39] Steele, untitled, STE 3/1/5, no. 5.

While rambling thro' this desert land"; she considers the depth of her distress and wonders where God is to be found.⁴⁰ The poem turns, then, to address this absent God, even while she continues to seek his "absent face."⁴¹ Her questions pile up, one on another:

> Hast thou not call'd me by thy Grace
>   To seek thy promis'd Love...
> And shall I seek thy aid in vain...
> Are thy ears deafen'd to my cry
>   That will not hear my moan...
> Why dost thou then withhold thy strength...
> Lord shall I seek and seek in vain
>   And still no answer have...⁴²

But the crux of Steele's searching surely is located in a brief question lodged in the middle of a verse, in the middle of the poem: "Why must I anguish feel."⁴³ If God is a loving God, as she faithfully affirms that he is, why does she experience this physical and emotional anguish? And why, she asks, as so many have asked, is God silent in the face of that suffering?

Steele's experience of God's absence resulted in her expression, at times, of doubt, despair, and uncertainty. She admits to a "complaining, doubting heart" and, though she claims God as her own, she does so with "wavering fear."⁴⁴ She laments the weakness of her faith, which is eroded by "distressing fears" related to her experience of pain and sorrow on earth; she is troubled by her "feeble trust," and prays that God would "raise [her] from the dust" where her faith languishes.⁴⁵ The "springs of doubt" are lamentably "ever near" and take the form of "gloomy clouds which rise and hide [God's] lovely face."⁴⁶ Caleb Ashworth, after visiting Steele at Broughton in 1763, wrote her a letter in which he refers, with concern, to "some expressions you dropt of doubt."⁴⁷ Steele

---

⁴⁰ Ibid.
⁴¹ Ibid.
⁴² Ibid. The theme of God's absence is similarly expressed in other verse:
> Absent from thee, my guide, my light,
>   Without one cheering ray,
> Through dangers, fears, and gloomy night,
>   How desolate my way!

Steele, "Absence from God," *Poems on Subjects Chiefly Devotional*, I, 111.
⁴³ Steele, untitled, STE 3/1/5, no. 5.
⁴⁴ Steele, "Submission to God under Affliction," *Poems on Subjects Chiefly Devotional*, I, 148; Steele, "God My Only Happiness," *Poems on Subjects Chiefly Devotional*, I, 142.
⁴⁵ Steele, "Desiring to Trust in God," *Poems on Subjects Chiefly Devotional*, I, 78.
⁴⁶ Steele, "The Faithfulness of God," *Poems on Subjects Chiefly Devotional*, II, 85.
⁴⁷ Caleb Ashworth to Steele, 31 August 1763, STE 3/13 (x).

responded quickly, though did little to alleviate his concern: "The thoughts which occasioned those expressions of doubt which you observed, frequently occur."[48] It is noteworthy that this discourse occurred in the context of Steele's "afflictions" and "sufferings"; her experiences of earthly sorrow, and her perception of God's silence, had troubling ramifications for her faith and her ability to affirm her experience of God in verse.[49]

Steele, in fact, relates her experiences of suffering with her ability to articulate praise. She writes, for example:

> Oppress'd with pain my feeble powers decay,
> The springs of life wear out, the vital flame
> Seems quivering near its exit. Is the day
> At hand which shall dissolve this mortal frame?[50]

Painful illness causes her "powers" to lose vitality, so that even as her body languishes so too does her ability to write hymns in praise of God. In an unpublished hymn in which Steele sets the praise of heaven beside earthly praise, she notes that when all is well, when she feels the love of God, she rises "On wings of Faith" and sings "In Heav'nly strains"; but when "the Glories fade," when "billows roll, / And thunder on the shore," and she finds herself "helpless and forlorn," her praise falters.[51] The movement is from heaven, where she sings of "Th'amazing pow'r of Grace Divine," to earth, where sorrows "o'erwhelm [her] Soul" and she waits in silence for understanding.[52] God's ways are fundamentally incomprehensible to her. While Steele hopes that God will, in his mercy, "ease the anguish of the throbbing heart," she concedes that "we in vain / Attempt to trace" the "steps of providence."[53] It is to a more thorough exploration of the sources and scope of Steele's understanding of God's incomprehensibility—as well as the related themes of divine sovereignty and transcendence—that we now turn.

Incomprehensibility and Anne Steele

As we have seen, Anne Steele's experiences of personal suffering resulted in significant hesitancy and uncertainty on her part, effectively complicating her attempt to articulate praise to God. Her experiences of suffering and her perception of God's silence in the face of that suffering, led her to think about

---

[48] Steele to Caleb Ashworth, 9 September 1763, STE 3/13 (ix).
[49] Caleb Ashworth to Steele, 31 August 1763, STE 3/13 (x); Steele to Caleb Ashworth, 9 September 1763, STE 3/13 (ix).
[50] Steele, "Written in a Painful Illness," *Poems on Subjects Chiefly Devotional*, III, 55.
[51] Steele, untitled, STE 3/1/1, no. 57.
[52] Ibid.
[53] Steele, "To a Friend in Trouble," *Poems on Subjects Chiefly Devotional*, I, 230.

God as someone who is fundamentally incomprehensible. Here, we will consider possible sources for Steele's introspective reflection on the incomprehensibility of God, and will contextualize her particular literary style and tone by introducing the writings of several other eighteenth-century writers. Along the way, we will ask questions about the significance of God's incomprehensibility to the hymn as a genre.

Steele's perception of God as essentially incomprehensible surely traces its roots to the Particular Baptist theology she learned in the Broughton church. The 1644 Baptist Confession states: "That God as he is in himselfe, cannot be comprehended of any but himselfe, dwelling in that inaccessible light, that no eye can attaine unto, whom never man saw, nor can see."[54] The picture of God "dwelling in that inaccessible light" finds clear echoes in Steele's depiction of God dwelling in "Accessless light."[55] The analogy is developed in her description of humanity's "weak eyes / Dim'd with surrounding mists," which prevent them from being able to discern God's perfect glory.[56] The dim light of earth permits only a dim understanding of God and his ways, and this, according to Steele, allows for only imperfect praise on earth.[57]

As we saw in the previous chapter, in her verse, Steele most often located God in the celestial light of heaven while situating sinful humanity in darkness on earth. This distinction in location, which emphasizes the distance between God and people, between divine perfection and human sin, inability, and incomprehension, reflects Steele's Calvinistic emphasis on God's transcendence. Steele understood God to transcend, to be exalted above and distinct from, the sinfulness pervading "this nest of worms."[58] This distance can be ascribed to the utter sinfulness of humanity. Alternatively, the distance can be attributed to the complete otherness of God—an otherness that makes God impossible to define and difficult to comprehend.

A connection should be drawn between Steele's emphasis on God's transcendence and her understanding of the ineffability of God. Ineffability, as we saw in the previous chapter, recognizes the limits of language, and this recognition implies an awareness of God as transcendent since the transcendent is logically beyond words and description. Michael Sells defines the relationship simply: "The transcendent," he writes, "must be beyond names,

---

[54] Lumpkin, *Baptist Confessions of Faith*, 156.
[55] Steele, "The Condescension of God," *Poems on Subjects Chiefly Devotional*, I, 65.
[56] Steele, "A Prospect of Life," STE 3/3/2, p. 26.
[57] See the discussion of Steele's poem, "On Being Desired to Write on the Death of Dr. Watts," in the previous chapter. Here, Steele laments the fact that her "languid pow'rs" and "lifeless heart" are held captive by the "surrounding shades" of earth, rather than being free to rise "to those bright Worlds Above." Steele, "On Being Desired to Write on the Death of Dr. Watts," STE 3/3/2, pp. 13-14.
[58] Steele, "Desiring a Taste of Real Joy," *Poems on Subjects Chiefly Devotional*, I, 112.

ineffable."[59] Henri de Lubac agrees, stating, "The ineffability of God is only another name for absolute transcendence."[60] Thus, Steele's consistent emphasis on the transcendence of God contributed to her difficulties in articulating meaning about God and the devotional experience, for a transcendent or ineffable God is beyond human understanding and expression.

Particular Baptist theology similarly emphasized God's sovereignty, a theme that can be traced through Steele's hymnody as well.[61] Throughout her verse, Steele's expression of God's sovereignty relates to how she experienced and understood his supreme power in the world. God's implication in personal suffering is expressed starkly by Steele; she indicates that God "deals the pains we feel."[62] She accepts this, humbly, and affirms that human "cares and pains / Fulfil whate'er his sacred will ordains."[63] In a letter to Philip Furneaux, for example, Steele asserts that a "sovereign hand" disperses "Afflictive as well as smiling providences."[64] The personal ramifications of this belief are clarified in a letter to her brother, William Steele, where she writes, first, that she is "yet in a poor state of health" and, then, that she desires "to depend only on that sovereign Hand which dispenses Afflictions & Comforts in infinite Wisdom and Goodness."[65] And, given the preponderance of references to illness and death in Steele's letters and verse, this belief—that a sovereign God both allows and uses afflictions—is oft-repeated, even as it is repeated in the verse of other eighteenth-century writers.[66]

---

[59] Michael Sells, *Mystical Languages of Unsaying* (Chicago: University of Chicago Press, 1994), 20.

[60] de Lubac, *The Discovery of God*, 121.

[61] In fact, Calvinistic theology is conspicuous for its adherence to the doctrine of God's sovereignty. And, since Calvinistic hymnody is typically doctrinal in nature, it is no surprise to find frequent indications of this belief in their hymnody. Erik Routley measures Isaac Watts as "the great singer of the Sovereignty of God." Erik Routley, *I'll Praise My Maker: A Study of the Hymns of Certain Authors Who Stand In or Near the Tradition of English Calvinism 1700-1850* (London: Independent Press, 1951), 13.

[62] Steele, "To a Friend in Trouble," *Poems on Subjects Chiefly Devotional*, I, 230.

[63] Ibid.

[64] Steele to Philip Furneaux, undated, STE 3/13 (ii). This belief is reiterated throughout her letters and verse.

[65] Steele to William Steele, 4 February 1762, STE 3/8 (ix).

[66] Steele often quotes Alexander Pope (1688-1744) who wrote, in his *Essay on Man*, "whatever is, is right," a principle which is repeated, in various forms, in the work of many eighteenth-century writers. Alexander Pope, *An Essay on Man, Being the First Book of Ethic Epistles. To Henry St. John, L. Bolingbroke* (London: John Wright, 1734), 20. The reasons for this eighteenth-century deference to God's providential use of earthly suffering are various. Karen Smith notes, for example, that for Particular Baptists, "illness, disease, poverty or misfortune, and even national disasters were all seen as a providential means by which people would be warned of the dangers of not believing and would thereby be brought into the community of faith." Smith goes on to cite Steele's father, William Steele, who in a sermon claims that "'publick calamities'

Other hymn-writers also were troubled by their perception of God's implication in their personal afflictions and similarly wrote hymns to probe this mystery. Susannah Harrison (1752-1784), for example, published a slim volume of hymns entitled *Songs in the Night, by a Young Woman under Deep Afflictions* (1780). Harrison's life was marked by various sorrows, including a spinal disease which left her incapacitated at the age of twenty, and her suffering can be traced throughout her hymnody. Harrison asks why God has given her such sorrow:

> What is it that provokes thine Ire?
> Is there some idol I must yield?

and searches herself, wondering if she may have brought her afflictions on herself:

> There's surely some beloved Sin,
>   Could I but find the deadly Foe,
> Has crept and lurks securely in;
>   Fain would I mourn and hate it too.[67]

---

were often used by God to 'awaken sinners to the need for reformation and to give warning to prepare for the general judgment that is coming.'" Smith, "The Community and the Believer," 238, citing William Steele sermon on Isaiah 26:9.

[67] Susannah Harrison, "XXVI," *Songs in the Night, By a Young Woman under Deep Afflictions* (London: R. Hawes, 1780), 26. Harrison (1752-1784), a Congregationalist, was born to poor parents and entered domestic service at the age of sixteen, after the early death of her father. By twenty she was permanently invalided and, having taught herself to read and write, began the composition of those hymns for which she would be remembered. M.G. Watkins records that Harrison sang these hymns "at home while awaiting death." Her verse was popular and reached a fifteenth edition by 1823. Maison, "'Thine, Only Thine!' Women Hymn Writers in Britain, 1760-1835," in *Religion in the Lives of English Women*, 19, 23; M.G. Watkins, "Harrison, Susannah (1752-1784)," rev. Rebecca Mills, *Oxford Dictionary of National Biography* (Oxford: Oxford University Press, 2004 [http://www.oxforddnb.com/view/article/12446, accessed 14 August 2006]). See also John Condor, preface to *Songs in the Night*, by Susannah Harrison, iii-iv.

The hymn included here is based on Job 10:2, which reads, "I will say to God, Do not condemn me; let me know why you contend against me" (ESV). Indeed, Harrison seems to have identified with Job; the title of her book is taken from Job 35:10: "But none says, 'Where is God my Maker, who gives songs in the night.'" Many of Harrison's hymns have a feeling of lament. See, for example:

> from Day to Day I'm left to mourn
> Beneath Thy Frown, by Unbelief enslav'd,
> Shut up in Darkness, where my gloomy Thoughts
> Are hov'ring on the Borders of Despair.

Harrison, "VIII," *Songs in the Night*, 140.

Steele and Harrison's more famous counterpart, William Cowper, is well known to have suffered from recurring bouts of mental anguish in the form of suicidal depression, as well as anxiety over whether God had damned him irrevocably. This suffering can be discerned in some of his verse, which also elucidates Cowper's deference to God's sovereign will. In one of his best-known hymns, "God Moves in a Mysterious Way," Cowper writes that while God may appear to have a "frowning providence," he remains a God of love.[68] In Cowper's more optimistic "Joy and Peace in Believing" (or, "Sometimes a Light Surprizes"), Donald Davie points out that the "crucial word" is the first word: "Sometimes." Davie writes, "only by first suffering through afflictions and desolations—the 'season of clear shining' comes only 'after rain,' only 'when comforts are declining'; and there is no guarantee that it will come, even then."[69] Cowper's personal sorrow dampened the experience of joy he felt when he first came to faith, leaving him with only an inexplicable "aching void."[70]

As noted previously, Edward Young was particularly admired by Steele, so where Harrison and Cowper's writings add scope to the discussion, Young's reflection on suffering more specifically provides a source of influence on Steele's verse.[71] Hoxie Neale Fairchild locates Young in the then-current aesthetic milieu: "By 1742, when *The Complaint, or Night Thoughts* began to appear, sensibility was becoming a badge of moral and aesthetic distinction."[72] Fairchild's reference to sensibility might offer some explanation for Steele's

---

[68] William Cowper, "God Moves in a Mysterious Way," *Olney Hymns*, 328.

[69] Davie, introduction to *The New Oxford Book of Christian Verse*, xxv, citing Cowper, "Joy and Peace in Believing," *Olney Hymns*, 367.

[70] Cowper, "Walking with God," *Olney Hymns*, 4. Earlier in this hymn, Cowper asks, "Where is the blessedness I knew / When first I saw the Lord?"

[71] Young's influence on Steele can be seen in part in similarities in language which serves to convey a particular melancholy tone. Earlier in this chapter we noted Steele's reference to life as "a mazy Wild," a "dark Wilderness," and a "vale of tears." Steele, "A Prospect of Life," STE 3/3/2, p. 26. Harry Clark records Young's reference to the world as a "miry vale" and a "nest of pain." Harry Clark, "A Study of Melancholy in Edward Young: Part I," *Modern Language Notes* 39, no. 3 (March 1924): 135.

[72] Fairchild, *Religious Trends in English Poetry*, 2: 137. Harry Clark positions Young in an "important period of transition" from "the rational Augustans" to "the sentimentalism which resulted from the philosophy of Shaftesbury and Rousseau, of which Richardson's *Clarissa Harlowe* (1748), Sterne's *Sentimental Journey* (1768), and MacKenzie's *Man of Feeling* (1771), are examples." Clark adds, "Young's work contains the seeds of many significant tendencies which reached fruition in the great romantic poets later,—for instance, his subjective tone, his vague aspiration and escape from the present, his fondness for solitude and gloomy meditation, and his doctrine of original genius with all its consequences." Clark, "A Study of Melancholy in Edward Young: Part I," 130-131. Northrop Frye defines this period between the Augustan age and the Romantic movement as the "age of sensibility." Northrop Frye, "Towards Defining an Age of Sensibility," *Journal of English Literary History* 23, no. 2 (June 1956): 144.

introspective, deeply-felt approach to writing about suffering. According to Fairchild, between 1740 and 1780—precisely the time during which Steele wrote much of her verse—we find "poetry which represents in varying proportions a blend of Christianity and sentimentalism."[73] An essential feature in sentimental poetry is the prevalence of feeling; beginning in the eighteenth century, the term sensibility denoted, according to Janet Todd, "the faculty of feeling, the capacity for extremely refined emotion and a quickness to display compassion for suffering."[74] Donald Davie adds that some commentators describe the style of the Age of Sensibility as "decadent" and that its adherents are "thought to evince an enjoyment of feeling 'for its own sake.'"[75] Davie further characterizes the style of sensibility as "complicated and ambiguous," and notes the use of "oxymoronic states of sentiment—grief crossed with pleasure, mournfulness with joy."[76]

Young's verse exemplifies these characteristics of the poetry of sensibility and, as Steele greatly admired Young's poems, it is reasonable that her verse also might bear the marks of sensibility. Porter and Porter, in their study of sickness in eighteenth-century England, argue that in the Age of Sensibility

> the real hallmark of the superior person became his—or, in particular, *her*—capacity for exquisite feeling....This could take many forms; one, obviously, could be the ability to sustain and even nourish intense suffering, emotional or physical, to radiate as a man or woman of feeling. The sensitive soul was the suffering soul, and suffering was, after all, ennobling.[77]

Much of Young's poetry is distinctively melancholic in tone, an observation that can also be made of Steele's verse. In fact, Steele's poem, "Ode to Melancholy," begins with an invocation to melancholy:

---

[73] Fairchild, *Religious Trends in English Poetry*, 2: 191.

[74] Janet Todd, *Sensibility: An Introduction* (London: Methuen and Co., 1986), 7. Susan Manning further characterizes the Age of Sensibility: "Literary history has placed Sensibility as a transitional phase of mid eighteenth-century writing, between the decline of neo-classical 'Reason' and the eruption of Romantic 'Imagination.' It identifies characteristic features including anti-rationalism, a focus on emotional response and somatized reactions (tears, swoons, deathly pallor), a prevailing mood of melancholy, fragmentation of form, and set-piece scenes of virtue in distress." Susan Manning, "Sensibility," in *The Cambridge Companion to English Literature 1740-1830*, ed. Thomas Keymer and Jon Mee (Cambridge: Cambridge University Press, 2004), 81.

[75] Davie, *The Eighteenth-Century Hymn in England*, 126. J.R. Watson marks the distinctive features of the "cult of sensibility" as a time when "religious and ethical questions...became more and more associated with feeling, with the tender heart and the sensitive mind." Watson, *The English Hymn*, 298.

[76] Davie, *The Eighteenth-Century Hymn in England*, 126.

[77] Porter and Porter, *In Sickness and In Health*, 202 (italics in original).

> Daughter of grave reflection, gentle power,
> Whose dictates oft improve the lonely hour,
> Kind melancholy come!⁷⁸

In this poem, Steele spurns earthly distractions, suggesting that her reader is better occupied in contemplating the life to come. Her language appears representative of the Age of Sensibility; she writes of "the starting tear / That trembles in my eye," "the involuntary sigh," asks, "Did not the bosom heave a sigh," and exclaims, "Let me meditate the tomb!"⁷⁹

Yet, where Fairchild argues that Young's melancholic style was consistent with current taste, he concedes that after various personal losses, Young's "sorrow and solitude and contemplativeness had become for him much more than literary fashions."⁸⁰ The same might be said of Steele, whose verse might be in keeping with the fashion of the day, but certainly her personal suffering offers fair reason for her tone, regardless of that fashion. Steele's devotional and literary reflection on her experience of earthly sorrow was therefore understandably and, perhaps, appropriately subjective.⁸¹

We see in Porter and Porter's comments a connection being made between the language of sensibility and the experience of women: they write, "the real hallmark of the superior person became his—or, in particular, *her*—capacity for exquisite feeling."⁸² The comment alludes to the eighteenth-century

---

⁷⁸ Steele, "Ode to Melancholy," *Poems on Subjects Chiefly Devotional*, III, 13.

⁷⁹ Ibid., 14-15. An argument could also be made that the emotion and depth of feeling present in Steele's hymnody signals a coming Romantic Age; the influence of the Romanticism on eighteenth-century hymnody will be considered in the following chapter.

⁸⁰ Fairchild continues, "Young exaggerates and dramatizes his woe; he disposes himself in affecting attitudes; he savors his own tears. Yet the glycerine of those tears is mingled with human brine." Fairchild, *Religious Trends in English Poetry*, 2: 137-138. The losses Young endured included, within three months, the deaths of his stepdaughter, son-in-law, and wife. Harry Clark further attributes Young's melancholy to "his solitary habits" and to "the surroundings which he chose to remind him of the transitory nature of human life"—that is, he made a habit of walking in graveyards. Clark, "A Study of Melancholy in Edward Young: Part I," 132.

Significantly, another of Steele's favourite authors, James Hervey, also reflected at length on earthly death, and his writings similarly have an affected, melancholic tone. See especially *Meditations among the Tombs. In a Letter to a Lady* (London: J. and J. Rivington, and J. Leake, 1746).

⁸¹ Harry Clark, with reference to Edward Young, finds it significant that "the return of 'I' to literature,—the subjective, introspective tone—should be inseparably linked to the return of melancholy." Harry Clark, "A Study of Melancholy in Edward Young: Part II," *Modern Language Notes* 39, no. 4 (April 1924): 202.

⁸² Various other critics have similarly associated the Age of Sensibility with literature written by and for women. Amanda Vickery, for example, relates the language of sensibility to gender: "The mid-eighteenth century saw the phenomenal success of the

assumption that women were more naturally emotional than men, and that therefore the Age of Sensibility was supportive of their instinctive inclination to feel deeply. Richard Allestree (1621/2-1681), an Anglican divine and author of the very popular conduct book, *The Ladies Calling* (1673), argues that women are predominantly emotional, that they have a "native Softness and Gentleness," adding that their lack of reason or their "easy credulity," is actually used by God, who "converts their natural infirmities into a means of Spiritual strength."[83] Steele's emotional temperament—Caleb Evans referred to her "exquisite sensibility," adding that she was "apt to feel too often to a degree too painful for her own felicity," while Louis Benson claims, "the depth and sincerity of feeling in Miss Steele's hymns made…even Watts seem cold"— was therefore in keeping with current cultural and religious expectations of women.[84] Significantly, the hymn, which we have seen to have a requisite emotional element, thereby introduced possibilities for feminine expression in the eighteenth century. Indeed, while Steele was the eighteenth century's first significant woman hymn-writer, as the century progressed we find an

---

novels of sensibility, which glorified the supposedly female qualities of compassion, sympathy, intuition and 'natural' spontaneous feeling." Amanda Vickery, *The Gentleman's Daughter: Women's Lives in Georgian England* (New Haven: Yale University Press, 1998), 41. An example of this kind of novel is found in Samuel Richardson's (1689-1761) *Sir Charles Grandison* (1753-1754), which Steele teased her sister for reading while her fiancé, Portius, was away. Portius is a pseudonym of Joseph Wakeford. See Steele, "On Amira's Reading *Grandison* in the Absence of Portius," STE 3/3/1, pp. 67-68.

Leslie Stephen also relates sensibility to gender, though in an opposite way. He writes that sentimentalism "is the name of the mood in which we make a luxury of grief, and regard sympathetic emotion as an end rather than a means—a mood rightly despised by men of masculine nature." Leslie Stephen, *History of English Thought in the Eighteenth Century* (London: Smith, Elder, and Co., 1876), 2: 436.

[83] Richard Allestree, *The Ladies Calling* (1673; Oxford: n.p., 1720), 2, 89-90. Allestree's work is representative of the then-popular genre of the conduct book; conduct books were "books of moral instruction" that included "discussions of the purpose of marriage and the proper ordering of domestic relations." Robert B. Shoemaker, *Gender in English Society 1650-1850: The Emergence of Separate Spheres?* Themes in British Social History (London: Addison Wesley Longman, 1998), 21. *The Ladies Calling* was first published in 1673, with at least twelve additional editions appearing by 1787. Allestree is likely also the author of the popular devotional handbook, *The Whole Duty of Man* (1657). Another popular eighteenth-century conduct book, the anonymous *The Whole Duty of a Woman* (1737), likewise argues that women are less naturally reasonable—and more naturally emotional—than men; the author claims that nature, "having allotted to Women a more smooth and soft Composition of Body, infers thereby her Intention, that the Mind should correspond to it." *The Whole Duty of a Woman*, 41.

[84] Evans, "Advertisement," in *Poems on Subjects Chiefly Devotional*, III, ix; Benson, *The English Hymn*, 214.

increasing number of hymns written by women.[85]

Yet Steele's emotional expression cannot be attributed solely to her identity as a woman, despite Louis Benson's claim that the intensely emotional tone, the "plaintive, sentimental note," in Steele's hymns was due to her introducing a "feminine standpoint" to the eighteenth-century English hymn.[86] For Steele's hymnic efforts were coincident with the beginnings of the Evangelical Revival, and the eighteenth-century feminine virtue of emotion was similarly a virtue of early evangelicalism. The developing values of the evangelical movement included a heartfelt religious devotion and the honest expression of personal piety. A distinction was made between nominal or "almost" Christians and real or "serious" Christians, where the faith of the former was based on lifeless piety while that of the latter was "experimental." In the eighteenth-century, "experimental" was a term used to describe a religion known by experience and by genuine, earnest feelings. It is significant to note several references in Anne Cator Steele's diary: on 20 February 1752, she records that she and Steele "are often communicating our Experience to each other," while on 15 August 1752, she notes that she spent the day listening to Steele reading and talking with her about "Experimentall things."[87] Within this context, the hymn presented itself as an ideal form with which to articulate a sincere spiritual emotion, a religion of the heart, since the eighteenth-century hymn was intended to give voice to both doctrine and personal devotion.

Furthermore, we should note that while Steele's hymns would come to be sung widely in both England and America, she wrote initially for private devotional reflection, rather than public use. Watts's and Wesley's hymns, on the other hand, were intended primarily for public use: Watts intended his for the edification of the corporate worshipping community, those who "sing the Praises of our God in his Church," while Wesley's were used to fuel the fire of the Evangelical Revival.[88] In contrast, Steele was freer to express her emotion as she reflected on her own spiritual experience and attempted to comprehend the activity of God in her life.[89] Steele's articulation of her personal devotional

---

[85] Janet Todd suggests that the "cult of sensibility" brought opportunity for "poetical women who could express themselves with perfect propriety in its conventional diction and could exalt their own sensibility without appearing improperly self-centred." With reference to the common theme of suffering in the literature of sensibility, Todd writes that women "wrote much of the physical manifestations of sensibility noted within themselves, their own tremblings, palpitations, blushes and tears, which proved the sentimental worth of the sufferer as well as forming a proper sentimental subject." Todd, *Sensibility*, 60-61.

[86] Benson, *The English Hymn*, 214.

[87] Anne Cator Steele diary, 20 February 1752, 15 August 1752, STE 2/1/2.

[88] Isaac Watts, preface to *Hymns and Spiritual Songs*, iii.

[89] Karen Smith postulates that the "intense personal response" which is "clearly part of all of Anne Steele's hymns" may explain why her hymnody was popular well into the

experience was recognized by Louis Benson as something new in eighteenth-century hymnody and labelled, by him, "the Hymn of Introspection." In Benson's view, Steele's "fervid terms of heightened emotion" were a result of her "exchanging the common ground for the feminine standpoint," though perhaps this "feminine" introspection was more closely related to Steele's writing in private than to her identity as a woman.[90] The distinction is difficult to make, as Steele's writing in private had much to do with her identity as a woman, since the eighteenth century did not favour female public expression. Writing in private, attempting to make sense of her experiences of personal suffering, Steele was made to confront her inability to comprehend fully the nature and ways of God.

The consequences of Steele's sustained reflection on suffering and God's silent response to human sorrow are considerable in that her chosen genre, the hymn, principally is intended to serve in worshipping God. J.R. Watson indicates that hymns "are designed to be a part of worship, they make up one element of the praise of God in church services, and they have to be easily and quickly comprehended; and as a result their content and expression are limited."[91] Steele's contemplation of the incomprehensibility of God would seem to complicate that intention, since it is difficult to convey meaning succinctly, within the constraints of the hymn form, when one is inhibited by problems of understanding. How indeed was Steele able to use the form of the hymn genre to communicate content which persistently eluded her?

Whereas in the previous chapter we saw how Steele was able to work within the confines of the hymn form in order to articulate particular content, despite the problem of language as she experienced it, now we find that Steele utilized the form of the hymn in particular ways in her effort to articulate painful truths pertaining to the problem of suffering. By making careful use of questions and tone—and thus defining her own unique style as a hymn-writer—Steele was able to communicate difficult content while remaining within the standard form of the hymn. Having traced the sources and scope of Steele's reflection on the problem of suffering, and considered her writings in the light of contemporary religious and literary concerns, let us now turn to a more thorough exploration of several of Steele's hymns in which we see how she meaningfully conveyed her experience and understanding of God, despite ongoing problems of comprehension.

Tracing the Theme of Incomprehensibility in Anne Steele's Hymns

In writing hymns in which she attempted to give voice to her experience of God

---

nineteenth century, as it appealed to changing aesthetic tastes. Smith, "The Community and the Believer," 254.

[90] Benson, *The English Hymn*, 214.

[91] Watson, *The English Hymn*, 1-2.

and her perception of God's purposes in human life, Steele had to contend with her own inability to understand the ways of God; this experience of the incomprehensibility of God can be seen most clearly when set against the background of Steele's personal experiences of suffering. The problem of suffering as it relates to the hymn genre might be expected to inhibit the hymn-writer as it prevents her from being able to make confident statements about the involvement of God in the human experience. Steele, as we will see via a close reading of several of her hymns, effectively confronts the incomprehensibility of God, "The Great Unsearchable," by using the form of the hymn in particular ways.[92]

One of the first things one notices when reading Steele's verse together is a certain lack of confident assertions. While she does, in keeping with other eighteenth-century hymn-writers, take care to pass along doctrine as she understands it—and as such, certain of her hymns have a decidedly didactic character—the form that her verse most often takes is that of questions and open-ended, probing verse. The tone this engenders is set early in the first volume of her published poems—and is established in relation to her task as a hymn-writer—where she asks, "But may my song with Angels join? / Nor sacred awe forbid the joy?"[93] She repeats her question in the next verse, emphasizing her uncertainty: "Then how shall mortals dare aspire / In thought, to try th' unequal strain?"[94] The questions are left to linger as Steele presses forward, hesitant and "trembling," yet certain that she must at least try. She does not suggest answers to her questions, nor even appear to expect them.

Compare Steele's tentative tone with that of Charles Wesley, whose "note of confidence, heavenly and inviolable confidence," Bernard Manning identifies as the "*one* note in his hymns which rings out clear above all the rest."[95] As a point of comparison, let us consider hymns that both Wesley and Steele modelled after Watts's very popular, then as now, "Crucifixion to the World by the Cross of Christ" (which we remember as "When I Survey the Wondrous Cross"). Wesley's version is certainly personal, in that he begins by posing a question to himself—"Where shall my wandering soul begin?"—as he considers how best to communicate the grace he has received from God.[96] The question is soon overtaken by a rush of enthusiasm, as Wesley is overwhelmed by the knowledge that he has been saved and has felt his sins forgiven:

---

[92] Steele, "The Pleasures of Spring," *Poems on Subjects Chiefly Devotional*, I, 225.
[93] Steele, "Desiring to Praise God," *Poems on Subjects Chiefly Devotional*, I, 1.
[94] Ibid., 2.
[95] Manning, *The Hymns of Wesley and Watts*, 73.
[96] Wesley, "Hymn XXIX," *A Collection of Hymns, for the Use of the People Called Methodists* (1780), 34. J.R. Watson notes that this hymn was written after Wesley's conversion experience of 21 May 1738. Watson, *The English Hymn*, 221.

> Oh! how shall I thy goodness tell,
>   Father, which thou to me hast showed,
> That I a child of wrath and hell,
>   I should be called a child of God!
> Should know, should feel my sins forgiven,
> Blest with this antepast of heaven![97]

Wesley soon concludes that he cannot hide his experience "within his heart" and turns the focus outward, urging his audience to consider how they also might come to experience the saving grace of God. He writes:

> For you the purple current flowed,
>   In pardons from his wounded side,
> Languished for you the eternal God,
>   For you the prince of glory died,
> Believe, and all your sin's forgiven,
> Only believe, and yours is heaven![98]

Wesley's confidence is exuberant and his enthusiasm infectious. He draws his readers or singers along, bolstering their faith with his emphatic assertions that they must only "Believe...believe" and they will similarly know the joy of salvation.

Steele's tone is strikingly different. Her hymn begins with clear echoes of Watts's original:

> Stretch'd on the cross the Saviour dies;
> Hark! his expiring groans arise!

---

[97] Wesley, "Hymn XXIX," *A Collection of Hymns, for the Use of the People Called Methodists*, 34. The *Oxford English Dictionary* defines an antepast as "something taken before the meal to whet the appetite; a foretaste."

[98] Wesley, "Hymn XXIX," *A Collection of Hymns, for the Use of the People Called Methodists*, 35. Compare this verse to Watts's:
> His dying Crimson, like a Robe,
> Spreads o'er his Body on the Tree,
> Then am I dead to all the Globe,
> And all the Globe is dead to me.

Watts, "Crucifixion to the World by the Cross of Christ," *Hymns and Spiritual Songs*, 189. Watts's version is grander; according to Marshall and Todd, he creates a tableau: a "highly dramatic presentation of religious material." Marshall and Todd, *English Congregational Hymns of the Eighteenth Century*, 10. Wesley's version is, according to Watson, a "complex echo of Isaac Watts" in which the focus has become the possible conversion of those hearing or reading Wesley's words. Watson, *The English Hymn*, 222. Note also the change from Watts's Long Metre to Wesley's less conventional and more complex metre.

> See, from his hands, his feet, his side,
> Runs down the sacred crimson tide!
>
> But life attends the deathful sound,
> And flows from every bleeding wound;
> The vital stream, how free it flows,
> To save and cleanse his rebel foes!
>
> To suffer in the traitor's place,
> To die for man, surprizing grace!
> Yet pass rebellious angels by—
> O why for man, dear Saviour, why?[99]

The confidence pervading Wesley's hymn is missing in Steele's version. Where Wesley proclaims God's saving grace:

> Outcasts of men, to you I call,
>   Harlots, and publicans, and thieves!
> He spreads his arms to embrace you all,
>   Sinners alone his grace receives

Steele wonders at the divine sacrifice:

> And didst thou bleed, for sinners bleed?
> And could the sun behold the deed?[100]

Both hymns are personal, certainly, but Wesley's in a hearkening, rousing way and Steele's a more tender, introspective way that becomes, in the end, self-chastising, as she is cognizant of how her own hard heart has wounded her Saviour:

> Can I survey this scene of woe,
> Where mingling grief and wonder flow;
> And yet my heart unmov'd remain,
> Insensible to love or pain!
>
> Come, dearest Lord, thy power impart,
> To warm this cold, this stupid heart;

---

[99] Steele, "A Dying Saviour," *Poems on Subjects Chiefly Devotional*, I, 180.
[100] Wesley, "Hymn XXIX," *A Collection of Hymns, for the Use of the People Called Methodists*, 35; Steele, "A Dying Saviour," *Poems on Subjects Chiefly Devotional*, I, 180.

> Till all its powers and passions move,
> In melting grief and ardent love.[101]

J.R. Watson notes that by this final verse Steele "gently detaches herself from the situation in order to consider the appropriate devotional response to it," which is, at once, characterized by both grief and love.[102] Recall that Donald Davie characterized the literature of the Age of Sensibility as that which exhibited "oxymoronic states of sentiment"; Steele's "melting grief and ardent love" offers a fine example of that sentiment described by Davie.[103]

Steele's hymn, "Mourning the Absence of God, and Longing for His Gracious Presence," is a personal and sensitive composition emanating from her experience of suffering. In the first verse, Steele establishes the distance she perceives between herself and God:

> My God, to thee I call—
> Must I for ever mourn?
> So far from thee, my life, my all?
> O when wilt thou return![104]

The distance she senses effectively clouds the face of God, making him indistinct and enigmatic:

> Dark as the shades of night
> My gloomy sorrows rise,
> And hide thy soul-reviving light
> From these desiring eyes.[105]

Steele goes on to set her "Expiring hope" and "distressing fears" against God's

---

[101] Ibid. Several manuscript copies of this hymn survive, with slight variants to the published version; see Steele, STE 3/1/1, no. 101 and STE 3/1/2 (iii). Note that Steele, like Watts, writes in Long Metre. This hymn is a good example of the direct influence Watts's hymns had on Steele's composition. Compare her lines, "Can I survey this scene of woe, / Where mingling grief and wonder flow," to Watts's "When I survey the wondrous cross.... / Sorrow and love flow mingled down." Compare also Steele's lines, "See, from his Hands, his Feet, his Side, / Runs down the sacred crimson tide!" to Watts's "See from his Head, his Hands, his Feet.... / His dying crimson, like a robe." Watts, "Crucifixion to the World by the Cross of Christ," *Hymns and Spiritual Songs*, 189.
[102] Watson, *The English Hymn*, 193.
[103] Davie, *The Eighteenth-Century Hymn in England*, 126.
[104] Steele, "Mourning the Absence of God, and Longing for His Gracious Presence," *Poems on Subjects Chiefly Devotional*, I, 143.
[105] Ibid. This divine-human distance, described via the dichotomy of light and dark, is characteristic of Steele, as seen in the previous chapter.

"healing ray," which provides the only answer to her precipitating sorrows.[106] The hymn concludes:

> Dear source of all my joys,
> And solace of my care,
> O wilt thou hear my plaintive voice
> And grant my humble prayer!
>
> These envious clouds remove,
> Thy cheering light restore,
> Confirm my interest in thy love
> 'Till I can doubt no more.
>
> Then if my troubles rise,
> To thee, my God, I'll flee,
> And raise my hopes above the skies,
> And cast my cares on thee.[107]

Her tone is "plaintive," as she herself notes, adding that her sorrow draws a veil of cloud before God, resulting in troubling doubts which exacerbate her inability to understand the nature and ways of God.[108]

Steele's particular tone is clarified further by her frequent use of questions. Earlier, we noted the predominance of the exclamation mark as a form of punctuation in Wesley's hymns; in the same way that one might characterize Wesley's hymns by the exclamation point, Steele's hymns could be characterized by the question mark. Watson points out that it is typical of Steele to use "a question to probe more deeply than a statement would do," and cites as example the following verse from "A Dying Saviour":

> To suffer in the traitor's place,
> To die for man, surprizing grace!
> Yet pass rebellious angels by—
> O why for man, dear Saviour, why?[109]

Watson argues that the "question 'why...why,' dramatically repeated, is a searching, not just for motives, or for an answer, or for a whole world-view; it is a question which is unanswerable, and therein lies its point: God's ways and

---

[106] Ibid.
[107] Ibid., 144.
[108] Ibid.
[109] Watson, *The English Hymn*, 192; Steele, "A Dying Saviour," *Poems on Subjects Chiefly Devotional*, I, 180.

purposes are beyond our comprehension."[110] Here, Watson notes something significant in relation to Steele's way of understanding and articulating her experience of the world. Her hymns are riddled with questions as she probes the edges of her various sorrows and her experience of God's silence in the face of that suffering. Her faith in a sovereign God who dwells "in inaccessible light" allows her only to continue to search, probing the periphery of her pain, struggling to articulate what is incomprehensible.

Steele's style can be distinguished further in her hymn, "Christ the Life of the Soul." Here, she again relies on personal experience, beginning her hymn in that time

> When sins and fears prevailing rise,
> And fainting hope almost expires[111]

The tone is thus set early on, as Steele creates a feeling of tenderness and vulnerability. As we saw in the previous chapter, in these times that verge on despair, Steele doubts her ability even to speak, instead opting to "breathe" her "soul's desires."[112] By the second verse, Steele begins to pose her questions, which invoke the difficulties created by her "fainting hope" and her distant Saviour:

> Art thou not mine, my living Lord?
> And can my hope, my comfort die,
> Fix'd on thy everlasting word,
> That word which built the earth and sky?[113]

The answers to these rhetorical questions seem obvious: first yes, then no. But Steele intends the diverse possibilities to linger, as can be seen in the following verse:

> If my immortal Saviour lives,
> Then my immortal life is sure[114]

The hesitancy is subtle, as it is possible to understand the initial "If" as a more certain "Since." But the "If" is intentional, and clarifies Steele's tentative posture—a posture in marked contrast to Wesley's more boisterous confidence. The final verse of Steele's hymn incorporates these hesitant tendencies:

---

[110] Watson, *The English Hymn*, 192.
[111] Steele, "Christ the Life of the Soul," *Poems on Subjects Chiefly Devotional*, I, 138.
[112] Ibid.
[113] Ibid.
[114] Ibid.

> Here, O my soul, thy trust repose;
> If Jesus is for ever mine,
> Not death itself, that last of foes,
> Shall break a union so divine.[115]

The effect here is sensitive and introspective, as it hearkens back to the vulnerability of the scene as it was set in the first verse, where Steele tells us that she is overwhelmed with "sins and fears" and that her hope is fainting such that it "almost expires."

In her hymn, "The Mysteries of Providence," Steele begins by stating more pointedly than usual her understanding of God: "Lord, how mysterious are thy ways!"[116] But she quickly withdraws from such a direct statement and recedes into her more common posture, which is that of questioning: "Thy steps can mortal eyes explore?"[117] The hymn continues:

> Thy deep decrees from creature sight
> Are hid in shades of awful night;
> Amid the lines, with curious eye,
> Not angel minds presume to pry.
>
> Great God, I would not ask to see
> What in futurity shall be;
> If light and bliss attend my days,
> Then let my future hours be praise.
>
> Is darkness and distress my share?
> Then let me trust thy guardian care;
> Enough for me, if love divine,
> At length through every cloud shall shine.[118]

God's ways, his "deep decrees," are hidden from her, and while she affirms that she "would not ask to see / What in futurity shall be," by the next verse she does just that, asking, "Is darkness and distress my share?" Again, throughout this hymn, Steele's tone is plaintive and personal as she uses questions to search for meaning in the "shades of awful night" that hide God from her and leave her with her sorrow.[119] Hesitation and uncertainty would seem to prevail

---

[115] Ibid., 139. The "Here" in this verse points back to Steele's line, "His word a firm foundation gives," thus reiterating the scriptural basis for many of her hymns. Ibid., 138. Notice also the language of love introduced in the final line of this hymn.

[116] Steele, "The Mysteries of Providence," *Poems on Subjects Chiefly Devotional*, I, 131.

[117] Ibid.

[118] Ibid., 132.

[119] Ibid.

in this hymn but for the final verse, where Steele affirms that she will be content to live in "darkness and distress" if she could be assured of Christ's love:

> Yet this my soul desires to know,
> Be this my only wish below,
> "That Christ is mine!"—this great request
> Grant, bounteous God,—and I am blest.[120]

This survey of several of Steele's hymns has shown how she was able to uniquely use the form of the hymn in order to explore difficult and personally painful content related to the incomprehensibility of God, and thus to communicate her understanding and experience of God. Steele makes adept use of tone to convey her uncertainty, and poses questions rather than more simply stating her beliefs. J.R. Watson judges Steele to be

> at her best when she is able not just to make statements...but to use questions or exclamations. She employs them to probe further than the statements themselves can do, because they gesture towards the unanswered, the mysterious, and the unknown. Through them her hymnody celebrates not just the doctrine of grace, but the application of that grace to human experience.[121]

The result is that Steele is able to articulate content which is problematic in that it must take into account the seeming silence of God in the face of great personal suffering. But it might have been otherwise. Steele's experience of suffering and her sense of the incomprehensibility of God might have resulted instead in her silence.

The Incomprehensible and Silence

In view of the preceding discussion, it is conceivable that Steele's response to the problem of suffering would be silence, for experiences of great loss naturally test the limits of language. And how much more will language show its inadequacies when we consider Steele's perception of God's incomprehensible silence in the face of that suffering? George Herbert states the problem eloquently:

> When my devotions could not pierce
> Thy silent ears;
> Then was my heart broken, as was my verse[122]

---

[120] Ibid.
[121] Watson, *The English Hymn*, 198.
[122] Herbert, "Denial," *The Complete English Poems*, 73.

Thus, we see that the problem of suffering illuminates our understanding of the ineffability of God, for suffering, and God's response to it, can elude both human comprehension and expression.

The frontispiece of volume III of *Poems on Subjects Chiefly Devotional* (see Figure 7), offers an evocative depiction of the human inability to comprehend the nature of God. The illustration shows the figure of a woman approaching a large urn. The woman is veiled, a detail meant to signify that life contains mysteries that are "impenetrable and inscrutable" and, more specifically, that "Religion contains mysteries far above human understanding."[123] The scene is shrouded in darkness, and the dominating urn suggests the certainty of death. Beneath the picture we read these words:

> Forgive the wish that would have kept thee here,
> Fond wish! have kept thee from the seats of bliss.

The couplet is by Steele and originally published in her poem, "On the Death of Mr. Hervey," in volume II of *Poems on Subjects Chiefly Devotional*.[124] Words and picture together focus the mind and heart on earthly loss.

It is noteworthy that Steele prepared the manuscript for this third volume of *Poems on Subjects Chiefly Devotional* during the final years of her life, a time in which she was confined to bed and in very poor health, and it is likely that death would have figured prominently in her thoughts during this time. This inference is substantiated by the lines by Edward Young which appear on the title page of this volume:

> One labor more indulge, then sleep my strain,
> 'Till haply wak'd by Raphael's golden lyre,
> To bear a part in everlasting lays;
> Tho' far, far higher set, in aim, I trust,
> Symphonius to this humble prelude here.[125]

It seems likely that Steele was conscious that volume III represented her final poetic efforts, her "One labor more," and that as she prepared its manuscript for publication she contemplated her imminent death and the

---

[123] Richardson, *Iconology; or, A Collection of Emblematical Figures*, 2: 98, 136.
[124] The verse reads:
> O Hervey, honoured name, forgive the tear,
> That mourns thy exit from a world like this;
> Forgive the wish that would have kept thee here,
> Fond wish! have kept thee from the seats of bliss.

Steele, "On the Death of Mr. Hervey," *Poems on Subjects Chiefly Devotional*, II, 71.
[125] Edward Young, *The Complaint: or, Night-Thoughts on Life, Death, & Immortality*, 7th ed. (Dublin: P. Wilson, 1747), 236.

Figure 7: Frontispiece of the third volume of *Poems on Subjects Chiefly Devotional*

completion of the literary task she had accepted from God.

Certainly the greatest threat to language is death, the moment when all human expression is finally suspended. Steele's perception of this ultimate silencing is reflected in her frequent reference to the "silent grave." The phrase is a trope, common in eighteenth-century prose and verse, yet it casts some light on Steele's thoughts regarding human language and loss. In her unpublished poem, "A Walk in a Churchyard," we observe Steele meditating on her own approaching death. The poem begins:

> Here whilst I wander thro' the silent tombs
> & on the Grass grown Grave I lonely tread
> the Silent Tomb reminds me of my Doom
> & tells me I must mingle with the Dead
>
> Death levels Princes with the meanest Slave
> They rest alike & no Distinction know
> In the bold Chambers of the Silent Grave
> & Shortly there must my frail Body go[126]

Throughout this book we have traced Steele's efforts to articulate her knowledge and experience of God, yet here we perceive her acknowledging that when her "frail Body" dies she will enter the "Silent Tomb" and thus finally surrender her literary efforts to silence.

Yet in the face of this impending death, this final silence, we have a reminder of Steele's strongly-felt poetic vocation, for at the base of the urn in the frontispiece of volume III rests a lyre, symbolic of music and lyric poetry.[127] In a scene centring on the certainty of death, the lyre serves as a reminder of Steele's earthly efforts to articulate praise to God. Despite being troubled by an inability to understand God's nature and ways, Steele continued to attempt expression, to pursue meaning where it eluded her. Her persistence confirms that she approached her task with hope, and this because she did not believe God to be ultimately incomprehensible, but merely hidden by human sin. Northrop Frye tells us that "the mystery behind knowledge is not darkness but shadow," and this surely is what kept Steele attempting to translate her sorrow, and her experience of God, into imperfect human language.[128] In light of the problem of understanding, Augustine poses a probing question: "'How,' you ask, 'shall I praise Him?'" And gives a less than satisfying answer: "I cannot now explain the small amount which I can perceive in part, through a glass

---

[126] Steele, "A Walk in a Churchyard," STE 3/3/6, no. 7.

[127] Richardson, *Iconology; or, A Collection of Emblematical Figures*, 1: 73, 77, 108.

[128] Northrop Frye, *The Double Vision: Language and Meaning in Religion* (Toronto: University of Toronto Press, 1991), xvi.

darkly."[129] Steele's vision of God was similarly obscured by shadow—a shadow cast by human suffering and divine silence—but she faithfully continued to attempt expression. Having considered the related problems of language and suffering in Steele's life and hymnody, in the next chapter we will turn our attention to how she was able to resolve these significant problems in order to articulate meaningful praise to God.

---

[129] Augustine, *Enarratio in Psalmum* XCIX, 6, *CC*, 39, 1396-1397, quoted in Colish, *The Mirror of Language*, 34-35.

Chapter 5

"Teach the Breathings of My Heart Dependence and Desire": Anne Steele's Faith in an Ineffable God

Faith in an ineffable, incomprehensible God would hardly be expected to elicit lyrical affirmations about God and the spiritual life, yet this is, in fact, what we find in the hymnody of Anne Steele. Steele begins many of her hymns tentatively, conscious of the limitations of human language and the challenges of articulating praise to a God who, in his incomprehensible sovereign will, allows suffering to burden frail humanity. Yet this hesitancy does not fully represent her hymnody nor adequately encapsulate her spirituality, for Steele concludes just as many of her hymns by making faithful affirmations about God and her experience of the spiritual life. While one of the questions which arises from a study of Steele's hymnody is whether her sense of loss and limitations will lead her to despair, her verse reveals a spirituality which is essentially hopeful, as she anticipates the day when her understanding of God will be complete, and when her praise will be perfected.

In the previous chapters, we considered the problems of language and suffering as they are revealed in Steele's writings and as they relate to her attempts to write hymns in praise of a God who eluded both her understanding and her verbal capacity. Her voice might understandably have been silenced. Yet Steele is remembered as a popular and successful writer of devotional verse, and of hymns in particular. In the present chapter, we will consider the particular facets of Steele's spirituality which enabled her to make affirmations about God in her hymnody. But before turning to the hymns themselves, we will explore the seemingly paradoxical themes of resignation and longing in Steele's writings, to show how they reveal key facets of her particular spirituality.

Anne Steele and Resignation

A prevailing theme in Steele's letters and verse, and a noteworthy aspect of her spirituality, is her faithful resignation to God's will. Her faith in God's sovereignty required her to trust that in his providence he also used her experiences of inarticulacy and suffering; indeed, her willingness to submit to what she recognized as a perfect, divine will influenced her response to the limitations she experienced in relation to human language and loss. She trusted God's power to transfigure her experiences of pain and her imperfect attempts to praise him. While Steele was certainly not alone in the eighteenth century in her meditation on the theme of resignation, as will be shown, the theme is reflected on repeatedly throughout her letters and verse and thus significantly clarifies her particular spirituality.

Steele's devotional and theological reflections on the theme of resignation are set in starkest relief when considered in light of the suffering she experienced in her own life and witnessed in the lives of those whom she loved. The theme is exemplified in her writing to and about her brother's first wife, Mary Bullock Steele, who died in 1762 after a lengthy and painful illness. In January 1762, her sister-in-law's health, long fragile, had begun to decline seriously, causing Steele to write to her brother, William Steele, communicating earnest concern for his wife's health; in this letter, Steele expresses her hope that "the great Physician in whose hand are the springs of Life" might "direct to and bless means for her recovery."[1] To this prayer for Mary Bullock Steele's recovery, Steele adds her belief that God is in sovereign control: "his wise & gracious hand...sometimes sends great afflictions for the exercise of Faith & Patience! It is good both to hope & quietly wait for his Salvation."[2] Despite this hope, her sister-in-law's health continued to decline, and by the following week Steele starkly advises her brother, "Resignation is our indispensable duty."[3]

Steele's willingness to resign herself to God's will was supported by her belief that his will was necessarily good and right; even the pain which she experienced was attributed to God, whose "gracious Hand...sends no affliction in vain, & whose dispensations are all right."[4] Her certainty that resignation is the appropriate response to that "affliction" sent by God's "gracious Hand" is developed in a final extant letter written to her brother before his wife's death:

> A Christian in the exercise of Faith and Hope has the greatest reason to be contented with the dispensations of Providence, even tho' they are painful and distressing; since they are all, not only just and right, but good and kind: and if afflictions are sanctified to wean us from Earth (which we know cannot be our Rest) and to raise our thoughts, our hopes and our hearts to Heaven; we may justly account them Blessings. When the Mind is preserved by the influences of divine Grace from sinking into a gloom of dejection, how many Mercies may we find mingled with every Affliction which demand our thankful acknowledgements,

---

[1] Steele to William Steele, 22 January 1762, STE 3/8 (vii).
[2] Ibid.
[3] Steele to William Steele, 31 January 1762, STE 3/8 (viii).
[4] Steele to William Steele, 5 January 1763, STE 3/8 (xi).

and tend to promote a chearful acquiescence, and encourage our hope and trust in the care of that heavenly Father who sends afflictions for our proffit.[5]

While the tone of Steele's letter to her brother is markedly didactic, as she works through the theological implications of her beliefs, when she writes to Mary Bullock Steele, her tone is more personal and tender: "I know that faintness and dejection of spirit often attends long-protracted pain and weakness; but while the Eternal God is our Refuge, and underneath are the Everlasting Arms, we can never be utterly cast down."[6] Having thus empathized with her sister-in-law's suffering, she repeats her advice regarding resignation: "It was a good saying of Dr. Watts in his Sickness 'The Business of a Christian is to bear the Will of God as well as to do it.'"[7] Steele's conclusion is consistent: since God is sovereign and his will perfect, believers must submit themselves, in faith, to the circumstances of their lives, trusting that God's will is good and right, and that he will work "painful and distressing...afflictions" to their profit.

This act of resignation must be motivated by trust, because while God's view of life is comprehensive, human sight is severely restricted. Steele reflects on the human incapacity to comprehend God's will in her poem, "To Delia Pensive" and, as Delia is a pseudonym for Mary Bullock Steele, this poem clarifies Steele's response to her sister-in-law's prolonged sickness and suffering. In language reminiscent of Pope's "whatever is, is right," Steele begins by reiterating her belief that whatever God wills is just and good:

> Say, Delia, whence these cares arise,
> These anxious cares which rack your breast?

---

[5] Steele to William Steele, 4 March 1762, STE 3/8 (x). The idea that joy and sorrow mingle, working together, under God's direction, for her good is repeated throughout Steele's letters and verse, as in her letter to Philip Furneaux: "When opprest with pain and grief he only can raise the dejected spirit and teach us to relish present enjoyments in the blessings of Providence.
> Who mingles sweets in every bitter draught
> And strews the thorny path with fragrant flow'rs
Afflictive as well as smiling providences are properly ingredients in Happiness if we can see the sovereign hand that disperses them." Steele to Philip Furneaux, undated, STE 3/13 (ii).

[6] Steele to Mary Bullock Steele, 16 M 1762, STE 3/9 (v). Steele's encouragement has its source in Scripture, where Deuteronomy 33:27, "The eternal God is your dwelling place, and underneath are the everlasting arms."

[7] Ibid.

> If heaven is infinitely wise,
> What heaven ordains, is right, is best.[8]

Yet while God's will is sovereign, people are limited in their ability to understand that will or to recognize the good in it. Steele believes that this narrow human perspective is a result of human sinfulness. She writes:

> From diffidence our sorrows flow;
> Short-sighted mortals, weak and blind,
> Bend down their eyes to earth and woe,
> And doubt if providence is kind.[9]

The answer, according to Steele, is to submit the weak human will to the greater will of God, for while our perspective is limited to "earth and woe," God's perspective is absolute. She concludes that if believers would resign themselves to God's greater will, they would realize that the circumstances of their lives are used by God to accomplish his perfect will in their lives; their own inability to understand is eclipsed by the light of God's perfect knowledge and sovereign will:

> Were once our vain desires subdu'd,
> The will resign'd, the heart at rest;
> In every scene we should conclude,
> The will of heaven is right, is best.[10]

For Steele, resignation to God's will was not an act of despair, but was, rather, consistently hopeful, as seen in her poem, "To Philander." Philander is a pseudonym for her brother, William Steele, and Steele wrote the poem for him after Mary Bullock Steele's death. The poem begins with Steele expressing her

---

[8] Steele, "To Delia Pensive," *Poems on Subjects Chiefly Devotional*, II, 28. As we saw in the previous chapter, this belief that "whatever is, is right" is in keeping with popular eighteenth-century thought. See Pope, *An Essay on Man*, 20.

[9] Steele uses the word diffidence, in this case, to refer to a lack of confidence or faith in God, which prevents "Short-sighted mortals" from perceiving how human suffering might be used by God in accordance with his perfect will. Steele, "To Delia Pensive," *Poems on Subjects Chiefly Devotional*, II, 28. In a letter to Mary Bullock Steele, Steele repeats her belief that those who suffer doubt God's goodness because of human ignorance and an inability to understand how God can will or use human suffering. She writes, "All the dispensations of Providence (however painful to sense) are exactly as they ought to be, and even as we our selves would wish them, were we capable of judging what is best for us. how can it be otherwise? since (diffident and short-sighted as we are) we must confess that they are the effect of infinite Wisdom and unalterable Goodness." Steele to Mary Bullock Steele, 16 March 1762, STE 3/9 (v).

[10] Steele, "To Delia Pensive," *Poems on Subjects Chiefly Devotional*, II, 29.

desire to ease her brother's sorrow after the loss of his wife:

> While in the arms of death your Delia sleeps
> And o'er her ashes fond remembrance weeps;
> In tender grief let friendship claim a share,
> Friendship, that fain would ease Philander's care.[11]

But Steele's efforts cannot mitigate her brother's grief; consequently, she urges him to rely on hope, that "Celestial comforter," which will turn the eye toward heaven where his wife now rests, healed of "long-continued pain & weakness," finally in perfect health.[12] According to Steele, faith and hope are able to shift a person's focus from the suffering inherent in earthly life to the promise of perfect joy and health in heaven:

> In all her force may hope celestial glow
> Till heaven's fair dawn beam o'er the shades of woe;
> Till faith shall with seraphic ardour rise,
> And claim the promis'd glories of the skies;
> Till that illustrious, that transporting hour,
> When death for ever shall resign his power;
> When joy shall wipe the tear from every eye
> And faith and hope in perfect vision die.[13]

On earth, human vision is clouded by sinfulness; "earthly vapours cloud [the] sight" of those who would wish to see and understand God.[14] In heaven, "fair

---

[11] Steele, "To Philander," *Poems on Subjects Chiefly Devotional*, III, 32.

[12] Ibid.; Steele to William Steele, 4 March 1762, STE 3/8 (x).

[13] Steele, "To Philander," *Poems on Subjects Chiefly Devotional*, III, 33-34.

[14] In a poem in which she likens the mind to a bird that would, if it could, rise to her "native skies," Steele laments the fact that "earthly vapours" "hang with cold oppressive weight / Upon [the] drooping wings" of the mind. Steele, "The Fettered Mind," *Poems on Subjects Chiefly Devotional*, I, 227. The image is expanded in her poem, "The Desire of Knowledge a Proof of Immortality," where she again writes of the mind as a bird making attempts to rise to heaven. Yet "soon she tires, and droops her feeble wing, / Oppress'd with heavy clay, and sinks to earth"; she "Sinks down amid the shades of mortal night, / And mourns her fetters, and her feeble wings." Again hope is offered as a remedy:
> But hope, dear comforter, relieves her care,
> Celestial hope! her smiling presence cheers
> The sable gloom, and beams a healing ray;
> Her gentle, peace-inspiring whisper, bids
> Look forward to a nobler happier state;
> When minds releas'd from all the chains of flesh,
> And all the toys of sense shall rise enlarg'd

dawn" will "beam o'er the shades of woe," and she will see God and hope to understand his ways; there, she will no longer rely on faith and hope, which can, now that she has attained "perfect vision," safely "die."[15] Until then, until her sight is perfected, she will resign herself, in hope and faith, to what she trusts is the perfect will of God.[16]

Reflecting on her own suffering, Steele's resignation remains both faithful and hopeful. In a poem in which she meditates on her physical afflictions, Steele asks question after question regarding the "painful illness" she experiences and about God's implication in her suffering. She is "Oppress'd

---

> To perfect freedom, and unbounded bliss.

Steele, "The Desire of Knowledge a Proof of Immortality," *Poems on Subjects Chiefly Devotional*, II, 37-38.

[15] Steele, "To Philander," *Poems on Subjects Chiefly Devotional*, III, 34. Faith and hope are consistently seen to fuel resignation, as in:

> Come Faith, and Hope, celestial pair!
> Calm Resignation waits on you.

Steele, "Resignation," *Poems on Subjects Chiefly Devotional*, II, 10. Steele thus invokes two of the three classic Christian virtues, which are faith, hope, and charity.

The suggestion that hope will someday die is found also in her hymn, "Hope in Darkness." Here, Steele likens hope to a candle shining in the dark:

> Hope, in the absence of my Lord,
> Shall be my taper; sacred light,
> Kindled at his celestial word,
> To cheer the melancholy night.

Hope provides the light by which to see in this "melancholy night," yet Steele longs for the "joyful day" when her Lord will no longer be absent, when the feeble ray of her candle of hope will be lost in the brilliant light of God's presence—"When hope shall in assurance die!" Steele, "Hope in Darkness," *Poems on Subjects Chiefly Devotional*, I, 126-127.

[16] While I have used the circumstances of Mary Bullock Steele's ill health and death to demonstrate Steele's reflection on the theme of resignation, the idea can be traced throughout her letters and verse. See, for example, the poem addressed to her sister after the death of their mother, Anne Cator Steele. In it, Steele prays for the grace to be calm in this emotional storm and to resign herself humbly to God's sovereign, "wise and good" will:

> At length my dear Amira, be our griefs
> Restrain'd, obedient to the voice divine
> Which calms the winds and seas, that sovereign voice
> Which bids the tempest of the mind—"Be still."
> Reflection now returning, may our souls
> Adore submissive his disposing hand,
> Who gives and takes our comforts as he pleases,
> Still wise and good in all.

Steele, "To Amira on the Sudden Death of Her Mother," *Poems on Subjects Chiefly Devotional*, III, 39.

with pain" and considers that her "frail tottering mansion soon should fall."[17] Yet she ends the poem in a posture of humble resignation, waiting in "patient silence," listening for God's voice bidding "every anxious thought 'be still,'" and chastising herself for her inability to trust God more completely. She asks herself:

> What mean these questions?—all depends on thee
> My Saviour God: speak to my trembling heart:
> Say "thou art mine," that word is life to me,
> And I can smile at death's tremendous dart![18]

Her poem, "Desiring a Cheerful Resignation to the Divine Will," similarly is framed with worrying questions:

> Why breathes my anxious heart the frequent sigh?
> Why from my weak eye drops the ready tear?
> Is it to mark how present blessings fly?
> Is it that griefs to come awake my fear?[19]

Again Steele makes a deliberate effort to still the questions in favour of faithful submission to God's will:

> Nor let me curious ask if dark or fair
> My future hours, but in the hand divine
> With full affiance leave my every care,
> Be hope, and humble resignation mine.[20]

Steele was not unique in eighteenth-century England in her readiness to resign herself to the will of God. In fact, in advocating resignation, she aligned herself with many others who likewise made sense of their earthly sorrow by appealing to God's sovereign will. Amanda Vickery traces the theme of resignation in the records of various eighteenth-century families and records "phrases which abound in the correspondence of the bereaved and their commiserators":

"we must endeavour to submit to the will of providence," "joy and afflictions are both dispensed by the same divine providence, your own good sense will teach

---

[17] Steele, "Written in a Painful Illness," *Poems on Subjects Chiefly Devotional*, III, 55.
[18] Ibid., 55-56.
[19] Steele, "Desiring a Cheerful Resignation to the Divine Will," *Poems on Subjects Chiefly Devotional*, III, 96.
[20] Ibid.

you to submit to the one as well as the other," "who the lord loveth, he chastitheth and scourgeth."[21]

The eighteenth century, as we observed in the previous chapter, was a time during which the threat of sickness cast a pall over daily life. Porter and Porter, in their study of sickness in the eighteenth century, judge resignation to be a common and particularly Christian response to the experience of physical suffering. They write:

> However difficult, resignation was the Christian's duty. Therein lay wisdom, according to the Quaker, Isabella Harris. For when He, "in infinite wisdom," killed off her son with scarlet fever in 1796, she could reflect "that my dear children are taken from a world of sorrow and suffering to a place of inconceivable happiness"—a thought that "enables me to be resigned to the will of my Heavenly Father." This gave her further comfort in the next year, for when her mother fell mortally sick she "was enabled calmly to resign herself as being in the Lord's Hand."[22]

The tone of Porter and Porter's comments may be somewhat disparaging, but their research remains helpful in clarifying the meaning of resignation in the thought of ordinary men and women in the eighteenth century.

Furthermore, many pastors took as their theme resignation in their attempts to contend with the problem of suffering in the lives of their congregants. Thomas Adam (1701-1784), a Church of England clergyman, who himself suffered both physically and emotionally, repeatedly offered resignation as the appropriate response to human loss and limitations. In his diary, in which he meditates on the role of pain and suffering in his life, Adam reveals that he consistently and faithfully surrendered himself into the hands of God; he writes, "The very point and top of resignation, is to submit quietly to the leading of God in the want of sensible support and comfort."[23] At times of death, the

---

[21] Vickery, *The Gentleman's Daughter*, 319, n. 124.

[22] Significantly, Harris continued to trust in God, "the Physician of value," for healing. Porter and Porter, *In Sickness and In Health*, 236-237, 174, quoting Harris, *Family Memorials: Chiefly the Memoranda left by Isabella Harris with Some Extracts from the Journal of her Mother* (n.p., 1869), 22-23, 16.

[23] Thomas Adam, *Private Thoughts on Religion, and Other Subjects Connected with it, Extracted from the Diary of the Rev. Thomas Adam, Late Rector of Wintringham. To which is Prefixed a Short Sketch of his Life and Character*, 2nd ed. (York: G. Peacock, 1795), 233. Adam served his parish in Wintringham for fifty-eight years, never seeking preferment, despite some pressure to do so. From 1759, he suffered recurring pain from kidney stones (referred to in his diary rather starkly as "the stone"), and in 1760 his wife died. A prominent theme in his writing is that of resignation to the will of God. A.B. Grosart, "Adam, Thomas (1701-1784)," rev. D. Bruce Hindmarsh, *Oxford Dictionary of National Biography* (Oxford: Oxford University Press, 2004 [http://www.oxforddnb.com/view/article/106, accessed 17 September 2006]).

theme seems to have been picked up particularly, as evidenced by the many published funeral sermons that urge mourners to cope with their grief by resigning themselves to the will of God.[24] In fact, when Steele herself died in 1778, the sermon preached at her funeral included the following appeal to her mourning family and friends: "May he incline you to submit with the most perfect resignation to this stroke of his hand."[25]

Steele's devotional and theological notions regarding resignation likely were sharpened by the thoughts of those authors she read who similarly considered the theme. In 1761, for example, Edward Young published a lengthy poem entitled *Resignation*.[26] In it, he urges his reader to maintain "A calm, unshaken Mind" in the midst of "the Storms of Life," and encourages resignation in the face of earthly suffering.[27] For her part, Elizabeth Singer Rowe, after her husband's and father's deaths, resigned herself to the will of God and penned

---

[24] See, for example, Stephen Addington, *Resignation the Duty of Mourners. A Sermon Preached at Coventry, Nov. 22, 1772, on the Death of Mr. Thomas Dawson; who Departed this Life November 15, 1772. In the Twenty-eighth Year of his Age* (Coventry: J.W. Piercy, 1773); John Barker, *Resignation to the Will of God, Consider'd, in a Funeral Sermon for the Late Reverend Mr. John Newman, Who Departed this Life, July 25, 1741. In the 65th Year of his Age. Preached at Salters Hall, August 2, 1741* (London: R. Hett, 1741); Samuel Lowell, *The Nature and Importance of Resignation: A Sermon Occasioned by the Christian Triumph Displayed in the Peaceful Departure of Mrs. Sizer, of Woodbridge, Suffolk; Who Died the 1st February, 1797, in the 27th Year of her Age* (London: C. Whittingham, 1797).

[25] Josiah Lewis, *A Pious Memorial*, STE 3/15. Lewis's sermon was copied for Steele's family into a manuscript volume to which was later added the sermon preached at the funeral of her brother, William Steele. The title of the sermon preached at Anne Steele's funeral was "The Mourners Consolation: A Discourse Occasioned by the Decease of Mrs. [sic] Anne Steele of Broughton," and it was based on the text John 14: 2-3, as she had requested. In his sermon, Lewis appealed to his listeners to prepare themselves for the judgment they surely would face. Lewis was the pastor of the Broughton church from 1777; Samuel Stennett preached his ordination sermon. Smith, "The Community and the Believer," 106, 241.

[26] Edward Young, *Resignation, &c. In Five Parts. To Mrs. B******* including a Funeral Epithalamium, Occasioned by a New Marriage-Act* (London: n.p., 1761). Hoxie Neale Fairchild writes, "*Resignation* was written at the request of Mrs. Elizabeth Montagu for Admiral Boscawen's widow, who had found in *Night Thoughts* her only source of consolation. The Advertisement provides a clear summary: 'God Almighty's infinite power, and marvelous goodness to man, is dwelt on, as the most just and cogent reason for our cheerful and absolute resignation to his will.'" Fairchild, *Religious Trends in English Poetry*, 2: 140. Elizabeth Montagu (1718-1800), who has been called the "queen of the blue stockings," was at the centre of an influential literary circle, which included Frances Boscawen (1719-1805). Boscawen was married to Edward Boscawen (1711-1761), an admiral in the navy who died at the age of forty-nine, leaving his wife a long-time widow.

[27] Young, *Resignation*, 5.

the following poem:

> Oh be thy int'rest safe, thy cause secure!
> Whatever clouds hang on my future hours,
> I pass them all.—Thy sacred will be done!
> I am of no importance to myself;
> I could resign my being[28]

Henry Stecher notes that Rowe "demonstrated an extraordinary confidence in God when, with Job-like humility, she submitted to the will of Providence" after these grave losses.[29]

Closer to home, in a notebook containing "Hymns by Miss Scott," Steele transcribed some verse by Mary Scott Taylor (1751/2-1793), a friend of the Steele family and a particular friend of Steele's niece, Mary Steele Dunscombe. One of these hymns, entitled "Resignation to the Divine Will," echoes Steele's own verse on the subject.[30] Within the Steele family circle, Mary Scott Taylor

---

[28] Elizabeth Singer Rowe, "Letter LXXIV," in *The Miscellaneous Works in Prose and Verse of Mrs. Elizabeth Rowe* (London: R. Hett and R. Dodsley, 1739), 2: 135.

[29] Stecher, *Elizabeth Singer Rowe, the Poetess of Frome*, 204.

[30] Mary Scott Taylor, "Resignation to the Divine Will," STE 3/6/1, p. 15. In 1774, Scott published *The Female Advocate*, written in response to John Duncombe's *The Feminead* (1754), which celebrated female learning and women poets in particular. In writing *The Female Advocate*, Scott hoped to update Duncombe's work and praise those poets whom he had omitted. Scott's poem was dedicated to Mary Steele, whom Scott credits with having encouraged her to write even when she thought herself "unequal to the task." Mary Scott Taylor, *The Female Advocate; A Poem Occasioned by Reading Mr. Duncombe's Feminead* (London: Joseph Johnson, 1774), v. Scott and Mary Steele were long-time friends, encouraging each other's poetic gifts and engaging in a lengthy epistolary relationship. See STE 5/14. "In their correspondence," Moira Ferguson writes, "Scott and Mary Steele avidly discuss their role and concerns as authors while lauding women writers, especially their beloved Anne Steele." Moira Ferguson, *Eighteenth-Century Women Poets: Nation, Class, and Gender*, SUNY Series in Feminist Criticism and Theory (New York: State University of New York Press, 1995), 32. Mary Steele was herself an accomplished poet, anonymously publishing *Danebury: or The Power of Friendship* in 1779; in addition, there are more than fifty of her unpublished poems in the Steele Collection. See STE 5/1-5/3. She appears to have been part of a literary circle which included Scott, the abolitionist Elizabeth Heyrick (1769-1831), and the poet Susanna Watts (*bap.* 1768, *d.* 1842). Mary Steele was also an acquaintance of Hannah More (1745-1833), who accompanied her on an outing to the ancient site of Danebury, the setting of her published poem, which was located only a few miles from Broughton. See STE 5/15; Reeves, *Pursuing the Muses*, 135; Reeves, "Literary Women in Eighteenth Century Nonconformist Circles," in *Culture and the Nonconformist Tradition*, 17-20. More wrote a poem to commemorate the occasion, which was later published in William Jay's autobiography. George Redford and John Angell James, eds.,

assumed the pseudonym, Myra, and in Steele's poem, "To Myra," she notes that she and Scott are "In suffering and in sentiment allied."[31] Here, Steele again encourages resignation as the appropriate response to personal suffering:

> Oh train'd to virtue in affliction's school,
> Long since convinc'd what heaven ordains is best;
> Still, still adhere to this unerring rule,
> Be resignation still a welcome guest.[32]

Clearly, the theme was near to Steele's heart and the source of ongoing meditation.

Steele's prolonged reflection on resignation as the appropriate response to human loss and limitations will in some part be explained as the reiteration of a spiritual theme which was prevalent in the eighteenth century, encouraged, perhaps, by the preponderance of ill health during that period. Certainly Steele's own ill health and the suffering she encountered in the lives of those she loved required a theological response. And we can see that her response to that suffering reflects her Calvinistic convictions, which emphasized divine sovereignty and transcendence. As we observed earlier, Steele had a prevailing view of God's immensity and a corresponding view of her own smallness. Her inclination toward resigning herself to the will of God therefore likely also was a result of her Calvinistic theology, for Calvinism preached the innate sinfulness of humanity and humanity's utter dependence on God.

Yet Steele's understanding of resignation should not be understood as a passive abandoning of one's self to God's will, such as was characteristic of

---

The Autobiography of William Jay (1854; reprint, Carlisle, PA: Banner of Truth Trust, 1974), 343 (page citations are to the reprint edition).

In *The Female Advocate*, Scott includes a tribute to Anne Steele:
> When Theodosia tunes her Heav'n-taught lyre,
> What bosom burns not with seraphic fire?...
> There, resignation smiles on care and pain,
> And rapt'rous joy attunes the grateful strain.
> O yet may Heav'n its healing aid extend,
> And yet to health restore my valued friend:
> Long be it ere her gentle spirit rise,
> To fill some glorious mansion in the skies.

Scott, *The Female Advocate*, 25. The influence of the Steele family on Scott's poetic endeavours is further revealed in her appreciation of the encouragement of Steele's brother, William Steele ("Philander! generous, affable, sincere"). Ibid., 39-40. William Steele, in a letter to his daughter, Mary Steele, is enthusiastic when he hears that "Miss Scott's poem has the applause of the Gentlemans Magazine." William Steele to Mary Steele Dunscombe, 17 September 1774, STE 4/5.

[31] Steele, "To Myra," *Poems on Subjects Chiefly Devotional*, III, 128.

[32] Ibid.

seventeenth-century Quietism, though this movement also had a strong sense of the fallen nature of humanity and humanity's essential dependence on God. Quietist writers such as François Fénelon (1651-1715) and Madame Guyon (1648-1717) counselled such utter passivity that they attempted to quiet their own wills completely, aspiring toward a kind of "holy indifference."[33] As Fénelon wrote to Guyon on 11 August 1689, "The soul is transformed, for the life and the will of God have been substituted for its own."[34] So complete was this forsaking of the will that the Quietists were willing to abandon all hope of heaven if this was the will of God. The writings of Quietist authors did find popular appeal in England during the eighteenth century—John Wesley read a biography of Fénelon, while William Cowper translated Guyon—but there is no link discernable between their writings and Steele.[35] Furthermore, Steele distinguishes herself from the submission promoted by the Quietists in several important ways.

Chiefly, Steele's faith cannot be characterized as passive. While she did encourage those burdened by loss to submit their hearts and minds to the will of God, she consistently acknowledged the role of the intellect in the life of faith. Whereas Quietism instructed that the mind should rest inactive in order to be ruled instead by God, Steele never relinquished human activity or responsibility in matters of faith. Indeed, for Steele, resignation had much to do with maintaining a calm heart and mind in the face of suffering, and this required an active faith, fuelled by reason as much as emotion. In fact, consistent with the opinion of a period labelled the Age of Reason, Steele affirms her confidence in

---

[33] Michael Richards, "Guyon, Jeanne-Marie Bouvier de la Motte," in *The SCM Dictionary of Christian Spirituality*, 184. Fénelon and Guyon are likely the most well-known figures in seventeenth-century Quietism. Fénelon was a French bishop who met Guyon after her release from prison, where she had been sentenced for her controversial ideas regarding completely abandoning oneself to God through mental prayer. Fénelon was attracted to Guyon's spiritual vitality, and attempted to give her ideas an orthodox foundation by educating her in classic spiritual literature. Despite this, a Quietism controversy developed in France, implicating Fénelon because of his relationship with Guyon. Quietism advocated a complete denial of the will in favour of the will of God, no matter what that will contained. See Elfrieda Dubois, "Fénelon and Quietism," in *The Study of Spirituality*, 408-415.

[34] Quoted in ibid., 412.

[35] A version of seventeenth-century Quietism can be discerned in the "stillness" of the eighteenth-century Moravians. John Wesley referred to the Moravians as "the still brethren," and was openly critical of their "Quietist type of gentle piety." Wesley, quoted in Ronald A. Knox, *Enthusiasm: A Chapter in the History of Religion, with Special Reference to the Seventeenth and Eighteenth Centuries* (Oxford: Oxford University Press, 1950; reprint, Westminster, MD: Christian Classics, 1983), 410 (page citations are to the reprint edition).

the power of the mind: "Surely, the mind must be akin to heaven."[36]

The active nature of Steele's faith is, of course, witnessed most compellingly in her efforts as a writer. For it was precisely in the act of writing that Steele attempted to work out her faith as well as the implications of those beliefs. And writing is inherently active; as Steele was well aware, it involved a deliberate searching for words, a conscious labour to articulate what eluded expression. Despite Steele's frequent appeals to the muse, she did not passively await its inspiration. Steele's self-conscious reflection on the activity of writing makes this clear, as does her active effort to understand God by conveying her experience and her understanding of God in words. Steele undertook this activity in faith—believing that God had given her a vocation as a writer—and actively attempted to translate her experience of God into language, itself burdened by human limitations.

Another way in which Steele's notion of resignation differs from that preached by the Quietists is that Steele's version is marked by a persistent hopefulness. For if a person is willing to resign himself to damnation if this should be the will of God, there is little room for hope in redemption or eternal salvation. In Steele's view, resignation was neither fatalistic nor stoic, as if all things are predetermined by fate, rendering it useless to resist, or as if one were merely indifferent to pain or pleasure. Her faith was characterized by intense longing, rather than a suppression of desire, as was characteristic of Stoicism. Rather than impassively accepting the good or ill which might come from God, Steele placed her hope in the salvation which comes from Christ.

We should note as well that this humble and faithful yielding of one's life to the purposes of a transcendent God has ample precedence in classic Christian spirituality. John of the Cross, for example, judges the willingness to resign oneself humbly to God to be the mark of a mature Christian. A less mature Christian, John explains, equates his own will with that of God; "the better way," he writes, "is that of humble resignation."[37] Teresa of Avila, for her part, in a discussion regarding prayer, urges her reader to "the greatest resignation to the will of God," cautioning her reader against forcing one's own will. She adds, more simply and directly, "Leave the soul in God's hands, let him do whatever he wants with it."[38] When Steele advises resignation as the appropriate response to God's incomprehensible nature and ways, she takes her place in a long line of Christian writers who have similarly expounded this classic spiritual theme.

---

[36] Steele, "The Desire of Knowledge a Proof of Immortality," *Poems on Subjects Chiefly Devotional*, II, 37.

[37] John of the Cross, *Dark Night of the Soul*, trans. and ed., with an introduction, by E. Allison Peers (New York: Image Books, 1959), 55-56.

[38] Teresa of Avila, *The Interior Castle*, trans. Kieran Kavanaugh and Otilio Rodriguez, intro. by Kieran Kavanaugh, preface by Raimundo Pinikkar, Classics of Western Spirituality (New York: Paulist Press, 1979), 80.

In Steele's case, resignation to God and his will found expression in her hymnody and went some way toward enabling her to overcome the problems pertaining to language and suffering which were explored in previous chapters. An ineffable, incomprehensible God eluded her powers of speech and understanding, yet she understood those limitations to result from her frail, broken humanity and resigned herself and her imperfect "powers" to the will of God. According to the theologian Karl Rahner, where people strain against the incomprehensibility of God, they are obligated, ultimately, to "be resigned to being trapped within [their] finite capacity of knowledge in the face of the incomprehensible God."[39] Steele's acceptance of her limitations and her powerlessness, coupled with her trust in God's enduring goodwill, enabled her to yield to the difficulties she faced with regard to her inability to understand fully or to articulate her experience of God. Her faithful resignation to the will of God and her confidence that God could transfigure the loss and limitations implicit in her frail humanity, including the weakness of human expression, helped her to overcome what might have silenced her in order to attempt devotional expression in her chosen genre, the hymn. Yet even while she waited in the silence, troubled by limitations and loss, she persistently longed for what eluded her: an understanding of the nature of God, the experience of his very near presence, and the ability to articulate meaningful praise.

Anne Steele and Longing

As much as Steele's spiritual identity can be described with reference to her faithful resignation to the will of God, it can also be characterized by her hopeful longing for God. At first glance, these two facets of her devotional life would appear to be at odds—Is it, in fact, possible for one to be resigned to what is, but long for more? Can acceptance and yearning simultaneously define the devotional life or, on the other hand, the active life of the writer? This would seem problematic, yet we will see that both resignation and longing informed Steele's spirituality, and together they shaped her work as a hymn-writer. While her resignation enabled her to accept her limited human capacity to articulate her understanding of God, her longing allowed her to hope for something greater, to challenge the limits of her abilities and to continue to strive toward more meaningful devotional expression. More than this, she yearned for the experience of God's presence, which provided both comfort in present afflictions and hope for the future perfection of her praise. Steele's faith was clearly reliant on an understanding of God's transcendence; she resigned herself to this fundamental divine-human distinction and its logical conclusions regarding God's ineffability. This results in obvious challenges for the hymn-writer, for she must shape fallen human language into praise of a transcendent

---

[39] Karl Rahner, *Theological Investigations*, vol. 16, *Experience of the Spirit: Source of Theology*, trans. David Morland (New York: Crossroad, 1983), 232.

and ineffable God. Yet Steele's letters and verse reveal her belief that while God is transcendent, he is also a God of grace who was made incarnate, and this compelled her to long for the experience of his presence, and with his presence the transformation of her praise.

A series of letters between Steele and her sister, Mary Steele Wakeford, introduces the theme of spiritual longing in Steele's thought.[40] In a letter to Wakeford, Steele clarifies her understanding of the spiritual life by introducing various images of the passing seasons; in her illustration, her faith begins as a seed, planted by God in her heart. While now Steele's faith languishes in "cold, joyless Winter," a scene which is "comfortless and desolate," she longs for the promise of spring.[41] In this schema, heaven is depicted as summer, a time when Steele's faith will reach "full maturity" and "bloom forever fragrant in the Paradise of God."[42] There is direction in Steele's illustration of the spiritual life; the movement is from the decay of fall to the hope of new life in the spring, from gloomy winter to the warmth and joy of summer—from immaturity to a fully mature faith. Steele longs for the time when her faith will be complete, when she will know God not only as the "God of Nature & Providence" but also as the "God of Grace."[43]

Very often Steele's longing is set in the context of her desire for relief from the earthly afflictions that she, and those she loved, experienced. While Steele consistently and honestly confronts the reality of human sorrow, often lingering over the problem and questioning God's role in that suffering, most often her verse does not remain in that place of desolation. See, for example, her poem, "To Amira on Her Mother's Illness," in which she considers the impending loss of her own stepmother, Anne Cator Steele. She begins this poem, as she does many others, by contemplating the common human experience of anxiety and loss:

> While o'er affliction's gloom, a deeper night
> Dark apprehension spreads, and woes unborn

---

[40] While these letters are undated, on 15 December 1757, Anne Cator Steele records in her diary that she is pleased with some "spiritual conversation by letter between our daughters." Perhaps these letters form part of that "conversation." Anne Cator Steele diary, 15 December 1757, STE 2/1/3.

[41] Steele's physical suffering sets the context for this reflection: "The declining year, as well as my weak state of body, reminds me that all things are tending to their dissolution." Steele to Mary Steele Wakeford, undated, STE 3/10 (vi).

[42] Ibid.

[43] Steele asks, "Why, my dear Amira, while we see his Almighty hand, and confess & adore the God of Nature & Providence, why are we so slow of heart to believe what he hath revealed as the God of Grace?" She continues, "We believe in the God of Nature and Providence; O may we believe with a more steady & cheerful affiance in the God of Grace!" Ibid.

> Rise visionary to the mental sight,
> The present grief we feel, the future mourn.[44]

But she does not remain there, instead focussing on God's promised love, the stimulus for her "vast desires."[45] She asks Amira (her sister, Mary Steele Wakeford) if "time's transient cares" should preclude the Christian's hope, and affirms that together, hope and faith give her a new vision, a vision of a future without pain:

> The sorrow-shaded scenes that rise between
> Time's friendly wing will quickly bear away;
> And hope with placid air shall wait serene,
> While faith points forward to eternal day.[46]

God's promised presence helps her to "combat unbelief" and allows her to "rest, desire, expect, adore," longing for the day when she, and her stepmother, will fully know God's healing presence, and painful loss will be forgotten.[47]

The tension between Steele's earth-bound sinfulness and suffering, on the one hand, and her hope and faith in God's ability to redeem her from that suffering, on the other, is felt throughout her poetry. A Calvinistic sense of her inherent sinfulness causes her to "tremble low on earth," yet her past experiences of God's love enable her concurrently to "aspire, / Aspire to love."[48] She is conflicted and dissatisfied with herself: "I fear, yet hope, I doubt, and yet desire / ...—ah vile, ungrateful heart!"[49] She is worn down by pain and loss, acutely feeling the weakness and limitations of her own humanity, yet the result is a faithful and persistently hopeful yearning for God:

---

[44] Steele, "To Amira on Her Mother's Illness," *Poems on Subjects Chiefly Devotional*, III, 28.

[45] Ibid., 29.

[46] Ibid.

[47] Ibid., 30. In the surviving manuscript version of this poem, Steele crossed out diffidence and replaced it with unbelief; the corrected version is preserved in print. While diffidence, in this case, refers to a lack of trust or confidence, the word unbelief more specifically implies that the lack of faith to which Steele refers is a lack of faith in God. See STE 3/3/5, sheet 8, verses 4 and 10. The theme is developed further in Steele's hymn, "The Promised Land." In this hymn, Steele anticipates the "Unbounded glories" of heaven, where "pain and sickness never come" and where "Health triumphs in immortal bloom." Significantly, Steele associates her anticipation of perfected health with her anticipation of perfected praise. Even as she longs for eschatological healing, she prays, "bid our spirits rise and join / The chorus of the sky." Steele, "The Promised Land," *Poems on Subjects Chiefly Devotional*, I, 157, 159.

[48] Steele, "The Humble Claim," *Poems on Subjects Chiefly Devotional*, II, 14.

[49] Ibid.

> O may my panting heart to thee aspire,
> With restless wishes, with intense desire
> Till full assurance of thy love impart
> The dawn of heaven to my enraptur'd heart![50]

This yearning for God fuels Steele's literary efforts. While her "longing mind" seeks to understand God, her "longing heart" desires to praise him.[51] This longing is perceived in her desire to convey meaning using imperfect human language, as she strives against the innate limitations of language and knowledge. She recognizes that her striving is doomed to failure.[52] Still, she remains hopeful, trusting that God's grace will "guide every song, / And fill my heart and tune my tongue."[53] She affirms that God is the source and inspiration of her praise:

> My panting soul aspires to try;
> To sing the great the glorious name
> Who gives thee all thy pleasing art[54]

Her persisting hopefulness is witnessed further in her belief that, despite her limitations, God will translate her efforts to praise him. She asks:

> Where is my God? does he retire
> Beyond the reach of humble sighs?
> Are these weak breathings of desire
> Too languid to ascend the skies?

and then answers the question she poses:

---

[50] Ibid., 15. In a prose meditation, Steele elaborates on this spiritual yearning: "There is a desire implanted in the human mind, which no earthly enjoyment can ever satisfy, a restless, craving wish for some distant happiness, some good unpossest!" To support her view, she quotes Pope: "That something which still prompts th'eternal sigh, / For which we wish to live, and dare to die." Steele, "Acquaintance with God the Supreme Good," *Poems on Subjects Chiefly Devotional*, III, 165.

[51] Steele, "The Sickly Mind," *Poems on Subjects Chiefly Devotional*, III, 8; Steele, "Imploring Divine Influence," *Poems on Subjects Chiefly Devotional*, I, 2.

[52] Steele considers that her "fetter'd powers" will not be free—that is, she will not be able to write as she would wish—until she is released from the bounds of earth and "upward learn[s] to fly." Steele, "The Fettered Mind," *Poems on Subjects Chiefly Devotional*, I, 227.

[53] Steele, "Imploring Divine Influence," *Poems on Subjects Chiefly Devotional*, I, 3.

[54] Steele, "Ode on a Rural Prospect in June," *Poems on Subjects Chiefly Devotional*, III, 43.

> He hears the breathings of desire,
> The weak petition if sincere,
> Is not forbidden to aspire,
> And hope to reach his gracious ear.[55]

Steele's language—"desire," "aspire," "hope"—clarifies her longing for God as her poetic inspiration and the impetus for her continued attempts to express devotion.

Even as Steele awaited the future healing of her various infirmities, both physical and emotional, she anticipated the eschatological perfection of her praise. She longed for the time when she would be able to join the praise already taking place in heaven. In a poem written for her sister after her mother's death, Steele juxtaposes Anne Cator Steele's earthly appearance, where she was

> enfeebled, bent with years,
> Worn out with pains, her mental powers decay'd
> And lost to social joys

with her presence in heaven, where "she shines amid the blissful choir."[56] Steele found hope in the notion that now in heaven, Anne Cator Steele had joined the song of angels, her praise perfected. Healing, in Steele's view, is associated with this ability to articulate praise worthy of God. And so she persists in longing for the transformation of her praise which is promised in heaven.[57]

Throughout Steele's writings, the theme of longing can be understood, essentially, as a desire to be in the presence of God, for only there will she find relief from human sorrow and finally be able to offer fitting praise to God. Steele's faith is oriented toward heaven, where she longs to enjoy God's presence eternally:

> Yes, Lord, in thy divine abode
> My soul desires, and hopes a place,
> To dwell for ever near my God,
> And view unveil'd thy lovely face.

---

[55] Steele, "Breathing after God," *Poems on Subjects Chiefly Devotional*, III, 130, 131.

[56] Steele, "To Amira on the Sudden Death of Her Mother," *Poems on Subjects Chiefly Devotional*, III, 40.

[57] Throughout her verse, Steele contrasts the song of heaven with the silence of earth. In an untitled and unpublished hymn, Steele distinguishes between heaven, where "Th' amazing pow'r of Grace Divine, / ...I sing," and earth, where storms threaten, and "Sorrow and guilt o'erwhelm my Soul"; when she mounts to heaven she is able to sing, but when she returns to earth, her song is silenced. Steele, untitled, STE 3/1/1, no. 57.

> With all my powers renew'd, refin'd,
> To join the blissful choir above;
> In strains immortal, unconfin'd
> To celebrate my Saviour's love.[58]

In God's presence she will be able to "view serene the shades of woe," for, writes Steele, "Thy smile, my God, forbids my fears."[59] And in God's presence she will be able to overcome those problems related to language and suffering which impeded her ability to praise God.

This spiritual desire, this inexorable draw towards God, resulted in Steele's expression of a spiritual longing which has similarly been articulated by believers throughout the history of Christianity. We find evidence of this longing in Psalm 63, where we read David's words: "O God, you are my God; earnestly I seek you; my soul thirsts for you; my flesh faints for you, as in a dry and weary land where there is no water" (Psalm 63:1). And much later, Augustine memorably depicts this spiritual restlessness: "You made us for Yourself, our hearts are restless until they rest in You."[60] We read of this longing in the writings of the mystics, where Gregory of Nyssa speaks of the endless longing for God, where the author of *The Cloud of Unknowing* tells us of the obscuring cloud that veils God from human sight, a cloud which can only be pierced by "naked intent" and the "dart of your loving desire," and where John of the Cross writes of "yearnings for God" that "become so great in the soul that the very bones seem to be dried up by this thirst."[61] And we encounter

---

[58] Steele, "Faith and Hope in Divine Goodness, Encouraged by Past Experience," *Poems on Subjects Chiefly Devotional*, III, 68. Similarly:
> Oh! could my weary spirit rise,
> And panting with intense desire,
> Reach the bright mansions in the skies,
> And mix among the blissful choirs.

Steele, "Desiring a Taste of Real Joy," *Poems on Subjects Chiefly Devotional*, I, 112.

[59] Steele, "Faith and Hope in Divine Goodness, Encouraged by Past Experience," *Poems on Subjects Chiefly Devotional*, III, 67.

[60] Augustine, *The Confessions of St. Augustine*, 11.

[61] The image Gregory uses to explain his vision of the spiritual life is that of Moses climbing Mount Sinai where he encounters God in darkness, but a darkness that elicits a truer experience of God than is possible from the light at the mountain's base. According to Gregory, a yearning for God is what motivates the seeker after God to climb the mountain, despite the difficulties inherent in the journey, in order to encounter God more truly. This notion of spiritual progression fuelled by desire is referred to in the thought of Gregory of Nyssa as *epiktasis*. Bernard McGinn clarifies that *epiktasis* is Gregory's teaching "that the goal of the Christian life, both here and in heaven, is the endless pursuit of the inexhaustible divine nature." McGinn, *The Foundations of Mysticism*, 1: 141.

The Cloud of Unknowing, 56, 55. The author of *The Cloud* offers Mary, of Mary and Martha, as a model of how we should fix our longing hearts on God: "She fastened her

this theme in the writings of later poets, including John Donne (c. 1572-1631), who writes of a "holy discontent" and his soul's "strong sober thirst," and George Herbert, who writes of the various blessings (strength, beauty, wisdom, honour, pleasure) that God has conferred on humanity, and who concludes, in God's voice:

> Yet let him keep the rest,
> But keep them with repining restlessness:
> Let him be rich and weary, that at least,
> If goodness lead him not, yet weariness
> May toss him to my breast.[62]

Clearly, in articulating her yearning not only for wholeness and understanding, but for the very near presence of God, Steele gave expression to a fundamental spiritual yearning which is at the heart of the Christian experience.

Writing as she did in the middle of the eighteenth century, Steele's literary efforts coincided with a time that has been called, by some, pre-Romanticism. The term suffers from problems of elasticity in definition as it is meant to signify a transitional literary period rather than a period characterized by any cohesive theory.[63] Still, it signals the advent of the Romantic Age, and as such is helpful in identifying and isolating Romantic tendencies in eighteenth-century writers. Pre-Romanticism is relevant to our present discussion since one of the distinguishing qualities of Romantic literature is, according to

---

love and longing on to that *cloud of unknowing* and learned to love him without seeing him in the clear light of reason or feeling his presence in the sensible delight of devotion." Ibid., 70 (italics in original).

John of the Cross, *Dark Night of the Soul*, 73.

While I have included Gregory of Nyssa, the author of *The Cloud of Unknowing*, and John of the Cross as representatives of this mystical longing, I might have included other mystical writers. Julian of Norwich, for example, tells us, "It is our task to live in longing and in penance until the time that we are led so deep into God that we verily and truly know our own soul." Julian of Norwich, *Revelation of Love*, 124. Julian, as do other classic mystical writers, positions human longing in the context of the prior longing of God for the human soul. The believer's yearning for God can only be in response to the initiating longing of God. Julian writes of God longing "to teach us to know him," "to have us with him in his bliss," and "to fill us full of bliss." Ibid., 163.

[62] Donne, "La Corona," *The Complete English Poems*, ed. A.J. Smith (London: Penguin Books, 1971), 310, 306; Herbert, "The Pulley," *The Complete English Poems*, 150.

[63] See Stone, *The Art of Poetry, 1750-1820*, 84-103; J.R. Watson, ed., *Pre-Romanticism in English Poetry of the Eighteenth Century: The Poetic Art and Significance of Thomson, Gray, Collins, Goldsmith, Cowper and Crabbe* (London: Macmillan Education, 1989), 102-117. Also, Stecher characterizes the pre-Romantics as having a "love for natural settings, melancholy, and solitude." Stecher, *Elizabeth Singer Rowe, the Poetess of Frome*, 195.

Corbin Scott Carnell, "a sense of aspiration and longing for the infinite."[64] Carnell likens this longing to a sense of alienation from that which is desired, and this estrangement finds echoes in Steele, for we have seen that her yearning was a result of her impression of God's absence and her desire to be in his presence. During the decades Steele was at work a shift was taking place from the clarity and rationality of the classical style to the more complex, because it allowed for mystery and emotion, style of Romanticism. Both can be traced in Steele's verse. We have seen that Steele's poetic efforts were classical in nature, and we have observed that her verse bore the marks of the Age of Sensibility. Here let us also note that her prolonged reflection on longing exhibits one of the key attributes of the coming Romantic Age.

To clarify the picture further, Steele's style should be considered not only with reference to then-current literary trends, but with an eye to her particular theological milieu. As we have noted, Steele's background was Calvinist, and this would find expression not only in the content of her hymnody, but also in its form. Donald Davie memorably depicts a Calvinist aesthetic as breathing "*simplicity, sobriety,* and *measure.*"[65] Thus, Isaac Watts's hymns, a product of "Old Dissent," have typically been described as having qualities of austerity and gravity and we have seen that he composed them with a view to making them accessible to a broad base of worshippers. According to J.R. Watson, Isaac Watts "eschews the dramatic and the emotional in favour of something finer, the controlled and reflective ordering of thought and passion."[66] As has already been noted, Steele fashioned her own verse after that of Watts, a fact

---

[64] Corbin Scott Carnell, *Bright Shadow of Reality: Spiritual Longing in C.S. Lewis* (Grand Rapids, MI: Eerdmans, 1974), 27. Carnell's book treats the theme of spiritual longing in the writings of C.S. Lewis, but is helpful in the current discussion of longing in Steele's hymnody. Carnell identifies Lewis as the first literary critic to name this sense of spiritual longing which features in so much literature. Lewis uses the word *Sehnsucht*, meaning "longing" or "yearning," but Carnell points out that the concept has the added element of "nostalgia," for, according to Carnell, "basic to its various manifestations is an underlying sense of displacement or alienation from what is desired." Ibid., 14-15. Karl Barth similarly correlates Romanticism with yearning. He writes, "Romanticism is pure as yearning, and only as yearning." Karl Barth, "Novalis," in *Protestant Theology in the Nineteenth Century: Its Background and History*, new ed., trans. Brian Cozens and John Bowden, intro. by Colin E. Gunton (Grand Rapids, MI: Eerdmans, 2002), 333.

[65] Davie explains: "The aesthetic *and* the moral perceptions have, built into them and near to the heart of them, the perception of licence, of abandonment, of superfluity, foreseen, even invited, and yet in the end denied, fended off. Art *is* measure, *is* exclusion; is therefore simplicity (hard-earned), is sobriety, tense with all the extravagances that it has been tempted by and has denied itself." Davie, *A Gathered Church*, 25-26 (italics in original). N.H. Keeble similarly notes that the style of seventeenth-century Puritanism set as its virtues "clarity, simplicity and plainness." Keeble, *The Literary Culture of Nonconformity*, 240.

[66] Watson, *The English Hymn*, 169.

that was discerned even by her contemporaries. Karen Smith records a letter from James Fanch to his brother-in-law, Daniel Turner; in it, Fanch comments on Steele's verse some years before its publication, comparing her work to that of Isaac Watts:

> Her poetical compositions, both of the serious and amusing kind are almost inimitable, much beyond anything I have yet seen since those of Dr. Watts. She aims not at the sublime or any high flights of imagination but her productions are admirably correct and delicate. I have several of them in my hands which she desired me to review, all which are truly delightful.[67]

Fanch's remarks, that Steele's verse "aims not at the sublime or any high flights of imagination" and that it is "admirably correct and delicate," find echoes in Davie's criteria of Calvinist art being marked by *"simplicity, sobriety,* and *measure."*

So while Steele's verse offers an extended meditation on longing, and in so doing signals the coming Romantic Age, she maintains the Calvinistic disposition typical of her heritage. In her hymns in particular, her tone is restrained and often plaintive and introspective. Conversely, we have the

---

[67] Smith, "The Community and the Believer," 251-252, citing Daniel Turner, *Brief Memoirs of the Revd. Mr. James Fanch late pastor of the church at Romsey, Hants.* (n.d.), 29. James Fanch (1704-1767) was born in Hertfordshire and moved with his sister, Ann, and brother-in-law, Daniel Turner, to Reading in 1741. In 1745, he accepted an invitation to serve the Baptist congregation at Romsey. Fanch had trouble at Romsey, but was supported by nearby ministers such as John Lacy, pastor of the church at Portsmouth, and Steele's father, William Steele, pastor at Broughton. Smith, "The Community and the Believer," 3, 84. Anne Steele encouraged Fanch to publish *Paraphrase of the Psalms of David, translated from the Latin* (1761). Reeves, "Literary Women in Eighteenth-Century Nonconformist Circles," in *Culture and the Nonconformist Tradition*, 12. John Lacy (1700-1781) was himself a hymn-writer, publishing his small volume, *Divine Hymns, Made on the Most Important Points of Christianity*, in 1776.

Daniel Turner (1710-1798) was called to be pastor of the Baptist church in Reading in 1741, and moved in 1748 to be the minister of the church at Abingdon. He was a friend and correspondent of the hymn-writers Robert Robinson, John Rippon, and Isaac Watts, and himself became well known for his hymns, four of which were published in Ash and Evans's "Bristol Collection," and eight in Rippon's *Selection*. He wrote "Beyond the Glittering Starry Skies" with James Fanch. S.L. Copson, "Turner, Daniel (1710-1798)," *Oxford Dictionary of National Biography* (Oxford: Oxford University Press, 2004 [http://www.oxforddnb.com/view/article/27845, accessed 1 May 2006]). After Steele's death in 1778, Turner wrote a letter of condolence to her niece, Mary Steele Dunscombe, which reads, in part, "Sweet was the Lyre she so often devoutly tuned to her melodious Songs amongst us here on Earth, but infinitely Sweeter that Golden Harp with which she is accompanying the *New Song* to *Him that Sits upon the Throne, & the Lamb that Was Slain*." Daniel Turner to Mary Steele Dunscombe, 19 November 1778, STE 5/16.

hymnody of Charles Wesley, whose enthusiasm is motivated by a spiritual confidence in keeping with his theological beliefs. Where Wesley believes that God can restore believers' hearts in their earthly lives, Steele is more inhibited by human finitude and sinfulness. Thus, for Steele, the restoration of the heart by divine grace was anticipated in the future. It was something for which to hope, because at present God's "radiant face" remained hidden behind a "veil of interposing night."[68] Therefore, while Steele's hymnody is marked throughout by a spiritual longing, it is distinguished from the more emotive longing of Methodism and Romanticism in being tempered by the more classically sober spiritual posture of the Calvinists.[69]

Steele's longing for God found expression in her hymnody both as a recurring theme and as her motivation itself, stimulating her as a poet to strive against the limitations of human language. According to Mark Burrows, there is a "longing inherent in language itself"; similarly, Paul van Buren argues that religious language, and religious poetry in particular, "is the result of a longing, an intensity of concern, a passion for some aspect of our linguistic existence."[70] The poet's task, the hymn-writer's task—indeed, Steele's task—is to challenge the limits of language in an attempt to convey religious meaning, even as she believes that she will fail in her task. It is not an easy task, to be sure, for language, according to Robert Shaw, is "the Christian poet's cross."[71] Steele's hymns reveal a longing for a presence that persistently eluded her, along with a related longing to put into words meaning that continually frustrated her attempts to convey. Language resists us because God is ineffable, but this fuelled Steele's poetic imagination and created the stimulus for her hymn-writing efforts.

Therefore, the problems Steele encountered with regard to language and suffering which might have prevented her from attempting to articulate praise to an ineffable God were overcome, in part, by her relentless longing to experience the presence of God, despite his felt absence, and to convey meaning about God, although she was encumbered by imperfect human language. Steele's faith was essentially hopeful, as she anticipated the day when her praise of God would be perfectly articulated. While on earth, writing hymns in the midst of her ongoing suffering, tormented by feelings of literary inadequacy—and resigned to these manifestations of human frailty and a

---

[68] Steele, "Christ the Supreme Beauty," *Poems on Subjects Chiefly Devotional*, I, 156.

[69] It is worth noting that Donald Davie correlates Methodistical evangelicalism and Romanticism, on the one hand, and, on the other, Calvinism and Classicism. Davie, *A Gathered Church*, 26.

[70] This longing, according to Burrows, is "the 'place' of our creativity." Mark S. Burrows, "'Raiding the Inarticulate': Mysticism, Poetics, and the Unlanguagable," in *Minding the Spirit*, 350; Paul M. van Buren, *The Edges of Language: An Essay in the Logic of a Religion* (New York: Macmillan Company, 1972), 115, 106.

[71] Shaw, "George Herbert: The Word of God and the Words of Man," in *Ineffability*, 92.

divinely sovereign will—Steele longed for the experience of God's promised presence and waited for that experience to translate itself into her hymnody. In the following section, we will see how the themes of resignation and longing found meaningful expression in several of Steele's hymns.

Tracing the Themes of Resignation and Longing in Anne Steele's Hymns

The themes of resignation and longing can be traced throughout Steele's hymnody: at times one or the other comprises the particular focus of a single hymn, while at other times both themes are developed in the same hymn. In those hymns in which the themes of resignation and longing coexist, we find meaningful insight into Steele's spirituality, which is marked by both a humble acceptance of her limited capacity to know God while confined to earth, as well as an unremitting desire to enjoy his presence in the future. Throughout, we see that despite her prolonged meditations on earthly suffering and human inarticulacy—despite her perception of God as ineffable—Steele's hymnody remains essentially hopeful, enabling her to make affirmations about God and the spiritual life.

Steele's hymn, "Desiring Resignation and Thankfulness," compellingly demonstrates how the theme of resignation found particular expression in her hymnody. She begins by acknowledging the coexistence of sorrow and joy in the world:

> When I survey life's varied scene,
>   Amid the darkest hours,
> Sweet rays of comfort shine between,
>   And thorns are mix'd with flowers.
>
> Lord, teach me to adore thy hand,
>   From whence my comforts flow;
> And let me in this desart land
>   A glimpse of Canaan know.[72]

Shafts of light pierce the oppressive dark; flowers emerge from amidst the threatening thorns. In this "varied scene," Steele prays that she will be able to recognize those moments of joy, of "health and ease," and praise God for

---

[72] Steele, "Desiring Resignation and Thankfulness," *Poems on Subjects Chiefly Devotional*, I, 134. According to J.R. Watson, Steele "contemplates the world as a place where good and evil happen (the deaths of children, her own loss of a fiancé), and recognizes its double nature feelingly: she is conscious of its beauty and fertility, but also of its unhappiness." Watson, *The English Hymn*, 198.

them.[73] Then, characteristically, Steele turns to contemplate the "griefs and pains" which recur with troubling frequency in her life.[74] She lingers over those times

> When present sufferings pain my heart,
>   Or future terrors rise,
> And light and hope almost depart
>   From these dejected eyes.[75]

For while it is natural to praise God when he gives her "delightful gifts," it is more difficult to articulate praise when she finds herself in a "desert land."[76]

In these dry times, in these times of trouble, Steele concludes that she must "wait resign'd," trusting that God has not abandoned her, despite her experience of his absence; she must have faith that he remains in sovereign control.[77] Her hymn therefore concludes:

> And O, whate'er of earthly bliss
>   Thy sovereign hand denies,
> Accepted at thy throne of grace,
>   Let this petition rise.
>
> "Give me a calm, a thankful heart,
>   "From every murmur free;
> "The blessings of thy grace impart,
>   "And let me live to thee.
>
> "Let the sweet hope that thou are mine,
>   "My path of life attend;
> "Thy presence through my journey shine,
>   "And bless its happy end."[78]

---

[73] Steele, "Desiring Resignation and Thankfulness," *Poems on Subjects Chiefly Devotional*, I, 135.

[74] Ibid.

[75] Ibid.

[76] Ibid., 135, 134.

[77] Ibid., 135. Susannah Harrison, whose hymns were introduced earlier, also encouraged resignation as the proper response to personal suffering. In a poem entitled "A Short Dialogue between Myself and My Soul," Harrison describes how she is "dispos'd to grieve" and how she spends her "Days and Nights in Tears." Her soul, in response, recommends "Resignation to His holy Will." Harrison, "A Short Dialogue between Myself and My Soul," *Songs in the Night*, 135-136.

[78] Steele, "Desiring Resignation and Thankfulness," *Poems on Subjects Chiefly Devotional*, I, 136. It has become part of the standard lore surrounding Steele's life that she composed this hymn in response to the drowning death of her fiancé. For example,

Steele's confidence that a sovereign God deals both joy and sorrow persuades her that the appropriate spiritual posture is consistently one of thankfulness and calm acceptance, whether life is characterized by "health and ease" or "griefs and pains." Thus, she resigns herself to the will of God, but she maintains the "sweet hope" that she will recognize God's presence in her earthly life and be rewarded with a more complete knowledge of his presence at the end of her life. This hope enables her to praise God, despite her "present sufferings" and the threat of "future terrors."

Steele's hymns are consistently more hopeful than the verse of her near contemporary, William Cowper. While Cowper also advocates resignation as the appropriate response to his experiences of personal suffering and God's consequent absence, his verse more often remains in a place of anxiety. See, for example, his hymn, "The Waiting Soul":

> I wish, thou know'st, to be resign'd,
>   And wait with patient hope;
> But hope delay'd fatigues the mind,
>   And drinks the spirit up.[79]

Cowper's extreme spiritual angst, issuing from his unrelenting view of God's impending judgement, impaired his ability to hope in God or in his own future redemption. Marshall and Todd argue that, while Cowper seemed to "ground his faith, in Wesleyan fashion, in...subjective experience," his theology created a problem for those feelings: he had no cause to hope for future happiness. They write, "The bridge to God, spun of one's own feelings, could not hold...if one retained a Calvinist fear of divine wrath and a conviction of total human

---

about that event and this hymn, Emma Pitman writes, "It was a tempest of sorrow at first; then it subsided, and she penned one of our sweetest hymns on resignation." Pitman, *Lady Hymn Writers*, 68. Moreover, this hymn is Steele's most frequently published. John Julian indicates that "Father, Whate'er of Earthly Bliss" is a cento, taken from "Desiring Resignation and Thankfulness." He states that the many centos taken from "Desiring Resignation and Thankfulness" put together to give it a wider circulation than any of Steele's other texts. Julian, *A Dictionary of Hymnology*, 2: 1269. In North America, "Father, Whate'er of Earthly Bliss" appeared 720 times between the years 1792 and 1969, in a wide variety of hymnbooks. The Dictionary of American Hymnology, Oberlin College, Ohio.

[79] Cowper, "The Waiting Soul," *Olney Hymns*, 322. In his hymn, "Submission," in which he asks God, "help me to resign, / life, health, and comfort to thy will," he begins to sound almost hopeful, but then ends on this gloomy note:
> But ah! my inward spirit cries,
>   Still bind me to thy sway;
> Else the next cloud that vails my skies,
>   Drives all these thoughts away.

Cowper, "Submission," *Olney Hymns*, 344-345.

depravity."⁸⁰ On the other hand, even the ordering of Steele's hymns reflects her desire to set her spiritual anxieties in the context of Christian hope. The poem, "Ode to Melancholy" is immediately followed by what would seem to be a companion piece, "Ode to Hope." Here, the hymn, "Desiring Resignation and Thankfulness" is followed by "Desiring the Presence of God," suggesting that while she faithfully resigns herself to the will of God, she longs with hope for the comfort of his presence, asking, "When will the mournful night be gone?"⁸¹

The theme of longing is considered more specifically in Steele's hymn, "Thirsting after God." Again the hymn begins in a scene of dryness and desolation as Steele portrays a soul "fainting in the sultry waste, / And parch'd with thirst extreme."⁸² Her "weary fainting mind" is "Oppress'd with sins and woes," making it difficult to praise God.⁸³ Yet the prevailing image in this hymn is of a soul longing for water that would refresh the "drooping spirits" of the "weary pilgrim," and this water is the presence of God.⁸⁴ Only these "flowing streams of life" can "ease the panting heart," just as only God's presence can satisfy Steele's spiritual longing.⁸⁵ She writes:

> O may I thirst for thee, my God,
>   With ardent, strong desire;
> And still through all this desert road,
>   To taste thy grace aspire.⁸⁶

This longing for the "soul-reviving spring" from "Whence heavenly comfort flows" derives from Steele's hope that her thirst might be quenched by God—that she might, she prays, "taste thy grace."⁸⁷ Where once her words caught in her throat for dryness, a taste of this life-giving water loosens her tongue:

> Then shall my prayer to thee ascend,
>   A grateful sacrifice;

---

⁸⁰ Marshall and Todd, *English Congregational Hymns in the Eighteenth Century*, 139.

⁸¹ Steele, "Desiring the Presence of God," *Poems on Subjects Chiefly Devotional*, I, 136. Steele does not question so much why she is made to endure suffering as she faithfully asks, with the psalmist, "How long, O Lord? Will you forget me forever? How long will you hide your face from me?" Psalm 13:1. The hymn is based, in actuality, on Isaiah 50:10, which reads, in part, "Let him who walks in darkness and has no light, trust in the name of the Lord and rely on his God."

⁸² Steele, "Thirsting after God," *Poems on Subjects Chiefly Devotional*, I, 28.

⁸³ Ibid., 29.

⁸⁴ Ibid., 29, 28.

⁸⁵ Ibid., 29.

⁸⁶ Ibid.

⁸⁷ Ibid.

> My plaintive voice thou wilt attend,
> And grant me full supplies.[88]

It is significant that Steele does not forget the place of desolation in which her hymn began; while her voice is lifted in praise, it remains a "plaintive voice." Yet her intense desire for God and the hope of her future redemption, despite her spiritual dryness on "this desert road," enable her to raise her voice in a "grateful sacrifice."

We sometimes see the theme of longing actually shape the form of Steele's verse. Most often, she exhibits the classical sobriety and conventional hymn form associated with her exemplar, Isaac Watts, but at these moments of spiritual yearning her verse sometimes assumes the more naturally broken speech often associated with the hymns of Charles Wesley.[89] While Steele's use of lyrical forms was normally anything but bold, she did write some hymns which exhibit what J.R. Watson depicts as "sharp, jagged interruptions to her otherwise even-toned and regular verses."[90] And these moments most often occur in the context of her devotion to Christ—that is, her joy as she hopes for redemption and her anticipation of spiritual fulfillment made possible by Christ's sacrifice. This distinctive characteristic is well illustrated in her hymn, "The Wonders of Redemption," which begins, typically, with a question:

> And did the holy and the just,
> The Sovereign of the skies,
> Stoop down to wretchedness and dust,
> That guilty worms might rise?[91]

Steele sets up the fundamental disparity between the divine and human: she contrasts "the holy and the just" with "wretchedness and dust"; the "Sovereign of the skies" is made to "Stoop down" to "guilty worms" on earth. Having thus set the scene, Steele meditates on the meaning of Christ's incarnation and subsequent death:

> Yes, the Redeemer left his throne,
> His radiant throne on high,
> (Surprizing mercy! love unknown!)
> To suffer, bleed and die.

---

[88] Ibid.
[89] Marshall and Todd notably judge the "two emotions that powered Wesley's hymns" to be "longing and ecstasy." Marshall and Todd, *English Congregational Hymns in the Eighteenth Century*, 131.
[90] Watson, *The English Hymn*, 194.
[91] Steele, "The Wonders of Redemption," *Poems on Subjects Chiefly Devotional*, I, 175.

> He took the dying traitor's place,
> And suffer'd in his stead;
> For man, (O miracle of grace!)
> For man the Saviour bled![92]

These parenthetical interjections interrupt the typically steady flow of her hymns, so that in creating this moment of suspense her verse effectively echoes the theme of longing: form follows content.[93] Having thus exclaimed, Steele again recedes into her more typical style of asking questions, and her more characteristic hesitancy regarding her own worthiness. She wonders, "And may I hope that love extends / Its sacred power to me?"[94]

It is also interesting to note the way in which Steele's use of repetition, "For man... / For man," causes the singer to linger over the cause of Christ's death, acknowledging her own role in requiring this sacrifice. We see this technique again in her hymn, "Praise to God for the Blessings of Providence and Grace," where we read:

> 'Tis here, I view with pleasing pain,
> How Jesus left the sky,
> (Almighty love! surprising scene!)
> For man, lost man, to die.[95]

Note also the typical juxtaposition between Jesus in heaven and "man, lost man" on earth. And, interestingly, notice the paradoxical "pleasing pain"—a sacrifice which is at once painful yet pleasing, in that through it her salvation is

---

[92] Ibid.

[93] See also her unpublished hymn, "On the Nativity of Christ":
> When Jesus left his glorious Throne
> (Amazing grace!) to dwell on Earth;
> The sons of harmony came down
> To celebrate his wond'rous birth.

Steele, "On the Nativity of Christ," STE 3/1/4, no. 2. For a variant form of this hymn, see Steele, untitled, STE 3/1/4, no. 18, where Steele departs from her almost exclusive use of quatrains to add a concluding couplet to each verse, as a kind of refrain, so that the verse just noted ends:
> Heav'n sent it's Envoys to proclaim
> Glory to God the Saviour's Name.

Here we again see the structure of the verse—her use of six lines rather than the usual four—shift in response to her subject.

[94] Steele, "The Wonders of Redemption," *Poems on Subjects Chiefly Devotional*, I, 176.

[95] The "here" with which Steele begins this verse points back to God's "sacred word," wherein she is able to see God, and "Where all thy glories shine." Steele, "Praise to God for the Blessings of Providence and Grace," *Poems on Subjects Chiefly Devotional*, I, 51-52.

won.[96] These antithetical emotions provide another compelling example of the crossed sentiments which Donald Davie marks as a sign of the literature of sensibility.[97] In their startling contrast, they also cause the reader to hesitate, so that again the form of Steele's hymn imitates its content.

While many of Steele's hymns take as their theme either resignation or longing, more interesting still are those hymns which consider the themes together. Steele begins her hymn, "Acknowledging His Goodness in Supporting and Restoring," by praying for the grace to accept humbly the "afflicting pains" which she understands to come from the hand of God.[98] Her grief emits merely a "plaintive sigh," and even as Steele resigns herself to the will of God, she acknowledges that while he chastens he also "pities and restores."[99] God's

---

[96] A similar paradox is found in an interjectory line in "The Excellency of the Holy Scriptures." Here, Steele writes:
> But when his painful sufferings rise,
>   (Delightful, dreadful scene!)
> Angels may read with wondering eyes
>   That Jesus died for men.

Steele, "The Excellency of the Holy Scriptures," *Poems on Subjects Chiefly Devotional*, I, 60. J.R. Watson surmises that Steele probably borrowed the phrase from Matthew Prior (1664-1721), who wrote of "the dear dreadful thought of a God crucified." Watson, *The English Hymn*, 194, quoting Matthew Prior, from a poem of 1685, "Advice to the Painter. On the Happy Defeat of the Rebels in the West, and the Execution of the Duke of Monmouth," in *Poems on Affairs of State* (1703). Steele repeats this phrase in her poem, "The Complaint and Relief": "Eternity—delightful, dreadful name!" Steele, "The Complaint and Relief," *Poems on Subjects Chiefly Devotional*, II, 114. While Steele may have been influenced directly or indirectly by Prior, it should be noted that the phrase is also found in Watts, as in "Bring that delightful, dreadful Day"—that is, judgment day. Watts, "A Happy Resurrection," *Hymns and Spiritual Songs*, 174.

[97] Note also that Steele's use of parenthetical references aligns these hymns with the verse characteristic of the Age of Sensibility which, according to Janet Todd, was characterized by "Exclamation marks, brackets, italics and capitals." Todd, *Sensibility*, 5.

[98] Steele, "Acknowledging His Goodness in Supporting and Restoring," *Poems on Subjects Chiefly Devotional*, III, 75.

[99] Steele notes that while God afflicts her, "His mercy holds the rod." Ibid., 75-76. The image of God disciplining with "the rod" is common in eighteenth-century hymnody, and has biblical precedence, as in Proverbs 29:15: "The rod and reproof give wisdom, but a child left to himself brings shame to his mother." In a hymn which clarifies both Steele's willingness to resign herself to the will of God as well as her Calvinistic piety, Steele writes, "Lord at thy feet I fain would lie, / And learn to kiss the rod." Steele, "Filial Submission," *Poems on Subjects Chiefly Devotional*, III, 132. Similarly, "Low at thy feet submissive I adore / Thy chastening hand, not murmur at the rod." Steele, "Written in a Painful Illness," *Poems on Subjects Chiefly Devotional*, III, 54. See also Maria Frances Cecelia Madan's poem, "The Consolation":
> With silent and submissive awe
>   Ador'd a chastening God,

mercy prompts her to praise him, yet she characteristically mourns her inability to compose worthy praise:

> Ah! how unequal to the theme
>   Our feeble efforts prove!
> Ye heavens resound his glorious name,
>   While we adore and love.
>
> Yet fain my grateful soul would bring
>   Her tribute to thy throne;
> Accept the wish, my God, my King,
>   To make thy goodness known![100]

She longs to praise God more fully and knows that her devotion would be more worthy if she could more fully experience God's presence. For now she trusts that God will mediate her desire. She concludes the hymn:

> O be the life thy hand restores
>   Devoted to thy praise!
> To thee, be sacred all my powers,
>   To thee, my future days!
>
> Thy soul-enlivening grace impart,
>   A warmer love inspire;

    Rever'd the terrors of his law,
        And humbly kiss'd the rod.

[Maria Frances Cowper], *Original Poems. On Various Occasions. By a Lady*, rev. William Cowper (London: J. Deighton, J. Mathews, R. Faulder, 1792), 22. Maria Madan (1726-1797), later Maria Cowper, published religious verse, and Margaret Maison notes that her life was "overshadowed by more than its fair share of 'dark events.'" Maison, "'Thine, Only Thine!' Women Hymn Writers in Britain, 1760-1835," in *Religion in the Lives of English Women*, 24, quoting Madan, "The Consolation," *Original Poems. On Various Occasions. By a Lady*, 22. She was the daughter of poet, Judith Madan (1702-1781), sister of Church of England clergyman, Martin Madan (1725-1790), and cousin of William Cowper. The Madan family was well connected with leading evangelicals such as Selina Hastings, Countess of Huntingdon and John Wesley. Martin Madan was himself a hymn-writer and published *A Collection of Psalms and Hymns* in 1760, which J.R. Watson considers "a robust, no-nonsense collection," indicating that in it Madan "aimed for plainness and simplicity." Watson, *The English Hymn*, 266. Despite his contribution to eighteenth-century hymnody, Madan is better remembered as an advocate of polygamy, the social benefits of which he argued in his book, *Thelyphthora* (1780).

[100] Steele, "Acknowledging His Goodness in Supporting and Restoring," *Poems on Subjects Chiefly Devotional*, III, 76.

> And teach the breathings of my heart
> Dependence and desire.[101]

In the end, she acknowledges that God must teach her to long for him more completely, even as he guides her to depend on him in humble resignation.

Steele's Calvinistic background resulted in her often positioning herself humbly at God's feet. References to this humility pervade her hymnody. She bends "Low at thy gracious feet."[102] She "wait[s] beneath thy feet."[103] She writes, "Here, at thy feet, I wait thy will."[104] In each case, she subjects her own will to the greater will of God, resigning herself to his will for her life. This typical stance, however, is countered in just as many instances by Steele's longing to glimpse the face of God, which symbolizes his very near presence. She exclaims, "My God, the visits of thy face / Afford superior joy."[105] She anticipates the day when she will be able to "view, unveil'd, thy radiant face."[106] She longs for his presence:

> But oh! to shew thy smiling face,
>   To bring thy glories near—
> Amazing and transporting grace
>   To dwell with mortals here![107]

When these corresponding images, of God's feet and face, are brought together we see how Steele was able to reconcile resignation and longing. The limitations of her humanity resign her to assume humbly a position "Low at thy feet," yet she longs for God's presence, symbolized by his face, where she will enjoy "True pleasure, peace, and rest."[108] She knows that when she is "absent from [her] Lord" she lives a life which is "Unsatisfy'd, unblest."[109] Yet when God looks on her with pity, "Then shall the mourner at thy feet, / Rejoice to seek thy face."[110] Though Steele positions herself at God's feet, faithful hope in

---

[101] Ibid.
[102] Steele, "Intreating the Presence of God in Affliction," *Poems on Subjects Chiefly Devotional*, III, 73.
[103] Steele, "God the Only Refuge of the Troubled Mind," *Poems on Subjects Chiefly Devotional*, I, 146.
[104] Steele, "Light and Deliverance," *Poems on Subjects Chiefly Devotional*, I, 20.
[105] Steele, "The Transforming Vision of God," *Poems on Subjects Chiefly Devotional*, I, 32.
[106] Ibid., 33.
[107] Steele, "The Condescension of God," *Poems on Subjects Chiefly Devotional*, I, 66.
[108] Steele, "Penitence and Hope," *Poems on Subjects Chiefly Devotional*, III, 79-80.
[109] Ibid., 80.
[110] Ibid.

God's mercy compels her to seek his face with longing love.[111]

At first glance, the themes of resignation and longing would appear to be incompatible, for, put simply, resignation implies the acceptance of what is, while longing suggests the desire for something more. Yet in Steele's hymns the themes do not contradict but instead are held together in a fruitful tension which illuminates her particular spirituality. In Steele's life and hymnody, the tensions accumulate: she resigned herself to chronic illness even while longing for the healing of Christ, the "Great Physician"; she accepted the various griefs of life even while desiring the comforting presence of God; she resigned herself to her own literary inadequacies and the insufficiency of language itself even while continuing to attempt to articulate meaningful praise to God. Paradoxically, Steele's persistent assertion that she is incapable of expressing truth about an ineffable God conveys rich meaning about the spiritual life, and about her spirituality in particular, with its concurrent attention to both the human need for redemption and the divine response to that need.

The Word Breaks the Silence

Through much of this book, we have considered Anne Steele's spirituality primarily in light of her prolonged reflection on God's transcendent nature, and we have observed her consequent deductions regarding the ineffability of God. But Steele's faith, and the expression of that faith in her hymnody, cannot be appreciated completely without some consideration given to her powerful devotion to the person of Christ. Hoxie Neale Fairchild makes the remarkable claim, "It would be difficult to find a writer of the period whose thought is more consistently Christ-centred than Theodosia's."[112] Certainly it is not

---

[111] This tension is felt throughout her writings, as when she pleads with God, "Forgive the boldness of a sinful worm, let me repeat my request, I beseech thee shew me thy glory!" Steele, "Longing for the Manifestations of Divine Love," *Poems on Subjects Chiefly Devotional*, III, 208. Compare Steele's vision of the spiritual life to that of Bernard of Clairvaux (1090-1135), who describes a formative spirituality as a series of kisses given to one's Lover: the beginner Christian's kiss on God's foot is replaced by a kiss on the hand which later reaches its height when it progresses to a kiss on the mouth. Bernard of Clairvaux, *Selected Works*, trans. and foreword by G.R. Evans, intro. by Jean LeClercq, preface by Ewert H. Cousins, Classics of Western Spirituality (New York: Paulist Press, 1987), 222-223. According to Bernard, the spiritual life moves from contrition, the kiss on God's foot, to intimacy, the final kiss on the mouth, which represents ultimate union with God. The imagery of a series of kisses as expressed by Bernard is representative of a long tradition in Christian spirituality in which the relationship between God and the soul is understood as that between a Lover and his beloved. The desire for this intimacy is expressed on the part of the beloved as an intense yearning for the Lover.

[112] Fairchild, *Religious Trends in English Poetry*, 2: 114. John Julian similarly notes Steele's "intense personal devotion to the Lord Jesus." Julian, *A Dictionary of*

unusual for Steele to locate the source of her hope in Christ's incarnation. With reference to Jesus's birth, she writes, for example, "Methinks I see some transient beams of hope dawning through the solid gloom," yet characteristically wonders, "can they reach a heart so impenetrably hard."[113] Christ's incarnation relates significantly to Steele's efforts to express the ineffable, for through Jesus, the Word made flesh, God is present to frail humanity; in Christ, God is no longer entirely transcendent and necessarily ineffable.

It is instructive to observe how Christ is portrayed in Steele's hymnody. Particularly compelling, given her chronic ill health, is her image of Christ as physician:

> Ye mourning sinners, here disclose
> Your deep complaints your various woes;
> Approach, 'tis Jesus, he can heal
> The pains which mourning sinners feel.
>
> To eyes long clos'd in mental night,
> Strangers to all the joys of light,
> His word imparts a blissful ray:
> Sweet morning of celestial day!
>
> Ye helpless lame, lift up your eyes,
> The Lord, the Saviour bids you rise;
> New life and strength his voice conveys,
> And plaintive groans are chang'd for praise.[114]

The "mourning sinners" who are afflicted with these "various woes" are clarified as the "helpless lame," those with "fatal leprosy," those suffering from a "burning fever" or "freezing palsy," and those in "mental night."[115] The range of maladies is as diverse as it is specific, and Steele stands with the variously

---

Hymnology, 2: 1089. Louis Benson echoes Julian, observing Steele's "intense devotion to Christ's person." Benson, *The English Hymn*, 214. J.R. Watson, for his part, judges Steele's solution to the suffering she experienced to be "to enter into a personal relationship with the Saviour, in a way which parallels the writing of her contemporary Charles Wesley." Watson, *The English Hymn*, 198.

[113] Steele, "Self Reflection," STE 3/4, no. 4.

[114] Steele, "The Great Physician," *Poems on Subjects Chiefly Devotional*, I, 15. Elsewhere, Steele uses the image of God as physician to convey an evangelical message of the need for salvation. Sin is likened to "a raging fever," a "dire contagion," and "poison"; the "great Physician," however, is able to provide "a sovereign cure" and reinstate "Life, health, and bliss" by means of "the Saviour's dying blood." Steele, "Christ the Physician of Souls," *Poems on Subjects Chiefly Devotional*, I, 63-64.

[115] Steele, "The Great Physician," *Poems on Subjects Chiefly Devotional*, I, 15-16.

afflicted. She continues:

> When freezing palsy chills the veins,
> And pale, cold death, already reigns,
> He speaks; the vital powers revive:
> He speaks, and dying sinners live.
>
> Dear Lord, we wait thy healing hand;
> Diseases fly at thy command;
> O let thy sovereign touch impart
> Life, strength, and health to every heart!
>
> Then shall the sick, the blind, the lame,
> Adore their Great Physician's name;
> Then dying souls shall bless their God,
> And spread thy wondrous praise abroad.[116]

Here is an image of Christ inhabiting the same space as a suffering humanity, of the Word itself dwelling among us, bringing wholeness and understanding. It is not surprising that Steele would find comfort in a vision of Christ's healing presence. Significantly, we notice that healing is depicted as resulting from the spoken word of Christ. For in Christ, the Word speaks into the silence of spiritual desolation which is caused by humanity's alienation from God. The incarnation thus breaks the silence caused by our separation from God.

The incarnation also has the power to break the silence caused by the incapacities of human language. For sin, Steele tells us, afflicts human language as it does the human soul. And in the same way in which Christ redeems humanity from sin, so is human language redeemed by Christ's incarnation. Across the centuries, Christians have found hope in this redemption of language. Marcia Colish observes that, according to medieval

---

[116] Ibid., 16. Compare Steele's deferential appeal to Christ's healing presence with Charles Wesley's more ecstatic and confident version:
> Hear him, ye deaf: his praise, ye dumb,
>   Your loosened tongues employ;
> Ye blind, behold your Saviour comes,
>   And leap ye lame for joy!

Wesley, "Hymn I," *A Collection of Hymns, for the Use of the People Called Methodists*, 8. Both hymns allude to the language of Isaiah 35:5-6, where we read, "Then the eyes of the blind shall be opened, and the ears of the deaf unstopped; then shall the lame man leap like a deer, and the tongue of the mute sing for joy." But where Steele reveals her prevailing sensitivity to human suffering and anticipates healing and fitting praise, Wesley locates God's healing in the present and proclaims a more immediate redemption.

thinkers, human language is "reborn through the Incarnation."[117] Similarly, Robert Shaw relays George Herbert's belief that "fallen language may be redeemed through the willingness of the Word to assume the burden of human utterance."[118] And, significantly, as the Word delivers human language from the strictures of sin, so it frees humanity to communicate the message of the Word to the world. Or, in Augustine's words, "He was made weak, so that He might be spoken by us, despite our weakness."[119]

Finally, the incarnation not only enables humanity's earthly praise, it provides the way for the eschatological perfection of our praise in heaven. Many of Steele's hymns thus anticipate the immortal song of heaven. By means of example, let us consider a final hymn, "The Joys of Heaven," in which we again perceive Steele's Christ-centred spirituality. Here we read:

> There on a throne, (how dazling bright!)
>   The exalted Saviour shines;
> And beams ineffable delight
>   On all the heavenly minds.
>
> There shall the followers of the Lamb
>   Join in immortal songs;
> And endless honours to his name
>   Employ their tuneful tongues.[120]

Now glorified, the Lamb inspires eternal worship in those whose powers of speech, and thus ability to praise, were once compromised by a persisting sinfulness. In Christ, God brought near, the Word breaks the silence, transfiguring human praise through the experience of divine love, and creating a way for the fulfillment of human longing—the promised presence of God and the eschatological perfection of praise.

---

[117] Colish, *The Mirror of Language*, 3.
[118] Shaw, "George Herbert: The Word of God and the Words of Man," in *Ineffability*, 90.
[119] Augustine, quoted in Colish, *The Mirror of Language*, 35.
[120] Steele, "The Joys of Heaven," *Poems on Subjects Chiefly Devotional*, I, 35-36.

CHAPTER 6

Conclusion

When Anne Steele published *Poems on Subjects Chiefly Devotional* in 1760, she made a distinctive contribution to the new and flourishing hymn genre, already rich with the compositions of Isaac Watts, Charles Wesley, and numerous others. Many of the hymns written during the eighteenth century are bolstered by a confidence of expression in keeping with the didactic ends to which their writers aspired, for we have seen that the hymn as a genre aimed not only to please, as a literary art form, but also to edify, as it provided a means by which to rehearse a particular theology. Yet in Steele's hymns we find evidence of an unanticipated tentativeness. We discover an introspective searching for answers to the questions that trouble her, and a self-conscious attempt to articulate praise despite the limitations of human language and understanding. In Steele's hymnody, we encounter a persistent effort to express the ineffable.

In tracing the themes of language and suffering in Steele's life and verse, it has become clear that there is no one cause responsible for the unique qualities we observe in her hymnody. Her Calvinistic tendency toward introspection is observed, as her theological convictions encouraged her to take sober stock of sin in her life while humbly acknowledging the immensity of God. At the same time, the emotion characteristic of the emerging Evangelical Revival and Romantic Age can also be perceived in her verse. Moreover, the literary milieu within which she wrote contributed to her style, as she sometimes assumed the affecting and melancholic tone characteristic of the Age of Sensibility. In addition to these theological and literary considerations we must take into account the particular circumstances of her life, for Steele's biography is marked by frequent illnesses and personal losses. Finally, we should consider the fact that her verse was written first for a private audience, and this perhaps a result of her being a woman, since the eighteenth century did not encourage women's writing on sacred subjects. Together, these factors created the conditions within which her spirituality was nurtured—a spirituality which we have seen is marked by both resignation and longing, as she accepts her human frailty and finitude while longing for wholeness and understanding. The effect is a powerful and compelling contribution to the eighteenth-century congregational hymn. And this contribution has continued to provide meaningful opportunities for worship long after the eighteenth century had passed.

We began this book by noting J. Cuthbert Hadden's nineteenth-century commendation of Steele's hymn, "Dear Refuge of My Weary Soul." As this hymn reveals not only the essential themes in Steele's hymnody but also her unique style and tone, it will be enlightening to take a closer look at it now by way of summary (see Figure 8). As is typical in Steele's hymns, this hymn begins in a place of spiritual hesitancy, recognizing the reality of human sorrow:

> Dear refuge of my weary soul,
>   On thee, when sorrows rise:
> On thee, when waves of trouble roll,
>   My fainting hope relies.
>
> While hope revives, though prest with fears,
>   And I can say, my God,
> Beneath thy feet I spread my cares,
>   And pour my woes abroad.
>
> To thee, I tell each rising grief,
>   For thou alone canst heal;
> Thy word can bring a sweet relief
>   For every pain I feel.[1]

Steele's language here is revealing: "waves of trouble," "prest with fears," "spread my cares," "pour my woes," "rising grief." We see that she does not merely acknowledge human suffering before proceeding hastily to praise God. Instead, she lingers over her grief, fully considering the implications of that suffering on her faith, for she admits that her hope is "fainting." Yet nonetheless she continues to look to God as her "refuge." She repeats, "On thee...On thee....To thee," clarifying that despite the sorrow which envelops her, her heart and mind remain fixed on God. The tone set at the beginning of this hymn is characteristically plaintive, as she meditates on her various troubles and the condition of her "weary soul."

Here also we have the first hints of the source of her reviving hope. We see Steele turn to the consoling image of God as healer, who attends to "each rising grief" that distresses her. The image of Christ, the "Great Physician," figures prominently in Steele's hymnody, and likely was meaningful on account of her ongoing physical and emotional trials. And here also we find evidence of Steele's Calvinistic deference to the authority of Scripture, for while it is God who brings release from suffering, Steele grants that she finds "sweet relief"

---

[1] Steele, "God the Only Refuge of the Troubled Mind," *Poems on Subjects Chiefly Devotional*, I, 144-145.

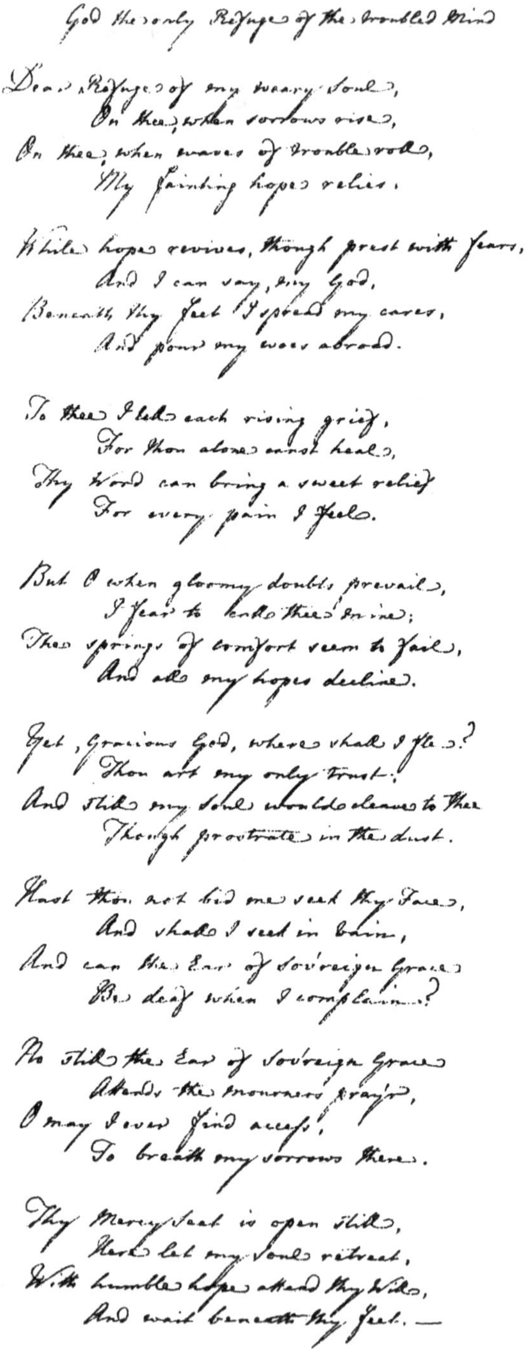

God the only Refuge of the troubled Mind

Dear Refuge of my weary Soul,
   On thee, when sorrows rise,
On thee, when waves of trouble roll,
   My fainting hope relies.

While hope revives, though prest with fears,
   And I can say, my God,
Beneath thy feet I spread my cares,
   And pour my woes abroad.

To thee I tell each rising grief,
   For thou alone canst heal;
Thy Word can bring a sweet relief
   For every pain I feel.

But O when gloomy doubts prevail,
   I fear to call thee mine;
The springs of comfort seem to fail,
   And all my hopes decline.

Yet, Gracious God, where shall I fle?
   Thou art my only Trust;
And still my soul would cleave to Thee
   Though prostrate in the dust.

Hast thou not bid me seek thy Face,
   And shall I seek in vain,
And can the Ear of Sov'reign Grace
   Be deaf when I complain?

No still the Ear of Sov'reign Grace
   Attends the mourners prayer,
O may I ever find access,
   To breath my sorrows there.

Thy Mercy Seat is open still,
   Here let my soul retreat,
With humble hope attend thy Will,
   And wait beneath thy feet. —

Figure 8: Manuscript copy of "Dear Refuge of My Weary Soul"

from her afflictions in the words of Scripture. While contemplating the full depths of her sorrow, Steele alludes to the solace she has found in God's healing presence and in Scripture.

Yet Steele will not resolve the problems she has presented so quickly. Her hymn continues:

> But oh! when gloomy doubts prevail,
>   I fear to call thee mine;
> The springs of comfort seem to fail,
>   And all my hopes decline.[2]

The resolution which had been suggested is undone, as the hymn turns with the word, "But," to descend into a state of spiritual dereliction. Here, Steele concedes that she is distressed by "gloomy doubts," that the "springs of comforts" sometimes fail her, that her "hopes decline," and, particularly poignant, that she fears to claim God as her own. She has reached the depths of her spiritual experience. Having journeyed from a place where she was cognizant of her sorrows but retained hope in God as her "refuge," she now is deprived of that comfort; spiritual doubts and uncertainty obscure God from her sight. She is desolate because God seems absent.

However, the hymn turns again, and concludes:

> Yet, gracious God, where shall I flee?
>   Thou art my only trust,
> And still my soul would cleave to thee,
>   Though prostrate in the dust.
>
> Hast thou not bid me seek thy face?
>   And shall I seek in vain?
> And can the ear of sovereign grace
>   Be deaf when I complain?
>
> No, still the ear of sovereign grace
>   Attends the mourner's prayer;
> O may I ever find access,
>   To breathe my sorrows there.
>
> Thy mercy-seat is open still;
>   Here let my soul retreat,
> With humble hope attend thy will,
>   And wait beneath thy feet.[3]

---

[2] Ibid., 145.
[3] Ibid., 145-146.

Having been brought low by her grief and doubts, she begins to pose questions. Wondering where she can turn in her sorrow, she confronts God, trusting that her search for him cannot be futile since it is God himself who asks believers to seek him and, indeed, establishes that longing in their hearts.[4] She is overwhelmed by earthly sorrow, and accepts this, humbly, but turns to God for comfort, cleaving to him in seeming desperation, despite the "gloomy doubts" which remain.

Steele considers whether God will listen to her cry of dereliction, and concludes that yes, if God is a God of "sovereign grace," he must hear the "mourner's prayer." And so she prays that even when her praise falters, even when language fails, God will continue to show his grace by attending to the sorrows that she is able merely to "breathe" to him. Here also we encounter further evidence of Steele's Calvinistic faith, for she locates herself "prostrate in the dust" and "beneath thy feet." Where this hymn began by engaging the full depth of human sorrow and then descended to a place of doubt, verging on despair, it makes a critical turn in order to focus again on God—a God who draws Steele forward in the spiritual life, a God of healing and grace, and a God full of mercy who consistently listens to her mourning prayer. And here is the source of Steele's "humble hope," which enables her to wait faithfully in the sorrow and silence, and long for a presence that persistently eludes her.

Long after Steele's death in 1778, her hymns maintained a remarkable level of popularity. Recall, for example, that in 1893, J. Cuthbert Hadden wrote, "there is no hymn I like better than 'Dear Refuge of My Weary Soul.'"[5] How can we account for this long-standing appeal when so many eighteenth-century hymns fell from popular usage with the turning of that century? Richard Arnold surmises that Steele's longevity might be related to her hymns being doctrinally neutral, so that in them she avoided taking a strong doctrinal stance.[6] This may bear some truth, though we have seen that Steele's hymns often betray her Calvinistic theology. Karen Smith wonders if Steele's "intense personal

---

[4] This is a common question in Steele's verse, as in, "Lord, shall the breathings of my heart / Aspire in vain to thee?" Steele, "The Presence of God, the Only Comfort in Affliction," *Poems on Subjects Chiefly Devotional*, III, 66. Also, "Hast thou not bid me seek thy face? / Hast thou not said, Return?" Steele, "Absence from God," *Poems on Subjects Chiefly Devotional*, I, 110. Similarly, "Hast thou not call'd me by thy Grace / To seek thy promised Love?" Steele, untitled, STE 3/1/5, no. 5.

[5] J. Cuthbert Hadden to Miss Bompas, 1 February 1893, STE 3/16 (xi). While "Dear Refuge of My Weary Soul" was certainly popular in Britain, it is interesting to trace the popularity of it in North America as well, where it was published 259 times between 1791 and 1939, and found a place in the hymnbooks of a wide variety of denominations, including Presbyterian, Lutheran, Christian and Missionary Alliance, and Mennonite Brethren. Almost a century after its initial publication, it was included in ten North American hymnbooks in 1843 and nine hymnbooks in both 1858 and 1859. The Dictionary of American Hymnology, Oberlin College, Ohio.

[6] Arnold, "A 'Veil of Interposing Night': The Hymns of Anne Steele," 383.

response" to life and her experience of God, subsequently articulated in her hymns, is the reason for her continued popularity well into the nineteenth century.[7] Perhaps Arnold and Smith identify the same quality in Steele's hymnody, for the real power of her hymnody is surely located in her honest, introspective searching for answers to the problems which inhibit her spiritual confidence—problems which, we have seen, are related to her reflections on language and suffering.

The hymns of Steele's contemporaries presented a powerful new means by which congregations were able to express their devotion to God, often in exuberant, confident tones as they made declarative statements about their theological beliefs. In Steele we have discovered something different, for in her hymns we encounter the possibility of spiritual uncertainty and doubt, of grappling with those moments of loss and limitation which are common to the human experience. And while Steele's hymns are little known at present, perhaps her spiritual candour explains why many of those who are familiar with her work today find something appealing in her vision of the life of Christian devotion. For while there is certainly a need for spiritual confidence and declarative hymn-singing, Steele's hymns temper a tempting triumphalism, reminding us of our human finitude and allowing for those moments of spiritual uncertainty which regularly occur in our lives. More than this, in Anne Steele's hymnody we encounter again the transcendent glory of God, beyond human powers of understanding and, but for the grace and mercy of God, beyond our finest efforts to praise.

---

[7] Smith, "The Community and the Believer," 254.

APPENDIX 1

Anne Steele's Family Tree

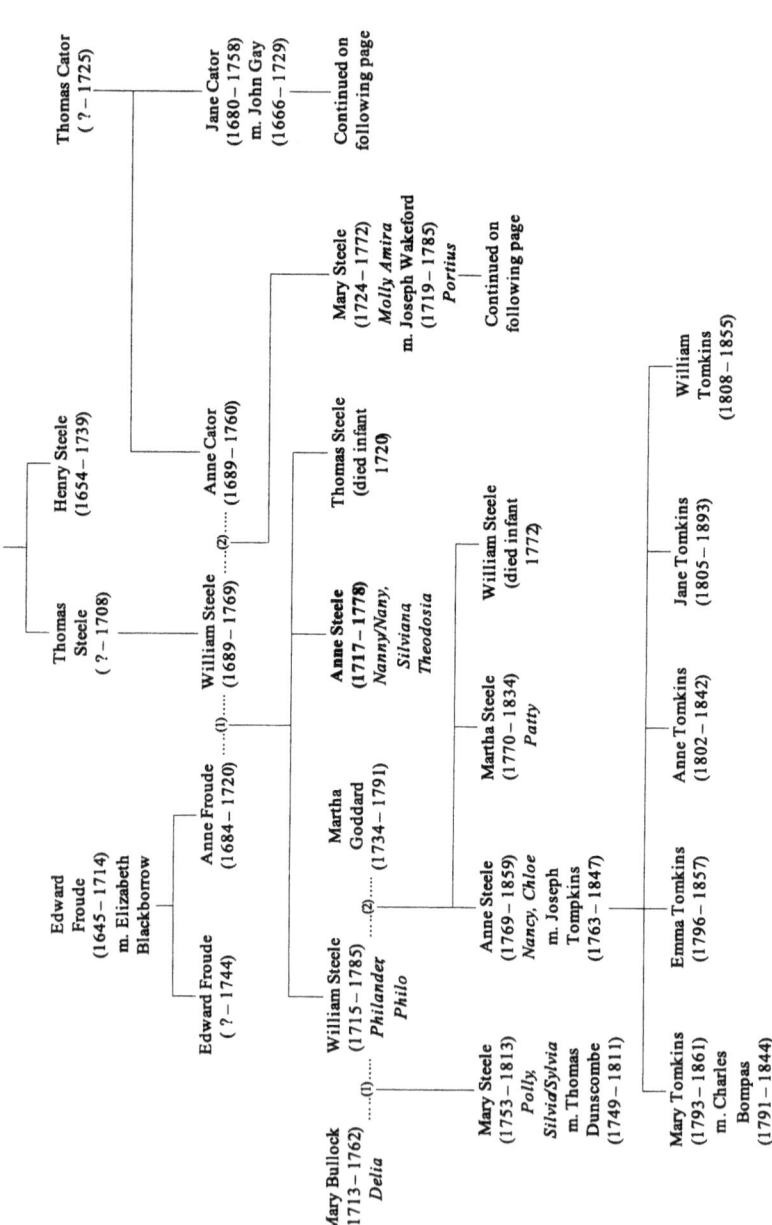

Nicknames and pseudonyms are in italics

Anne Steele's Family Tree

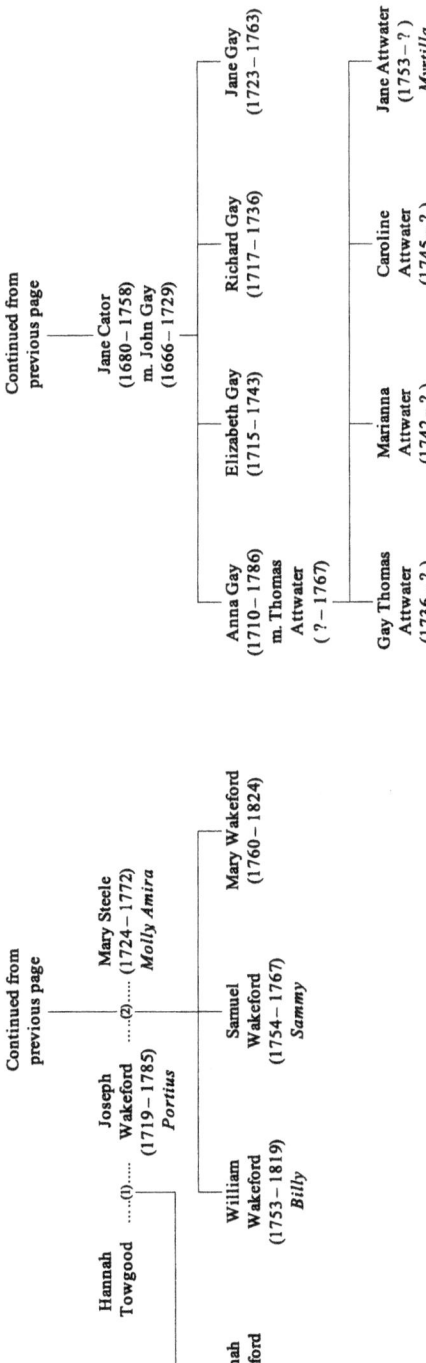

Nicknames and pseudonyms are in italics

APPENDIX 2

A Chronology of Anne Steele's Life

1717	April/May	Anne Steele born in Broughton.
1720	May	Death of Anne Froud Steele (mother); buried 7 May 1720.
1720	June	Death of Thomas Steele (infant brother); buried 1 July 1720.
1723	May	William Steele (father) marries Anne Cator.
1724	29 June	Steele's half-sister, Mary Steele born.
1729		Death of John Gay (uncle).
		Death of Aunt.
		Steele and Mary Steele (sister) at school in Trowbridge.
1730		William Steele (brother) joins William Steele (father) in timber business.
1732	8 June	William Steele (brother) baptised.
	10 June	Visits Henry Steele (uncle; pastor of Broughton church) to discuss baptism.
	11 June	Gives her experience, "to the full satisfaction of the church."
	9 July	Baptised, Broughton church.
1733		Steele and Mary Steele (sister) at school in Salisbury.
1734	September	Steele and Mary Steele (sister) stay with Jane Gay (aunt) at Haycombe.
1735	27-31 May	William Steele (brother) at meetings of the Western Association of Particular Baptist Churches.
	July	William Steele (father) thrown from horse and breaks his leg.
	6 August	Returns from Sarum; thrown from horse and hurts her hip.
1736		Death of Richard Gay (cousin).
	June	Staying with Joseph Cottle at Trowbridge.
1737	25 May	Drowning accident of James Elcombe.
1739	May-June	Steele and Mary Steele (sister) staying with Manfields at Ringwood.

	June	Death of Henry Steele (uncle).
1740	September	Steele and Mary Steele (sister) staying at Devizes.
1741	September	Steele and Mary Steele (sister) staying with Manfields at Ringwood.
1742		Steele and Mary Steele (sister) staying with Gays at Haycombe.
	23 December	Proposal of Benjamin Beddome.
1743		Death of Elizabeth Gay Phipps (cousin).
1745	December	Staying with Manfields at Ringwood.
1749		William Steele (brother) set up in timber business on his own.
	16 May	Mary Steele (sister) marries Joseph Wakeford; moves to Andover.
	17 May	William Steele (father) and Anne Cator Steele hear George Whitefield preach in Sarum.
1751	15 May	Visit from John Lavington, Philip Furneaux, and James Fanch, though Steele was absent, in Bath.
	May-June	Steele and Mary Bullock Steele (sister-in-law) staying at Bath.
1752	12 June	William Steele (father) and Anne Cator Steele hear George Whitefield preach in Whitchurch.
	11 July	Thrown from horse; shocked and ill with the experience.
1755	16 May	Philip Furneaux visits Broughton; he and Steele discuss the publication of her verse.
	late-May	Staying with Manfields at Ringwood.
1757		Philip Furneaux visits Broughton.
	July	Amira and Silviana letters regarding diffidence/difficulties of writing.
	July	Philip Furneaux visits Mary and Joseph Wakeford at Andover.
	October	Living with William Steele (brother) at "Broughton House."
	November	Joseph Wakeford delivers Steele's verse to Philip Furneaux.
	November	Amira and Silviana letters regarding the "gentle Swain" who proposed to Steele.
	29 November	Sends part of her verse to Andover for Joseph Wakeford to take to printers in London.
1758		Death of Jane Gay (aunt).
	5 May	Returns to live with parents.
1759	2 January	Ill; Mary Steele Wakeford (sister) takes Steele to Andover to get a physician's advice; stays at Andover and remains in poor health; returns to

		Broughton on 24 January.
	19 October	William Steele (brother) returns from printers with Steele's poems, not yet bound.
1760		Publication of *Poems on Subjects Chiefly Devotional, by Theodosia*.
	April-June	Several lengthy stays with Mary and Joseph Wakeford in Andover.
	28 June	Death of Anne Cator Steele.
1762		Death of Mary Bullock Steele (sister-in-law).
1763	August	Caleb Ashworth visits Broughton.
1767		Death of Sammy Wakefield (nephew).
1768		William Steele (brother) marries Martha Boddard.
1769	September	Death of William Steele (father). Goes to live with William Steele (brother); remains there until her death.
1770	July	Travels to Bodenham with Miss Waters.
1771-1778		Very poor health, often confined to bed.
1778	11 November	Death of Anne Steele, aged 61 years, 6 months.
1780		Second edition of *Poems of Subjects Chiefly Devotional, by Theodosia*.
1788		Publication of *Verses for Children, by Theodosia*.

APPENDIX 3

Anne Steele's Reading

A. Evidence exists in Steele's writings of her having read the following authors and, where indicated, specific works by those authors.

Benjamine Beddome (1717-1795), various hymns

John Byrom (1692-1763), "My Time, O Ye Muses" (first published in the *Spectator*, 1714)[1]

Philip Doddridge (1702-1751), various hymns, "Some Expressions of Dr. Dodridge [*sic*] to a Friend a few days before he embarked for Lisbon" (transcribed by Steele on the back of a letter to Marianna Attwater, undated, STE 3/12 [ii])

Bernard Foskett (1685-1758), various hymns

Thomas Gray (1716-1771), "Ode to Adversity" (1742)

George Herbert (1593-1633), "The Pulley" (1633)

James Hervey (1714-1758), *Meditations and Contemplations* (1746-1747), *Theron and Aspasio: Or, a Series of Dialogues and Letters, Upon the Most Important and Interesting Subjects* (1755)

John Milton (1608-1674)

Samuel Pike (1717?-1773), "Sermons on Sovereign Grace," (possibly *Saving Grace, Sovereign Grace: Lectures at Pinners' Hall* [1758]), *Some Important Cases of Conscience Answered, at the Casuistical Exercise, on Wednesday Evenings, In Little St. Helen's, Bishopsgate-Street* (1755)

Alexander Pope (1688-1744), "Ode on Solitude" (1717), *An Essay on Criticism* (1711), *An Essay on Man, Being the First Book of Ethic Epistles. To Henry St.*

---

[1] Byrom is also the author of the hymn, "Christians, Awake, Salute the Happy Morn."

John, L. Bolingbroke (1733-1734)

Samuel Richardson (1689-1761), *The History of Sir Charles Grandison, Published in a Series of Letters* (1753-1754)

Elizabeth Singer Rowe (1674-1737), various letters

William Shakespeare (1564-1616)

Jonathan Swift (1667-1745), various verses

Mary Scott Taylor (1751-1793), various hymns, *The Female Advocate; a Poem Occasioned by Reading Mr. Duncombe's Feminead* (1774)

James Thomson (1700-1748), *The Seasons* (1726-1744)

Isaac Watts (1674-1748), various hymns

Charles Wesley (1707-1788), various hymns

Edward Young (1681-1765), *The Complaint, or Night-Thoughts on Life, Death and Immortality* (1742-1746)

B. *Further evidence of the Steele family's reading can be found in a commonplace book compiled by Steele's brother, William Steele.* [2]

John Gay (1685-1732), "The Story of Arachne from the Sixth Book of Ovid's Metamorphoses" (1712), "An Epistle to the Right Honourable the Earl of Burlington. A Journey to Exeter" (1720)

Thomas Parnell (1679-1718), "The Hermit" (1722), "Hesiod, or the Rise of Woman" (1722)

---

[2] For William Steele's commonplace book, see STE 4/2. Only a selection of the poetry transcribed into this book is included here; the volume also contains a number of songs in a pastoral style, such as "A Song to the Tune of the Yellow Hair'd Laddie" and "A Song to the Tune of Gilder Roy," as well as, at the end of the volume, reversed, a selection of hymn tunes. For a fuller discussion of the content of William Steele's commonplace book, see Reeves, *Pursuing the Muses*, 35-38; Reeves, "Literary Women in Eighteenth-Century Nonconformist Circles," in *Culture and the Nonconformist Tradition*, 12.

William Pattison (1706-1727), "Strada's Nightingale Imitated" (1728), "The Court of Venus from Claudian" (1728)

Alexander Pope (1688-1744), *Messiah. A Sacred Eclogue in Imitation of Virgil's Pollio* (1712), *The Temple of Fame: A Vision* (1715), *Eloisa to Abelard* (1717)

C. Additional evidence of the Steele family's reading can be found in two printed volumes containing writings collected by William Steele and his daughter, Mary Steele Dunscombe.[3]

William Hayley (1745-1820), *The Triumphs of Temper: A Poem, in Six Cantos* (1781)

Samuel Marsh Oram (1765-1791), *Poems by the Late Mr. Samuel Marsh Oram, with an Introduction by Percival Stockdale* (1794)[4]

Anne Seward (1747-1809), *Louisa: A Poetical Novel, in Four Epistles* (1784), *Monody on Major André, to which are Added Letters Addressed to her by Major André in the Year 1769* (1781)

Mary Scott Taylor (1751-1793), *The Messiah: A Poem in Two Parts, Published for the Benefit of the General Hospital at Bath* (1788)

Helen Maria Williams (1762-1827), *An Ode on the Peace, by the Author of Edwin and Eltruda* (1783), *Peru: A Poem, in Six Cantos* (1784)

---

[3] For these volumes, see STE 14/2, 14/3. For a fuller discussion of the content of these books, see Reeves, *Pursuing the Muses*, 35-37; Reeves, "Literary Women in Eighteenth-Century Nonconformist Circles," in *Culture and the Nonconformist Tradition*, 12. While some of the works included in this volume were published after Steele's death in 1778, they do contribute to an understanding of her intellectual and literary background. See also commonplace book of Mary Steele Dunscombe, *c.* 1796; STE 5/4.

[4] Marsh was a local poet whose work was published posthumously. The subscription list at the end of his slim volume of poems includes Lady Carter and Mrs. Carter of Portsmouth, the Rev. J. Frowd of Chicklade in Wiltshire, Hannah More, Thomas Sandby (the painter and engraver) of Windsor Great Park, Miss Steele of Broughton (who ordered six copies), Miss Martha Steele and Mrs. Tomkins of Caldecot House in Berkshire (who ordered seven copies between them), and Mrs. Tomkins of Abingdon in Berkshire (who ordered six copies).

BIBLIOGRAPHY

Primary Sources

Manuscripts

ANGUS LIBRARY, REGENT'S PARK COLLEGE, OXFORD

Broughton Baptist Church Records
Porton and Broughton church book, 1655-1687.
Broughton church books, 1699-1730, 1730-1756 (including loose pages with record of baptisms 1708-1730 and deaths 1778-1786), 1759-1891.
Letter from Reuben Heffer to Miss Parsons, 1919.
Memorandum (undated) containing brief notes on Anne Steele, presumably once kept with her Bible.
Printed devotional books owned by the Steele family, including Anne Steele's Bible, previously owned by Anne Dutton.

Steele Collection
Letters from William Steele to Anne Froude Steele, 1712-1716; Anne Cator Steele, 1718-1733; unidentified relatives, 1761 and undated.
Letters from Anne Cator Steele to William Steele, 1722-1733.
Letter from James Manfield to William Steele, 1737.
Diaries of Anne Cator Steele, 1730-1736, 1749-1752, 1753-1760.
Volume of handwriting exercises of Anne Steele, 1728.
Hymns by Anne Steele (published and unpublished).
Psalms by Anne Steele (published and unpublished).
Poems by Anne Steele (published and unpublished).
Prose by Anne Steele (published and unpublished).
Letters from Anne Steele to Anne Cator Steele, 1729-1751.
Correspondence between Anne Steele and William Steele, 1736-1763.
Correspondence between Anne Steele and Mary Steele Wakeford, 1749-1757.
Letters from Anne Steele to Mary Bullock Steele, 1750-1762.
Letter from Anne Steele to William and Samuel Wakeford, *c.* 1760.
Letters from Anne Steele to Anna and Marianna Attwater, 1741 and undated.
Letter from Benjamin Beddome to Anne Steele, 1742.
Letters from Anne Steele to Philip Furneaux, undated.
Letter from Anne Steele to Mrs. Martin, 1757.
Letter from Anne Steele to anonymous man, undated.
Letter from Anne Steele to anonymous woman, 1761.

Correspondence between Anne Steele and Caleb Ashworth, 1763.
Draft dedication of Steele's hymns and poems to William Steele, *c.* 1760.
Works of others transcribed by Anne Steele, including notebook containing "Hymns of Miss Scott" (Mary Scott Taylor), poems by Mary Steele Wakeford, notebook containing hymns by Philip Doddridge.
Letter from Richard Pearsall to Joseph Wakeford, post-1760.
Letter from Joseph Wakeford to William Steele, 1767.
Manuscript volume entitled *A Pious Memorial*, containing "The Mourner's Consolation: A Discourse Occasioned by the Decease of Mrs. [*sic*] Anne Steele of Broughton" (1778) and "The Supports of Faith Delineated: A Discourse Occasioned by the Decease of William Steele esq. of Broughton" (1785), written by Josiah Lewis.
Later letters concerning Anne Steele, including letter from B.H. Draper to Anne Steele Tomkins, 1821; letter from John Green to Miss Bompas, 1878; letters from Robert Shindler to various members of the Steele family, 1875-1879; letter from William Stevenson to G. Buckeridge, 1887; letter from William Stevenson to Miss Bompas, 1887; letters from J. Cuthbert Hadden to Miss Bompas, 1893.
Miscellaneous verses and prose by contemporaries of Anne Steele, including verses transcribed by Benjamin Beddome, verses transcribed by Josiah Lewis, verses by John Lavington, letters from Elizabeth Singer Rowe transcribed by members of the Steele family.
Poems by William Steele.
Poems by Mary Steele Wakeford.
Poems by Mary Steele Dunscombe.
Commonplace book of William Steele.
Commonplace book of Mary Steele Dunscombe.
Printed volumes containing writings collected by William Steele and Mary Steele Dunscombe.
Letters from William Steele to Mary Steele Dunscombe, 1769-1777.
Letters from Mary Steele Dunscombe to Mary Scott Taylor, 1769-1786.
Letter from Daniel Turner to Mary Steele Dunscombe, 1778.
Letters from Caleb Evans to Mary Steele Dunscombe, 1778-1786.
Correspondence between Anne Steele Tomkins and John Sheppard, 1838-1842.
Printed books by or owned by the Steele family.
Research files of Hugh Steele-Smith.

Printed Works by Anne Steele

[Steele, Anne]. *Poems on Subjects Chiefly Devotional, by Theodosia.* London: J. Buckland and J. Ward, 1760.

[—]. *Poems on Subjects Chiefly Devotional, by Theodosia.* Bristol: W. Pine, 1780.

—. *The Works of Mrs. Anne Steele, Complete in Two Volumes. Comprehending Poems on Subjects Chiefly Devotional: and Miscellaneous Pieces in Prose and Verse: Heretofore Published under the Title of Theodosia.* Boston: Monroe, Francis and Parker, 1808.

—. *Hymns, Psalms, and Poems, by Anne Steele, With Memoir by John Sheppard.* London: Daniel Sedgwick, 1863.

—. *Hymns by Anne Steele*. Preface by J.R. Broome. London: Gospel Standard Baptist Trust, 1967.

Printed Works by Steele's Contemporaries

Adam, Thomas. *Private Thoughts on Religion, and Other Subjects Connected with it, Extracted from the Diary of the Rev. Thomas Adam, Late Rector of Wintringham. To which is Prefixed a Short Sketch of his Life and Character*, 2nd ed. York: G. Peacock, 1795.
Addington, Stephen. *Resignation the Duty of Mourners. A Sermon Preached at Coventry, Nov. 22, 1772, on the Death of Mr. Thomas Dawson; who Departed this Life November 15, 1772. In the Twenty-eighth Year of his Age*. Coventry: J.W. Piercy, 1773.
[Allestree, Richard]. *The Art of Contentment*. Oxford: n.p., 1705.
[—]. *The Ladies Calling*. 1673; Oxford: n.p., 1720.
Ash, John. *Sentiments on Education Collected from the Best Writers, Properly Methodized, and Interspersed with Occasional Observations*. London: Edward and Charles Dilly, 1777.
Ash, John, and Caleb Evans. *A Collection of Hymns Adapted to Public Worship*, 3rd ed. Bristol: W. Pine, 1778.
Barker, John. *Resignation to the Will of God, Consider'd, in a Funeral Sermon for the Late Reverend Mr. John Newman, Who Departed this Life, July 25, 1741. In the 65th Year of his Age. Preached at Salters Hall, August 2, 1741*. London: R. Hett, 1741.
Belknap, Jeremy. *Sacred Poetry, Consisting of Psalms and Hymns, Adapted to Christian Devotion, in Public and Private*, 2nd ed. Boston: Thomas and Andrews, 1797.
Browne, Simon. *Hymns and Spiritual Songs*. London: E. Matthews, 1720.
Cennick, John. *A Collection of Sacred Hymns*. Dublin: S. Powell, 1752.
[Cowper, Maria Frances]. *Original Poems. On Various Occasions. By a Lady*. Revised by William Cowper. London: J. Deighton, J. Mathews, R. Faulder, 1792.
Doddridge, Philip. *Hymns Founded on Various Texts in the Holy Scriptures*, 3rd ed. Preface by Job Orton. London: J. Buckland, et al., 1766.
[Dutton, Anne]. "A Letter to Such of the Servants of Christ, who have any Scruple about the Lawfulness of Printing any Thing written by a Woman." In *A Brief Account of the Gracious Dealings of God, with a Poor, Sinful, Unworthy Creature*. London: J. Hart, 1750.
—. *A Narration of the Wonders of Grace*. London: n.p., 1734.
Fanch, James. *A Paraphrase on a Select Number of the Psalms of David*. London: G. Keith, 1764.
Fawcett, John. *Hymns: Adapted to the Circumstances of Public Worship, and Private Devotion*. Leeds: G. Wright and Son, 1782.
Harrison, Susannah. *Songs in the Night, By a Young Woman under Deep Afflictions*. London: R. Hawes, 1780.
Harrison, Thomas. *Poems on Divine Subjects*. London: John Clark, E. Matthews, and T. Sanders, 1719.
Haywood, Eliza Fowler. *The History of Miss Betsy Thoughtless*, 2nd ed. London: T. Gardner, 1751.

Hervey, James. *Meditations among the Tombs. In a Letter to a Lady*. London: J. and J. Rivington, and J. Leake, 1746.

—. *Meditations and Contemplations*, 4th ed. London: John and James Rivington, 1748.

Hymns, Selected from the Most Approved Authors, for the Use of Trinity Church, Boston. Boston: Munroe, Francis and Parker, 1808.

Lacy, John. *Divine Hymns, Made on the Most Important Points of Christianity*, 2nd ed. Portsmouth Common: J. Whitewood, 1776.

Lowell, Samuel. *The Nature and Importance of Resignation: A Sermon Occasioned by the Christian Triumph Displayed in the Peaceful Departure of Mrs. Sizer, of Woodbridge, Suffolk; Who Died the 1st February, 1797, in the 27th Year of her Age*. London: C. Whittingham, 1797.

Newton, John, and William Cowper. *Olney Hymns*. London: W. Oliver, 1779.

Pope, Alexander. *An Essay on Man, Being the First Book of Ethic Epistles. To Henry St. John, L. Bolingbroke*. London: John Wright, 1734.

Richardson, George. *Iconology; or, a Collection of Emblematical Figures; Containing Four Hundred and Twenty-Four Remarkable Subjects, Moral and Instructive; in which are Displayed the Beauty of Virtue and Deformity of Vice. The Figures are Engraved by the Most Capital Artists, from Original Designs; with Explanations from Classical Authorities*. London: G. Scott, 1779.

Rippon, John. *A Selection of Hymns from the Best Authors, Intended to be an Appendix to Dr. Watts's Psalms and Hymns*. London: Thomas Wilkins, 1787.

Romaine, William. *An Essay on Psalmody*. London: n.p., 1775.

Rowe, Elizabeth Singer. *Devout Exercises of the Heart in Meditation and Soliloquy, Prayer and Praise*. Preface by Isaac Watts. London: R. Hett, 1738.

[—]. *Divine Hymns and Poems on Several Occasions, by Philomela*. London: R. Janeway, 1704.

—. *The Miscellaneous Works in Prose and Verse of Mrs. Elizabeth Rowe*. London: R. Hett and R. Dodsley, 1739.

Taylor, Mary Scott. *The Female Advocate; A Poem Occasioned by Reading Mr. Duncombe's Feminead*. London: Joseph Johnson, 1774.

Turner, Daniel. *Divine Songs, Hymns, and Other Poems*. Reading: S. Blackman and A. Ward, 1747.

Watts, Isaac. *Horae Lyricae*, 9th ed. Boston: Rogers and Fowle, 1748.

—. *Hymns and Spiritual Songs*. London: J. Humphreys, 1707.

—. *Hymns and Spiritual Songs*, 2nd ed., corrected and much enlarged. London: J. H[umphreys], 1709.

—. *The Psalms of David Imitated in the Language of the New Testament, and Apply'd to the Christian State and Worship*. London: J. Clark, R. Ford, and R. Cruttenden, 1719.

—. "A Short Essay Toward the Improvement of Psalmody: Or, An Enquiry how the Psalms of *David* ought to be translated into Christian Songs, and how lawful and necessary it is to compose other Hymns according to the clearer Revelations of the Gospel, for the Use of the Christian Church." In *Hymns and Spiritual Songs*, 233-276. London: J. Humphreys, 1707.

Wesley, John. *A Collection of Hymns, for the Use of the People Called Methodists*. London: J. Paramore, 1780.

—. *A Collection of Hymns, for the Use of the People Called Methodists*, a new edition. London: G. Whitfield, 1797.

Wesley, John, and Charles Wesley. *A Collection of Psalms and Hymns*, 2nd ed. London:

Strahan, 1743.
Western Association of Particular Baptist Churches. *The Elders and Messengers of the Several Baptist Churches, Meeting at Exon, Prescott, Wellington, Bridgwater,...Being Met in Association at Frome,...the 17th and 18th days of May, 1780. To the Several Churches They Represent Send Christian Salutation....*[Bristol: n.p., 1780].
The Whole Duty of a Woman: Or, an Infallible Guide to the Fair Sex. London: T. Read, 1737.
Young, Edward. *The Complaint: or, Night-Thoughts on Life, Death, & Immortality*, 7th ed. Dublin: P. Wilson, 1747.
—. *Resignation, &c. In Five Parts. To Mrs. B******* including a Funeral Epithalamium, Occasioned by a New Marriage-Act.* London:, n.p., 1761.

Secondary Sources

Abbey, Charles J., and John H. Overton. *The English Church in the Eighteenth Century*, 2nd ed. London: Longmans, Green, and Co., 1887.
Adey, Lionel. *Class and Idol in the English Hymn.* Vancouver, BC: University of British Columbia Press, 1988.
—. *Hymns and the Christian "Myth."* Vancouver, BC: University of British Columbia Press, 1986.
Alexander, James Waddel. "O Sacred Head, Now Wounded." The Cyber Hymnal (http://cyberhymnal.org/htm/o/s/osacredh.htm, accessed 13 January 2007).
Allen, Cecil J. *Hymns and the Christian Faith.* London: Pickering and Inglis, 1966.
Anderson, Howard, and John S. Shea, eds. *Studies in Criticism and Aesthetics, 1660-1800: Essays in Honor of Samuel Holt Monk.* Minneapolis, MN: University of Minnesota Press, 1967.
Appleby, Peter C. "Mysticism and Ineffability." *International Journal for Philosophy of Religion* 11, no. 3 (1980): 143-165.
Arnold, Richard. *English Hymns of the Eighteenth Century: An Anthology.* American University Studies, series 4, English Language and Literature, vol. 137. New York: Peter Lang, 1991.
—. "'The Hidden Life' of Hymnody: William Cowper's Use of a Genre." In *Tropic Crucible: Self and Theory in Language and Literature*, ed. Colin E. Nicholson and Ranjit Chatterjee, 271-296. Singapore: Singapore University Press, 1984.
—. "A 'Veil of Interposing Night': The Hymns of Anne Steele (1717-1778)." *Christian Scholar's Review* 18, no. 4 (June 1989): 371-387.
Augustine. *The Confessions of Saint Augustine.* New Kensington, PA: Whitaker House, 1996.
—. *On Christian Doctrine.* Edited and translated by R.P.H. Green. Oxford: Clarendon Press, 1995.
—. *The Trinity.* Translated by Stephen McKenna. The Fathers of the Church, vol. 45. Washington, DC: Catholic University of American Press, 1963.
Bailey, Albert Edward. *The Gospel in Hymns: Backgrounds and Interpretations.* New York: Charles Scribner's Sons, 1950.
Baird, J.L., and John R. Kane. *Rossignol: An Edition and Translation.* Kent, OH: Kent

State University Press, 1978.
Baker, Frank. *Charles Wesley's Verse: An Introduction.* London: Epworth Press, 1964.
Barth, Karl. "Novalis." In *Protestant Theology in the Nineteenth Century: Its Background and History,* new ed. Translated by Brian Cozens and John Bowden. Introduction by Colin E. Gunton. Grand Rapids, MI: Eerdmans, 2002.
Benson, Louis F. *The English Hymn: Its Development and Use in Worship.* New York: Hodder and Stoughton, 1915. Reprint, Richmond, VA: John Knox Press, 1962.
—. *Studies of Familiar Hymns.* Philadelphia: Westminster Press, 1903.
Bernard of Clairvaux. *Selected Works.* Translated and with a foreword by G.R. Evans. Introduction by Jean LeClercq. Preface by Ewert H. Cousins. Classics of Western Spirituality. New York: Paulist Press, 1987.
Bett, Henry. *The Hymns of Methodism in Their Literary Relations.* London: Charles H. Kelly, 1913.
Blumhofer, Edith L., and Mark A. Noll, eds. *Singing the Lord's Song in a Strange Land: Hymnody in the History of North American Protestantism.* Religion and American Culture. Tuscaloosa, AL: University of Alabama Press, 2004.
—. *Sing Them Over Again to Me: Hymns and Hymnbooks in America.* Religion and American Culture. Tuscaloosa, AL: University of Alabama Press, 2006.
Bonner, Carey. "Some Baptist Hymnists." *Baptist Quarterly* 8 (1936-1937): 256-262.
—. *Some Baptist Hymnists from the Seventeenth Century to Modern Times.* London: Kingsgate Press, 1937.
Brackney, William H. *A Genetic History of Baptist Thought: With Special Reference to Baptists in Britain and North America.* Baptists: History, Literature, Theology, Hymns. Macon, GA: Mercer University Press, 2004.
Brawley, Benjamin. *History of the English Hymn.* New York: Abingdon Press, 1932.
Breed, David R. *The History and Use of Hymns and Hymn-Tunes.* Chicago: Fleming H. Revell, 1903.
Briggs, John. "She-Preachers, Widows and Other Women: The Feminine Dimension in Baptist Life Since 1600." *Baptist Quarterly* 31, no. 7 (July 1986): 337-352.
Broome, J.R. *A Bruised Reed: The Life and Times of Anne Steele.* Harpenden, UK: Gospel Standard Trust Publications, 2007.
—. *The Friendly Companion* (February 1984).
Brown, Raymond. *The English Baptists of the Eighteenth Century.* A History of the English Baptists, no. 2. London: Baptist Historical Society, 1986.
Brown, Theron, and Hezekiah Butterworth. *The Story of the Hymns and Tunes.* New York: George H. Doran, 1906.
Burrage, Henry S. *Baptist Hymn Writers and Their Hymns.* Portland, ME: Brown Thurston and Company, 1888.
Burrows, Mark S. "'Raiding the Inarticulate': Mysticism, Poetics, and the Unlanguagable." In *Minding the Spirit: The Study of Christian Spirituality,* ed. Elizabeth A. Dreyer and Mark S. Burrows, 341-361. Baltimore: Johns Hopkins University Press, 2005.
—. "Words That Reach into the Silence: Mystical Languages of Unsaying." In *Minding the Spirit: The Study of Christian Spirituality,* ed. Elizabeth A. Dreyer and Mark S. Burrows, 207-214. Baltimore: Johns Hopkins University Press, 2005.
Carnell, Corbin Scott. *Bright Shadow of Reality: Spiritual Longing in C.S. Lewis.* Grand Rapids, MI: Eerdmans, 1974.
Champion, L.G. "Evangelical Calvinism and the Structures of Baptist Church Life."

Baptist Quarterly 28 (1979-1980): 196-208.
Christophers, S.W. *Hymn-Writers and Their Hymns.* London: S.W. Partridge, 1866.
Clark, Harry. "A Study of Melancholy in Edward Young: Part I." *Modern Language Notes* 39, no. 3 (March 1924): 129-136.
—. "A Study of Melancholy in Edward Young: Part II." *Modern Language Notes* 39, no. 4 (April 1924): 193-202.
Clement, A.S., ed. *Great Baptist Women, by Baptist Women.* London: Carey Kingsgate Press, 1955.
The Cloud of Unknowing. Edited and with an introduction by William Johnston. New York: Image Books, 1973.
Cohen, Ralph. "The Augustan Mode in English Poetry." *Eighteenth-Century Studies* 1, no. 1 (Autumn 1967): 3-32.
Colish, Marcia L. *The Mirror of Language: A Study in the Medieval Theory of Knowledge.* New Haven: Yale University Press, 1968.
Colligan, J. Hay. *Eighteenth Century Nonconformity.* New York: Longmans, Green, and Co., 1915.
Crawford, Patricia. *Women and Religion in England, 1500-1720.* Christianity and Society in the Modern World. London: Routledge, 1993.
Creed, John Martin, and John Sandwith Boys Smith. *Religious Thought in the Eighteenth Century: Illustrated from Writers of the Period.* Cambridge: Cambridge University Press, 1934.
Davie, Donald, ed. *Augustan Lyric.* London: Heinemann, 1974.
Davie, Donald. *Dissentient Voice: The Ward-Phillips Lectures for 1980 with Some Related Pieces.* University of Notre Dame Ward-Phillips Lectures in English Language and Literature, vol. 11. Notre Dame: University of Notre Dame Press, 1982.
—. *The Eighteenth-Century Hymn in England.* Cambridge Studies in Eighteenth-Century English Literature and Thought, no. 19. Cambridge: Cambridge University Press, 1993.
—. *A Gathered Church: The Literature of the English Dissenting Interest, 1700-1930.* The Clark Lectures 1976. New York: Oxford University Press, 1978.
—. Introduction to *The New Oxford Book of Christian Verse*, ed. Donald Davie, xvii-xxix. Oxford: Oxford University Press, 1981.
—. *Purity of Diction in English Verse.* New York: Schocken Books, 1952.
Davies, Horton. *Worship and Theology in England.* Vol. 3, *From Watts and Wesley to Maurice, 1690-1850.* Princeton: Princeton University Press, 1961. Reprint, Grand Rapids, MI: Eerdmans, 1996.
Dearmer, Percy, and Archibald Jacob. *Songs of Praise Discussed: A Handbook to the Best-Known Hymns and to Others Recently Introduced.* London: Oxford University Press, 1933.
de Lubac, Henri. *The Discovery of God.* Translated by Alexander Dru. Footnotes translated by Mark Sebanc and Cassian Fulsom. Grand Rapids, MI: Eerdmans, 1996.
The Dictionary of American Hymnology. Oberlin College, Ohio.
Dingley, R.J. "The Misfortunes of Philomel." *Parergon* 4 (1986): 73-86.
Dixon, Michael F., and Hugh F. Steele-Smith. "Anne Steele's Health: A Modern Diagnosis." *Baptist Quarterly* 32 (July 1988): 351-356.
Donne, John. *The Complete English Poems.* Edited by A.J. Smith. London: Penguin Books, 1971.

Donoghue, Denis. "On the Limits of a Language." *Sewanee Review* 85, no. 3 (Summer 1979): 371-391.
Doody, Margaret Anne. "Women Poets of the Eighteenth Century." In *Women and Literature in Britain, 1700-1800*, ed. Vivien Jones, 217-237. Cambridge: Cambridge University Press, 2000.
Duffield, Samuel Willoughby. *English Hymns: Their Authors and History*. New York: Funk and Wagnalls, 1886.
Duke, David N. "Giving Voice to Suffering in Worship: A Study in the Theodicies of Hymnody." *Encounter* 52, no. 3 (Summer 1991): 263-272.
Ebeling, Gerard. *Introduction to a Theological Theory of Language*. Translated by R.A. Wilson. London: William Collins Sons, 1973.
Eliot, T.S. *Four Quartets*. San Diego: Harcourt, 1943.
—. *On Poetry and Poets*. London: Faber and Faber, 1957.
—. *The Waste Land and Other Poems*. San Diego: Harcourt, Brace and Company, 1930.
Elliot-Binns, L.E. *The Early Evangelicals: A Religious and Social Study*. Greenwich, CT: Seabury Press, 1953.
Emurian, Ernest. *Living Stories of Famous Hymns*. Grand Rapids, MI: Baker Book House, 1955.
England, Martha Winburn, and John Sparrow. *Hymns Unbidden: Donne, Herbert, Blake, Emily Dickinson and the Hymnographers*. New York: New York Public Library, 1966.
Escott, Harry. *Isaac Watts Hymnographer: A Study of the Beginnings, Development, and Philosophy of the English Hymn*. London: Independent Press, 1962.
Eskew, Harry, and Hugh T. McElrath. *Sing with Understanding: An Introduction to Christian Hymnology*. Nashville, TN: Broadman Press, 1980.
Fairchild, Hoxie Neale. *Religious Trends in English Poetry*. Vol. 1, *Protestantism and the Cult of Sentiment*. New York: Columbia University Press, 1939.
—. *Religious Trends in English Poetry*. Vol. 2, *Religious Sentimentalism in the Age of Johnson*. New York: Columbia University Press, 1942.
Ferguson, Moira. *Eighteenth-Century Women Poets: Nation, Class, and Gender*. SUNY Series in Feminist Criticism and Theory. New York: State University of New York Press, 1995.
Findlay, George H. *Christ's Standard Bearer*. London: Epworth Press, 1956.
Fritz, Donald W. "The Prioress's Avowal of Ineptitude." *The Chaucer Review* 9, no. 2 (Summer 1974): 166-181.
Frye, Northrop. *The Double Vision: Language and Meaning in Religion*. Toronto: University of Toronto Press, 1991.
—. "Towards Defining an Age of Sensibility." *Journal of English Literary History* 23, no. 2 (June 1956):144-152.
Funk, Robert. *Language, Hermeneutic, and Word of God: The Problem of Language in the New Testament and Contemporary Theology*. New York: Harper and Row, 1966.
Gillespie, Katharine. *Domesticity and Dissent in the Seventeenth Century: English Women Writers and the Public Sphere*. Cambridge: Cambridge University Press, 2004.
Gillman, Frederick John. *The Evolution of the English Hymn: An Historical Survey of the Origins and Development of the Hymns of the Christian Church*. New York: Macmillan Company, 1927.
Goadby, J.J. *Bye-Paths in Baptist History: A Collection of Interesting, Instructive and*

Curious Information, Not Generally Known Concerning the Baptist Denomination. London: Elliot Stock, 1871. Reprint, Watertown, WI: Baptist Heritage Publications, 1987.

Goldhawk, Norman P. *On Hymns and Hymn-Books*. London: Epworth Press, 1979.

Greaves, Richard L., ed. *Triumph Over Silence: Women in Protestant History*. Contributions to the Study of Religion, no. 15. Westport, CT: Greenwood Press, 1985.

Greene, Donald. *The Age of Exuberance: Backgrounds to Eighteenth-Century English Literature*. New York: Random House, 1970.

Gregory, A.S. *Praises with Understanding: Illustrated from the Words and Music of the Methodist Hymn-Book*. London: Epworth Press, 1936.

Hamilton, Edith. *Mythology: Timeless Tales of Gods and Heroes*. New York: Warner Books, 1942.

Hardeman, James. "Caleb Ashworth of Cloughfield and Daventry." *Baptist Quarterly* (1936-1937): 200-206.

Harlan, Lowell B. "Theology of Eighteenth Century English Hymns." *Historical Magazine of the Protestant Episcopal Church* 48, no. 2 (June 1979): 167-193.

Hatfield, Edwin F. *The Poets of the Church: A Series of Biographical Sketches of Hymn-Writers with Notes on Their Hymns*. New York: Anson D.F. Randolph, 1884.

Hawkins, Peter S., and Anne Howland Schotter, eds. *Ineffability: Naming the Unnamable from Dante to Beckett*. AMS ARS Poetica, no. 2. New York: AMS Press, 1984.

Hay, Douglas, and Nicholas Rogers. *Eighteenth-Century English Society: Shuttles and Swords*. Oxford: Oxford University Press, 1997.

Hayden, Roger. "The Contribution of Bernard Foskett." In *Pilgrim Pathways: Essays in Baptist History in Honour of B.R. White*, ed. William H. Brackney, Paul S. Fiddes, and John H.Y. Briggs, 189-206. Macon, GA: Mercer University Press, 1999.

Haykin, Michael A.G. "The Baptist Identity: A View from the Eighteenth Century." *Evangelical Quarterly* 67, no. 2 (1995): 137-152.

—, ed. *The British Particular Baptists, 1638-1910*. Springfield, MO: Particular Baptist Press, 2000.

Herbert, George. *The Complete English Poems*. Edited by John Tobin. London: Penguin Books, 1991.

Hick, John. "Ineffability." *Religious Studies* 36, no. 1 (March 2000): 35-46.

Hindmarsh, D. Bruce. *The Evangelical Conversion Narrative: Spiritual Autobiography in Early Modern England*. Oxford: Oxford University Press, 2005.

—. *John Newton and the English Evangelical Tradition: Between the Conversions of Wesley and Wilberforce*. Oxford: Oxford University Press, 1996. Reprint, Grand Rapids, MI: Eerdmans, 2001.

Hobbs, June Hadden. *"I Sing for I Cannot Be Silent": The Feminization of American Hymnody, 1870-1920*. Pittsburgh Series in Composition, Literacy, and Culture. Pittsburgh: University of Pittsburgh Press, 1997.

Holt, Bradley P. *Thirsty for God: A Brief History of Christian Spirituality*, 2nd ed. Minneapolis, MN: Fortress Press, 2005.

Horder, W. Garrett. "Anne Steele and Her Hymns." *The Quiver* 60 (September 1900): 1040-1044.

—. *The Hymn Lover: An Account of the Rise and Growth of English Hymnody*. London: J. Curwen and Sons, 1889.

Hoyles, John. *The Edges of Augustanism: The Aesthetics of Spirituality in Thomas Ken, John Byrom and William Law*. The Hague: Martinus Nijhoff, 1972.

—. *The Waning of the Renaissance 1640-1740: Studies in the Thought and Poetry of Henry More, John Norris and Isaac Watts*. The Hague: Martinus Nijhoff, 1971.

Humphreys, A.R. *The Augustan World: Society, Thought, and Letters in Eighteenth-Century England*. New York: Harper and Row, 1954.

Ivimey, Joseph. *A History of the English Baptists: Including an Investigation of the History of Baptism in England from the Earliest Period to Which It Can Be Traced to the Close of the Seventeenth Century, to Which Are Prefixed Testimonies of Ancient Writers in Favor of Adult Baptism, Extracted from Dr. Gill's Piece Entitled, The Divine Right of Infant-Baptism Examined and Disproved*. London: n.p., 1811-1830.

James, Sharon. *In Trouble and in Joy: Four Women Who Lived for God*. Faverdale North, England: Evangelical Press, 2003.

Jarrett, Derek. *England in the Age of Hogarth*. New York: Viking Press, 1974.

Jeffrey, David Lyle. *English Spirituality in the Age of Wesley*. Grand Rapids, MI: Eerdmans, 1987. Reprint, Vancouver, BC: Regent College Publishing, 2000.

John of the Cross. *Dark Night of the Soul*. Translated and edited, with an introduction, by E. Allison Peers. New York: Image Books, 1959.

Johnson, Dale A. *Women in English Religion, 1700-1925*. Studies in Women and Religion, vol. 10. New York: Edwin Mellen Press, 1983.

Jones, Cheslyn, Geoffrey Wainwright, and Edward Yarnold, eds. *The Study of Spirituality*. New York: Oxford University Press, 1986.

Joyce, John J. "'These Filthy Rags of Speech': The Limits of Language and Robert Browning's Use of the Dramatic Monologue." *Cithara* 28, no. 2 (May 1989): 34-41.

Julian, John. *Dictionary of Hymnology: Origin and History of Christian Hymns and Hymnwriters of All Ages and Nations*, rev. ed. London: J. Murray, 1907. Reprint, Grand Rapids, MI: Kregel Publications, 1985.

Julian of Norwich. *Revelation of Love*. Edited and translated by John Skinner. New York: Image Books, 1996.

Keeble, N.H. *The Literary Culture of Nonconformity in Later Seventeenth-Century England*. Leicester, UK: Leicester University Press, 1987.

King, Winston L. "Negation as a Religious Category." *The Journal of Religion* 37, no. 2 (April 1957): 105-118.

Knox, Ronald A. *Enthusiasm: A Chapter in the History of Religion, with Special Reference to the Seventeenth and Eighteenth Centuries*. Oxford: Oxford University Press, 1950. Reprint, Westminster, MD: Christian Classics, 1983.

Lane, Belden C. *The Solace of Fierce Landscapes: Exploring Desert and Mountain Spirituality*. New York: Oxford University Press, 1998.

Lewis, Donald M., ed. *The Blackwell Dictionary of Evangelical Biography: 1730-1860*. Oxford: Blackwell, 1995.

Lonsdale, Roger, ed. *Eighteenth Century Women Poets: An Oxford Anthology*. Oxford: Oxford University Press, 1990.

Lorenz, Edmund S. *The Singing Church: The Hymns It Wrote and Sang*. Nashville, TN: Cokesbury Press, 1938.

Lovegrove, Deryck W., ed. *The Rise of the Laity in Evangelical Protestantism*. London: Routledge, 2002.

Lovelace, Austin C. *The Anatomy of Hymnody*. New York: Abingdon Press, 1965.

Lowther Clarke, W.K. *Eighteenth Century Piety*. London: Society for Promoting

Christian Knowledge, 1944.
Lumpkin, William L. *Baptist Confessions of Faith.* Valley Forge, PA: Judson Press, 1959.
Maison, Margaret. "'Thine, Only Thine!' Women Hymn Writers in Britain, 1760-1835." In *Religion in the Lives of English Women, 1760-1930,* ed. Gail Malmgreen, 11-40. Bloomington, IN: Indiana University Press, 1986.
Mallard, Ian. "The Hymns of Katherine Sutton." *Baptist Quarterly* 20 (1963-1964): 23-33.
Manley, Ken R. "'Sing Side by Side': John Rippon and Baptist Hymnody." In *Pilgrim Pathways: Essays in Baptist History in Honour of B.R. White,* ed. William H. Brackney, Paul S. Fiddes, and John H.Y. Briggs, 127-163. Macon, GA: Mercer University Press, 1999.
Manning, Bernard Lord. *Essays in Orthodox Dissent.* London: Independent Press, 1939.
—. *The Hymns of Wesley and Watts: Five Informal Papers.* London: Epworth Press, 1942.
Manning, Susan. "Sensibility." In *The Cambridge Companion to English Literature 1740-1830,* ed. Thomas Keymer and Jon Mee, 80-99. Cambridge: Cambridge University Press, 2004.
Manwaring, Randle. *A Study of Hymn-Writing and Hymn-Singing in the Christian Church.* Texts and Studies in Religion, vol. 50. Lewiston, NY: Edwin Mellen Press, 1990.
Mariani, Paul. "The Ineffability of What Counts: Some Notes on Poetry and Christianity." *Image* 5 (Spring 1994): 59-71.
Marshall, Madeleine Forell, and Janet Todd. *English Congregational Hymns in the Eighteenth Century.* Lexington, KY: University Press of Kentucky, 1982.
Martin, Hugh. "The Baptist Contribution to Early English Hymnody." *Baptist Quarterly* 19 (1961-1962): 195-208.
McGinn, Bernard. *The Foundations of Mysticism.* Vol. 1, *The Presence of God: A History of Western Christian Mysticism.* New York: Crossroads, 1991.
McIntosh, Mark A. "Lover Without a Name: Spirituality and Constructive Christology Today." In *Minding the Spirit: The Study of Christian Spirituality,* ed. Elizabeth A. Dreyer and Mark S. Burrows, 215-223. Baltimore: Johns Hopkins University Press, 2005.
—. *Mystical Theology: The Integrity of Spirituality and Theology.* Challenges in Contemporary Theology. Oxford: Blackwell Publishing, 1998.
McKibbens, Thomas R., Jr. "Our Baptist Heritage in Worship." *Review and Expositor* 80, no. 1 (Winter 1983): 53-69.
Michaelson, Patricia Howell. *Speaking Volumes: Women, Reading, and Speech in the Age of Austen.* Stanford, CA: Stanford University Press, 2002.
Miller, Josiah. *Our Hymns: Their Authors and Origin. Being Biographical Sketches of Nearly Two Hundred of the Principal Psalm and Hymn-Writers, with Notes on Their Psalms and Hymns.* London: Jackson, Walford, and Hodder, 1866.
Mistacco, Vicki. "The Metamorphoses of Philomel." *Women in French Studies,* special issue (2005): 205-218.
Moon, Norman S. "Caleb Evans, Founder of the Bristol Education Society." *Baptist Quarterly* 24 (1971-1972): 175-190.
Mowe, Richard J., and Mark A. Noll, eds. *Wonderful Words of Life: Hymns in American Protestant History and Theology.* Grand Rapids, MI: Eerdmans, 2004.

Music, David W. "Heroines of Baptist Hymnody." *Baptist History and Heritage* 29, no. 1 (January 1994): 37-44.
Nelson, Lowry, Jr. "The Rhetoric of Ineffability: Toward a Definition of Mystical Poetry." *Comparative Literature* 8, no. 4 (Autumn 1956): 323-336.
Newey, Vincent. *Cowper's Poetry: A Critical Study and Reassessment*. Liverpool: Liverpool University Press, 1982.
Noll, Mark A. *The Rise of Evangelicalism: The Age of Edwards, Whitefield and the Wesleys*. A History of Evangelicalism: People, Movements and Ideas in the English-Speaking World. Downers Grove, IL: InterVarsity Press, 2003.
Nussbaum, Felicity A. *The Autobiographical Subject: Gender and Ideology in Eighteenth-Century England*. Baltimore: Johns Hopkins University Press, 1989.
Nuttall, Geoffrey F. "John Ash and the Pershore Church: Additional Notes." *Baptist Quarterly* 22 (1967-1968): 271-276.
Ovid. *Metamorphoses*.
Parker, M. Pauline. "The Hymn as a Literary Form." *Eighteenth-Century Studies* 8 (1974-1975): 392-419.
Parry, Kenneth Lloyd, and Erik Routley. *Companion to Congregational Praise*. London: Independent Press, 1953.
Patterson, W. Morgan. "The Evangelical Revival and the Baptists." In *Pilgrim Pathways: Essays in Baptist History in Honour of B.R. White*, ed. William H. Brackney, Paul S. Fiddes, and John H.Y. Briggs, 243-262. Macon, GA: Mercer University Press, 1999.
Payne, Ernest A. *The Free Church Tradition in the Life of England*. London: SCM Press, 1944.
Pitman, Emma R. *Lady Hymn Writers*. London: T. Nelson and Sons, 1892.
Plomer, H.R., G.H. Bushnell, and E.R. McC. Dix. *A Dictionary of the Printers and Booksellers Who Were at Work in England, Scotland and Ireland from 1726 to 1775*. Oxford: Bibliographical Society at the Oxford University Press, 1930.
Pollard, Arthur. *English Hymns*. Bibliographical Series of Supplements to "British Book News" on Writers and Their Work. London: Longmans, Green, and Co., 1960.
Porter, Roy. *English Society in the Eighteenth Century*, rev. ed. London: Penguin Books, 1991.
Porter, Roy, and Dorothy Porter. *In Sickness and In Health: The British Experience 1650-1850*. London: Fourth Estate, 1988.
Prescott, Sarah. "Provincial Networks, Dissenting Connections, and Noble Friends: Elizabeth Singer Rowe and Female Authorship in Early Eighteenth-Century England." *Eighteenth-Century Life* 25 (Winter 2001): 29-42.
Pseudo-Dionysius. *The Complete Works of Pseudo-Dionysius*. Translated by Colm Luibheid. Classics of Western Spirituality. New York: Paulist Press, 1987.
Rahner, Karl. *Theological Investigations*. Vol. 16, *Experience of the Spirit: Source of Theology*. Translated by David Morland. New York: Crossroad, 1983.
Rattenbury, J. Ernest. *The Eucharistic Hymns of John and Charles Wesley*. London: Epworth Press, 1948.
——. *The Evangelical Doctrines of Charles Wesley's Hymns*. London: Epworth Press, 1941.
Redford, George, and John Angell James, eds. *The Autobiography of William Jay*. 1854. Reprint, Carlisle, PA: Banner of Truth Trust, 1974.
Reeves, Jeremiah Bascom. *The Hymn as Literature*. New York: Century Company,

1924.

Reeves, Marjorie. "Jane Attwater's Diaries." In *Pilgrim Pathways: Essays in Baptist History in Honour of B.R. White*, ed. William H. Brackney, Paul S. Fiddes, and John H.Y. Briggs, 207-222. Macon, GA: Mercer University Press, 1999.

—. "Literary Women in Eighteenth-Century Nonconformist Circles." In *Culture and the Nonconformist Tradition*, ed. Jane Shaw and Alan Kreider, 7-25. Religion, Culture, and Society. Cardiff: University of Wales, 1999.

—. *Pursuing the Muses: Female Education and Nonconformist Culture, 1700-1900*. London: Leicester University Press, 1997.

—. *Sheep Bell and Ploughshare: The Story of Two Village Families*. Bradford-on-Avon, UK: Moonraker Press, 1978.

Richardson, Paul. "Baptist Contributions to Hymnody and Hymnology." *Review and Expositor* 87, no. 1 (Winter 1990): 59-74.

—. Review of *"I Sing for I Cannot Be Silent": The Feminization of American Hymnody, 1870-1920*, by Jane Hadden Hobbs, and *Women of Sacred Song: Meditations on Hymns by Women*, by Margaret Partner and Daniel Partner. *The Hymn* 52, no. 2 (April 2001): 49-50.

Robinson, H. Wheeler. *The Life and Faith of the Baptists*, rev. ed. London: Kingsgate Press, 1946.

Rogers, Katharine M. *Feminism in Eighteenth-Century England*. Urbana, IL: University of Illinois Press, 1982.

Rolheiser, Ronald. *The Holy Longing: The Search for a Christian Spirituality*. New York: Doubleday, 1999.

Routley, Erik. *Hymns and Human Life*. London: John Murray, 1952.

—. *Hymns and the Faith*. Greenwich, CT: Seabury Press, 1956.

—. "The Hymns of Philip Doddridge." In *Philip Doddridge 1702-51: His Contribution to English Religion*, ed. Geoffrey F. Nuttall, 46-78. London: Independent Press, 1951.

—. *Hymns Today and Tomorrow*. New York: Abingdon Press, 1964.

—. *I'll Praise My Maker: A Study of the Hymns of Certain Authors Who Stand In or Near the Tradition of English Calvinism 1700-1850*. London: Independent Press, 1951.

—. *A Panorama of Christian Hymnody*. Collegeville, MN: Liturgical Press, 1979.

—. *A Short History of English Church Music*. Carol Stream, IL: Hope Publishing Company, 1997.

Russell, J. Stephen. "Song and the Ineffable in the *Prioress's Tale*." *The Chaucer Review* 33, no. 2 (1998): 176-189.

Ryden, E.E. *The Story of Christian Hymnody*. Rock Island, IL: Augustana Press, 1959.

Sambrook, James. *The Eighteenth Century: The Intellectual and Cultural Context of English Literature, 1700-1789*, 2nd ed. Longman Literature in English Series. London: Longman Group, 1993.

Sampson, George. "The Century of Divine Songs." In *Proceedings of the British Academy*, vol. 29, 37-64. London: Oxford University Press, 1943.

Sale, David M. *The Hymn Writers of Hampshire*. Winchester, UK: Winton, 1975.

Scharfstein, Ben-Ami. *Ineffability: The Failure of Words in Philosophy and Religion*. SUNY Series, Toward a Comparative Philosophy of Religions. Albany, NY: State University of New York Press, 1993.

Sells, Michael. *Mystical Languages of Unsaying*. Chicago: University of Chicago Press,

1994.

Sharpe, Eric. "Bristol Baptist College and the Church's Hymnody." *Baptist Quarterly* 28 (1979): 7-16.

Shaw, Jane. "Introduction: Why 'Culture and the Nonconformist Tradition'?" In *Culture and the Nonconformist Tradition*, ed. Jane Shaw and Alan Kreider, 1-6. Religion, Culture, and Society. Cardiff: University of Wales, 1999.

Shoemaker, Robert B. *Gender in English Society 1650-1850: The Emergence of Separate Spheres?* Themes in British Social History. London: Addison Wesley Longman, 1998.

Skedd, Susan. "Women Teachers and the Expansion of Girls' Schooling in England, c. 1760-1820." In *Gender in Eighteenth-Century England: Roles, Representations and Responsibilities*, ed. Hannah Barker and Elaine Chalus, 101-125. London: Addison Wesley Longman, 1997.

Smith, H. Augustine. *Lyric Religion: The Romance of Immortal Hymns*. New York: Century Company, 1931.

Smith, Karen Elizabeth. "Beyond Public and Private Spheres: Another Look at Women in Baptist History and Historiography." *Baptist Quarterly* 34 (April 1991): 79-87.

—. "The Community and the Believer: A Study of Calvinistic Baptist Spirituality in Some Towns and Villages of Hampshire and the Borders of Wiltshire, c. 1730-1830." DPhil diss., University of Oxford, 1986.

—. "The Covenant Life of Some Eighteenth-Century Calvinistic Baptists in Hampshire and Wiltshire." In *Pilgrim Pathways: Essays in Baptist History in Honour of B.R. White*, ed. William H. Brackney, Paul S. Fiddes, and John H.Y. Briggs, 165-183. Macon, GA: Mercer University Press, 1999.

—. "Forgotten Sisters: The Contributions of Some Notable but Un-Noted British Baptist Women." In *Recycling the Past or Researching History? Studies in Baptist Historiography and Myths*, ed. Philip E. Thompson and Anthony R. Cross, 163-183. Studies in Baptist History and Thought, vol. 11. Milton Keynes, UK: Paternoster, 2005.

Smith, William, ed. *A Dictionary of Greek and Roman Biography and Mythology*. London: Walton and Maberly, John Murray, 1862.

Spacks, Patricia Meyer. *The Poetry of Vision: Five Eighteenth-Century Poets*. Cambridge, MA: Harvard University Press, 1967.

Stecher, Henry F. *Elizabeth Singer Rowe, the Poetess of Frome: A Study in Eighteenth-Century English Pietism*. Frankfurt: Herbert Lang Bern, 1973.

Steele-Smith, Hugh. "The Steeles of Broughton: Some Notes on a Hampshire Family." Unpublished manuscript, Angus Library, Oxford, 1986.

Steiner, George. *Language and Silence: Essays 1958-1966*. London: Faber and Faber, 1967.

Stephen, Leslie. *History of English Thought in the Eighteenth Century*. London: Smith, Elder, and Co., 1876.

Stevenson, W.R. "English Baptist Hymnody." In *Dictionary of Hymnology: Origin and History of Christian Hymns and Hymnwriters of All Ages and Nations*, rev.ed., ed. John Julian, 110-113. London: J. Murray, 1907. Reprint, Grand Rapids, MI: Kregel Publications, 1985.

Stone, P.W.K. *The Art of Poetry, 1750-1820: Theories of Poetic Composition and Style in the Late Neo-Classic and Early Romantic Periods*. London: Routledge and Kegan Paul, 1967.

Sweet, Rosemary. *The English Town, 1680-1840: Government, Society and Culture*. New York: Pearson Education, 1999.

Tamke, Susan S. *Make a Joyful Noise Unto the Lord: Hymns as a Reflection of Victorian Social Attitudes*. Athens, OH: Ohio University Press, 1978.

Taylor, G.H. "The Reverend John Ash, LL.D., 1724-1779." *Baptist Quarterly* 20 (1963-1964): 4-22.

Temperley, Nicholas. *The Hymn Tune Index: A Census of English-Language Hymn Tunes in Printed Sources from 1535 to 1820*. Oxford: Oxford University Press, 1997.

—. *The Hymn Tune Index* (http://hymntune.music.uiuc.edu, accessed 13 January 2007).

Teresa of Avila. *The Interior Castle*. Translated by Kieran Kavanaugh and Otilio Rodriguez. Introduction by Kieran Kavanaugh. Preface by Raimundo Pinikkar. Classics of Western Spirituality. New York: Paulist Press, 1979.

Thomas, Gilbert. *William Cowper and the Eighteenth Century*, rev. ed. London: George Allen and Unwin, 1948.

Thomson, Ronald W. "Anne Steele, 1716-1778." *Baptist Quarterly* 21 (October 1966): 368-371.

—, ed. *The Baptist Hymn Book Companion*, rev. ed. London: Psalms and Hymns Trust, 1967.

Todd, Janet. *Sensibility: An Introduction*. London: Methuen and Co., 1986.

Underwood, A.C. *A History of the English Baptists*. London: Carey Kingsgate Press, 1947.

van Buren, Paul M. *The Edges of Language: An Essay in the Logic of a Religion*. New York: Macmillan Company, 1972.

Vickery, Amanda. *The Gentleman's Daughter: Women's Lives in Georgian England*. New Haven: Yale University Press, 1998.

Wakefield, Gordon S., ed. *The SCM Dictionary of Christian Spirituality*. London: SCM Press, 1983.

Watson, J.R. *The English Hymn: A Critical and Historical Study*. Oxford: Oxford University Press, 1997.

—, ed. *Pre-Romanticism in English Poetry of the Eighteenth Century: The Poetic Art and Significance of Thomson, Gray, Collins, Goldsmith, Cowper and Crabbe*. London: Macmillan Education, 1989.

Watts, Ann Chalmers. "*Pearl*, Inexpressibility, and Poems of Human Loss." *Publications of the Modern Language Association* 99, no. 1 (January 1984): 26-40.

Watts, Michael R. *The Dissenters*. Vol. 1, *From the Reformation to the French Revolution*. Oxford: Clarendon Press, 1978.

Whitley, W.T. "The First Hymnbook in Use." *Baptist Quarterly* 10 (1941): 369-375.

—. *A History of British Baptists*. London: Charles Griffin and Company, 1923.

—. "The Influence of Whitefield on Baptists." *Baptist Quarterly* 5 (1930-1931): 30-36.

Williamson, Marilyn. *Raising Their Voices: British Women Writers, 1650-1750*. Detroit: Wayne State University Press, 1990.

Wilson, John. "Looking at Hymn Tunes: The Objective Factors." In *Duty and Delight: Routley Remembered: A Memorial Tribute to Erik Routley (1917-1982), Ministry, Church Music, Hymnody*, ed. Robin A. Leaver and James H. Litton, 123-152. Carol Stream, IL: Hope Publishing, 1985.

Wright, Thomas. *The Lives of the British Hymn-Writers Being Personal Memoirs Derived Largely from Unpublished Materials*. Vol. 3, *Isaac Watts and Contemporary Hymn-Writers*. London: C.J. Farncombe and Sons, 1914.

Young, Robert H. *The History of Baptist Hymnody in England from 1612 to 1800*. PhD diss., University of Southern California, 1959.

INDEX

Adam, Thomas 143
Addington, Stephen 144
adynaton 84
Alexander, James Waddel 66–67
Allestree, Richard 121
Arminianism 14, 43, 60, 86
Arnold, Richard 2, 38, 66, 93, 176–177
Ash, John 16, 17, 20, 26, 27, 58, 60–63, 64, 157
  see also "Bristol Collection"
Ashworth, Caleb 107, 113–114, 182
Attwater, Anna 111, 179
Attwater, Caroline 22, 179
Attwater, Gay Thomas 87, 179
Attwater, Jane 22, 179
Attwater, Marianna 22, 67–68, 87, 107, 111, 179, 183
Augustanism 89–90, 94, 118–119
  see also classicism
Augustine 30, 79, 98, 101, 134–135, 154, 171

Bailey, Albert 2–3, 103, 105
Baker, Frank 44
Baptists
  1644 Baptist Confession 85–86, 115
  General Baptists 14, 86
  hymnody 2, 17, 20, 52, 55–56, 57–65, 92, 157
  ministers 12, 15, 16, 57, 58, 59–60, 62, 63, 103, 157
  Particular Baptists 6, 12, 13, 14, 16–17, 26, 28, 51, 55, 57, 58, 59–60, 62, 63, 72, 85–86, 92, 103, 115–116, 180
  see also Calvinism; Western Association of Particular Baptist Churches
Barker, John 144
Barth, Karl 156
Bath 11, 71, 75, 181
Beddome, Benjamin 16, 17, 20, 21, 29, 58–59, 63, 64, 181, 183

Beddome, Benjamin, hymns and poems
  "Resignation; or, God Our Portion" 59
Belknap, Jeremy 62–63
Benson, Louis 5, 30, 58, 59, 63, 121–122, 123, 169
Bernard of Clairvaux 66, 168
Bompas, Miss 1–2, 176
Boscawen, Edward 144
Boscawen, Frances 144
Boston 5, 63
Boswell, Elizabeth 21
Boswell, James 26
Brady, Nicholas 37, 43, 58
  see also New Version of the Psalms of David
Bristol 26, 43, 62
Bristol Baptist Academy 14, 16–17, 58, 62
"Bristol Collection" 17, 26, 60–63, 64, 157
Bristol Education Society 27, 62
  see also Bristol Baptist Academy
Broadmead Baptist Church (Bristol) 16–17, 62
Broome, J.R. 6, 10, 12, 13–14, 16
Broughton 10, 11, 13, 14, 16, 60, 68, 74–75, 83, 85, 105, 106, 107, 113, 145, 157, 180, 181, 182, 185
Broughton Baptist Church 6, 13–17, 64, 85, 115, 144, 157, 180
Burrage, Henry 9, 103
Burrows, Mark 158
Byrom, John 183

Calvin, John
  and psalm-singing 38
Calvinism 7, 13, 14, 50, 57, 60, 86, 115, 116, 146, 156, 157–158, 165, 167, 172, 173, 176
  and anxiety 43, 161
  and conception of sin 84–86, 95, 146, 151, 161–162, 172

Carnell, Corbin Scott 156
Catholicism 76, 86–87
Cator, Thomas 12, 178
Cecil, Lord David 34
Cennick, John 46
Cennick, John, hymns and poems
  "Hymn CXXVIII" ("Lo! he cometh, countless Trumpets") 46
Church of England 14, 33, 37, 43, 48, 52, 64, 121, 143, 166
Clark, Harry 118, 120
classicism 32, 70–74, 89–90, 100, 156, 158, 163
  see also neoclassicism
The Cloud of Unknowing 80, 154–155
Colish, Marcia 81, 101, 135, 170–171
conduct books 76, 121
Congregationalists 62, 117
  see also Independents
Cowper, Maria Frances Cecelia Madan 165–166
Cowper, Maria Frances Cecelia Madan, hymns and poems
  "The Consolation" 165–166
Cowper, William 2, 32, 47–51, 56, 59, 66, 118, 147, 161–162, 166
  see also Olney Hymns
Cowper, William, hymns and poems
  "The Contrite Heart" 48, 49–50; "God Moves in a Mysterious Way" 118; "Joy and Peace in Believing" ("Sometimes a Light Surprizes") 50, 118; "Submission" 161; "The Task" 47; "The Waiting Soul" 161; "Walking with God" 118

Danebury 11, 145
Dante Alighieri 81–82
Davie, Donald 29, 31–33, 34–35, 38, 39, 40, 41, 42, 43, 44, 46–47, 48–49, 50, 54, 118, 119, 127, 156–157, 158, 165
Davies, Horton 38, 42, 58–59
debate between hymns and psalms 37–39, 42, 57–58
de Lubac, Henri 94, 116
Dilly, Edward and Charles 26
Dissenters 2–3, 12–13, 14, 16, 23, 35, 41, 43, 45, 47, 48, 53, 55, 57, 64, 68, 86, 107, 156
hymnody 35, 52, 156
and women 51–52
Dixon, Michael 105, 106
Doddridge, Philip 2, 3, 33, 37, 55, 58–59, 60, 63, 64, 76, 107, 183
Donne, John 155
Duffield, Samuel Willoughby 2
Duncombe, John 145, 184
Dunscombe, Mary Steele 5, 14, 19, 22, 26–27, 62, 74, 107, 145–146, 157, 178, 185
Dutton, Anne 29, 51, 55–56, 77
Dutton, Anne, hymns and poems
  "The Mystery of the Trinity Reveal'd in Christ" 56

Ebeling, Gerard 102
Eckhart, Meister 80
Elcomb, James 21, 103, 104–105, 180
Eliot, T.S. 81–82, 89, 91–92, 101
Escott, Harry 40
Established Church, *see* Church of England
Ethridge, Sarah 15
evangelical, evangelicalism 2, 7, 46, 47, 50, 63, 90, 122, 158, 166, 169
Evangelical Revival 43, 44–45, 46, 48, 55, 60, 122, 172
Evans, Caleb 5, 6, 16, 17, 20, 23, 26–27, 28, 58, 60–63, 64, 75, 98, 107, 121, 157
  "Advertisement" in *Poems on Subjects Chiefly Devotional* 5, 23, 28, 75, 98, 107, 109, 121
  see also "Bristol Collection"
Evans, Hugh 16, 62

Fairchild, Hoxie Neale 90, 118–120, 144, 168
Fanch, James 60, 157, 181
fatalism 148
Fawcett, John 59
Fénelon, François 20, 147
Findlay, George 44
Foskett, Bernard 16–17, 58, 183
Francke, August Hermann 55
Froude, Edward 12, 13–14, 178

Froude, Elizabeth Blackborrow 14, 178
Froude, Sarah 111
Frye, Northrop 118, 134
Furneaux, Philip 20, 22, 23–24, 26, 62, 68, 74–75, 84–85, 116, 138, 181

Gay, Elizabeth 13, 179, 181
Gay, Jane Cator 12–13, 178, 179, 180, 181
Gay, John (author) 40, 184
Gay, John (uncle) 12–13, 178, 179, 180
Gay, Richard 12–13, 179, 180
General Baptists, *see under* Baptists
Gentleman's Magazine 74, 146
Gernhardt, Paul 66
Gifford, Andrew 12
Gill, John 63
girls' education 17–20
Gospel Magazine 64
Gray, Thomas 183
Gregory of Nazianzus 94
Gregory of Nyssa 79, 154–155
Guyon, Madame 147

Hadden, J. Cuthbert 1–2, 8, 173, 176
Hall, Robert 59
Harris, Howell 55
Harris, Isabella 143
Harrison, Susannah 117–118, 160
Harrison, Susannah, hymns and poems "VIII" ("While I am call'd to reason, Lord, with Thee") 117; "XXVI" ("Condemn me not, most gracious God") 117; "A Short Dialogue between Myself and My Soul" 160
Hatfield, Edwin 2, 8–9, 103
Haykin, Michael 16–17, 58
Hayley, William 185
Haywood, Eliza Fowler 78
health conditions 106, 108, 119, 143, 146
  medical treatment 106–107
  smallpox 13, 108
Herbert, George 83–84, 131, 155, 171, 183
Hervey, James 74–75, 76, 120, 132, 183
  Meditations among the Tombs 120
  Meditations and Contemplations 75, 183

Theron and Aspasio 75, 183
Heyrick, Elizabeth 145
Hindmarsh, Bruce 2, 16, 48, 50, 55, 106, 143
Hogarth, William 35
Hopkins, John 37, 43, 91
  see also Whole Booke of Psalmes
Hoyles, John 40, 89–90
Huntingdon, Lady Selina Hastings, Countess of 37, 166
hymns
  content of 20, 29–30, 33–35, 36, 41–42, 44–46, 50, 55, 91, 123, 131, 156, 164, 165
  definition of 30, 32, 48–49
  diction 30, 31–32, 40, 42, 50, 54, 90–91
  as didactic 41, 46, 48–49, 56–57, 90, 124, 172
  and doctrine 30, 33, 34, 35, 41, 46–47, 49, 55, 56, 65, 116, 122, 124, 131, 176
  form of 29–30, 31–33, 34–35, 36, 39–42, 43–44, 45–46, 50, 55, 56, 90–92, 123, 124, 131, 156, 163, 164, 165
  as literature 6, 29–33, 34–35, 36, 56, 65, 172
  metre 31, 37, 39, 42, 44, 46, 50, 90–91, 98, 112, 125, 127
  as poetry 30, 32–33, 34, 35, 40
  as sermon summaries 58–59
  as subjective 42, 43, 44–45, 46, 48–49, 54, 55, 56, 120, 122, 161, 176–177
  as theology 6, 7, 29–30, 33–35, 36, 41, 47, 56, 65, 172, 176
  and tunes 7, 39, 64, 184
  and women 2, 3, 51–57, 117, 121–123
  see also debate between hymns and psalms; plain style; psalms

iconography 72, 87, 132, 134
imagination 34, 39, 72, 76, 79, 119, 157, 158
inarticulacy 4, 6, 66, 77–84, 89–92, 94, 96, 99–100, 102, 114, 116, 129, 136, 148, 149, 158, 159, 160, 168, 172
Independents 2, 64
ineffability 4, 6–7, 66–67, 78, 79–99, 101, 115–116, 132, 136, 149–150, 158,

159, 158, 169, 171, 172
inexpressibility 66, 77–78, 80, 81, 90, 92–96, 99–101, 102, 116, 132, 148, 149, 168
Ivimey, Joseph 60, 103, 104, 105

Jay, William 145–146
John of the Cross 148, 154–155
Johnson, Samuel 26, 38, 52, 94
Julian, John 2–3, 5, 59, 63, 161, 168–169
Julian of Norwich 80, 155

Keach, Benjamin 12, 57–58
Keeble, N.H. 23, 35, 156
Kiffin, William 12, 57
Knollys, Hansard 12, 57

Lacy, John 157
Lane, Belden 80
Langdon, Edward 105
Lavington, John 24, 74–75, 181
Lewis, C.S. 156
  Sehnsucht 156
Lewis, Josiah 15, 144
London 1, 23, 24, 26, 28, 37, 43, 63, 86, 181
longing 44, 95, 127, 136, 148, 149–159, 162–168, 171, 172, 176
Lovelace, Austin 31, 42, 46
Lowell, Samuel 144
Luther, Martin
  and hymn-singing 38

MacKenzie, Henry 118
Madan, Judith 166
Madan, Martin 166
Maison, Margaret 51–52, 57, 104, 117, 166
Manfield, James 13, 104–105, 106, 180, 181
Manley, Ken 3, 63, 64–65
Manning, Bernard 44, 47, 124
Marshall, Madeleine Forell 30, 33, 35, 39, 41, 46, 48, 50, 125, 161–162, 163
Martin, Hugh 57, 58
McGinn, Bernard 102, 154
McIntosh, Mark 80, 86
Medley, Samuel 59

melancholy 7, 8, 28, 99, 101, 110, 118, 119–120, 141, 155, 162, 172
  see also Sensibility, Age of
Methodism 2, 35, 43, 45, 47, 48, 64, 158
  and assurance 43, 44, 158
  see also Evangelical Revival
Milton, John 74, 75, 183
Montagu, Elizabeth 144
Moravians 46, 147
  see also stillness
More, Hannah 145, 185
muse 24, 69, 70–74, 89, 110, 148

neoclassism, *see* Augustanism
Newton, John 2, 3, 48–49, 50
  see also Olney Hymns
New Version of the Psalms of David 37
Nonconformists, *see* Dissenters
Nuttall, Geoffrey 62

Olney Hymns 48, 49–50, 64, 118, 161
Oram, Samuel Marsh 185
Origen of Alexandria 86
Orton, Job 58–59

Parker, Pauline 31, 32, 42, 49
Parnell, Thomas 40, 184
Particular Baptists, *see under* Baptists
Pattison, William 185
Payne, Ernest 33, 52
Pearsall, Richard 76
Peterfreund, Stuart 81
Philomel 99–101
Pietism 54–55
Pike, Samuel 183
Pine, William 26
Pitman, Emma 9, 103, 161
plain style 32–33, 39–41, 54
Pope, Alexander 19–20, 33, 40, 52, 94, 116, 138–139, 152, 183–184, 185
  Essay on Man 19–20, 116, 139, 183–184
Porter, Dorothy 106, 107, 108, 119–120, 143
Porter, Roy 106, 107, 108, 119–120, 143
pre-Romanticism 155–156
Prior, Matthew 52, 165
psalms 4–6, 37–39, 42, 43, 57, 63, 91

see also debate between hymns and psalms; hymns; *New Version of the Psalms of David*; Scripture; *Whole Booke of Psalmes*
Pseudo-Dionysius 79–80
pseudonyms 5, 19, 22, 24, 52, 68, 69, 71, 74, 76, 77, 87, 100, 111, 121, 138, 139, 145–146, 178–179
Puritans 42, 54, 156

Quietism 147–148

Rahner, Karl 149
Rattenbury, Ernest 33
reason 18, 50, 70, 119, 121, 147–148, 155
Reeves, Jeremiah Bascom 31, 32
Reeves, Marjorie 12, 20, 21–22, 53, 145, 157, 184, 185
resignation 4, 28, 59, 136–149, 159–162, 165–168, 172
  funeral sermons 143–144
Richardson, George 72, 87, 132, 134
Richardson, Paul 2, 57, 60, 64
Richardson, Samuel 118, 121, 184
Rippon, John 59, 60, 63–64, 157
  Rippon's *Selection* 59, 60, 63–65, 157
Rivers, Isabel 37, 75
Robinson, Robert 59–60, 157
Rogers, Katharine 77
Romaine, William 37
Romanticism 8, 118, 119, 120, 155–158, 172
  see also pre-Romanticism
Rousseau, Jean-Jacques 118
Routley, Erik 2, 49, 116
Rowe, Elizabeth Singer 51, 52–55, 56, 77, 100–101, 144–145, 184
  and Isaac Watts 37, 52–53, 54
Rowe, Elizabeth Singer, hymns and poems
  "Hymn" ("Immortal Fountain of my Life") 53–54; "Letter LXXIV" 145
Ryland, John Collett 16

Salisbury 11, 13, 18, 108, 180
Sampson, George 29, 33, 49
Sarbiewski, Mathias Casimir 90
Scriblerus Club 40

Scripture 41, 42, 51, 53, 55, 56, 72, 87, 92, 130, 138, 164, 165, 173, 175
Sedgwick, Daniel 5, 6
Sells, Michael 115–116
Sensibility, Age of 7, 118–122, 127, 156, 165, 172
sentimental literature 118–119, 121, 122
  see also Sensibility, Age of
Seward, Anne 185
Shaftesbury, Third Earl of 118
Shakespeare, William 33, 184
Shaw, Robert 83–84, 92, 158, 171
Sheppard, John 5–6, 10, 14, 71, 105
smallpox, *see under* health conditions
Smith, Karen 10, 13–15, 51, 58, 76, 86, 116–117, 122–123, 144, 157, 176–177
sovereignty of God 2, 94, 99, 114, 116, 118, 129, 136–139, 141, 142, 146, 159, 160–161, 163, 169, 170, 175–176, 183
Spener, Philipp Jacob 55
Steadman, William 14
Stecher, Henry 54–55, 101, 145, 155
Steele, Anne
  baptism 15–16, 180
  church life 6, 13–17
  death 1, 5, 12, 28, 98, 107, 144, 176, 182, 185
  on death 107–109, 111–112, 116, 132, 134, 140–141, 142, 153, 176
  education 15, 17–20, 180
  family life 10–13, 19, 103–104
  on friendship 22, 24, 85, 140
  friendships with ministers 16, 20, 22, 26, 28, 60, 62, 107
  health 13, 15, 28, 103, 104, 105–107, 109–111, 112, 114, 116, 132, 141–142, 146, 150, 153, 168, 169–170, 172, 173, 181–182
  on heaven 72, 86–89, 95, 97–98, 114, 115, 137, 140–141, 150, 151, 153–154, 161, 164, 171
  hymn theory 35–36
  on language 3, 66, 67–78, 83–84, 93–99, 152, 168
  marriage proposals, engagements 8–9, 21, 69, 103, 104–105, 112, 160–161, 180, 181
  on nature 21, 69, 71, 96, 99

pseudonym, "Theodosia" 4–5, 36, 76, 77, 146, 168, 178
publication 2, 4–5, 12, 23–28, 62, 68, 74, 98, 132, 157, 172, 176, 181, 182
reading 19–20, 183–185
on sin 83–89, 115, 151, 163, 168, 169–170, 172
on singleness and marriage 69–70
studies of, writing on 2, 5–6, 8–9, 66, 103, 160–161
on suffering 1–2, 4, 103–114, 123, 127–131, 137–142, 146, 150–151, 153, 154, 159–161, 162, 168, 169–170, 173–176
vocation as writer 67–68, 69, 94, 101, 132, 134, 148
wealth of family 6, 10, 14–15, 26, 28
on writing 21, 22, 67–78, 148, 152
in writing circle 21–22, 53, 60, 62, 74

Steele, Anne, hymns and poems
"Absence from God" 113, 176; "The Absent Muse" 71; "Acknowledging His Goodness in Supporting and Restoring" 165–167; "The Blind Man's Petition" 87; "Breathing after God" 152–153; "By Mr. Lavington on Visiting Broughton with Dr. Furneaux" 75; "Christ the Christian's Life" 75; "Christ the Life of the Soul" 99–100, 129–130; "Christ the Physician of Souls" 169; "Christ the Supreme Beauty" 87, 158; "Cold Affections" 83; "The Complaint and Relief" 68, 85, 112, 165; "The Condescension of God" 97–98, 115, 167; "The Desire of Knowledge a Proof of Immortality" 140–141, 148; "Desiring a Cheerful Resignation to the Divine Will" 142; "Desiring a Taste of Real Joy" 115, 154; "Desiring Resignation and Thankfulness" 159–161, 162; "Desiring the Presence of God" 162; "Desiring to Praise God" 93–94, 124; "Desiring to Praise God for the Experience of His Goodness" 84; "Desiring to Trust in God" 113; "A Dialogue" (STE 3/3/1, pp. 25–37) 22; "A Dialogue" (STE 3/3/1, pp. 38–44), 69–70; "A Dying Saviour" 125–127, 128; "The Elevation" 90; "Eusebia and Urania, or Devotion and the Muse" 71, 72, 74; "An Evening Meditation" 99; "An Evening Walk" 96, 99; "The Exalted Saviour" 96; "The Excellency of the Holy Scriptures" 165; "Faith and Hope in Divine Goodness, Encouraged by Past Experience" 153–154; "The Faithfulness of God" 113; "The Fettered Mind" 140, 152; "Filial Submission" 165; "Friendship" 85; "God My Only Happiness" 113; "God the Only Refuge of the Troubled Mind" ("Dear Refuge of My Weary Soul") 1–2, 99, 167, 173–176; "God the Soul's Only Portion" 86; "The Great Physician" 169–170; "Hope in Darkness" 141; "Hope Reviving in the Contemplation of Divine Mercy" 78, 84; "Human Frailty" 67; "The Humble Claim" 151–152; "Humble Worship" 96–97; "A Hymn of Praise to God the Father, Son, and Spirit Praise to the Sacred Trinity" 98; "Imploring Divine Influence" 94–95, 152; "The Inconstant Heart" 83; "Intreating the Presence of Christ in His Churches" 96; "Intreating the Presence of God in Affliction" 167; "The Invocation" 72; "The Joys of Heaven" 171; "Light and Deliverance" 167; "A Meditation on Death" 111–112; "Mourning the Absence of God, and Longing for His Gracious Presence" 127–128; "The Mysteries of Providence" 98, 130–131; "The Nativity of Christ" 84; "Ode on a Rural Prospect in June" 75, 152; "Ode to Hope" 162; "Ode to Melancholy" 119–120, 162; "On a Day of Prayer for Success in War" 84; "On Amira's Reading *Grandison* in the Absence of Portius" 121; "On Being Desired to Send Some Verses to the Gentlemans Magazine" 74; "On Being Desired to Write on the Death of Dr. Watts" 75, 89, 115; "On Dr. Youngs Night Thoughts" 69, 75; "On Oct. 19th

1760. A Day of Thanksgiving for National Successes" 86–87; "On Reading Mr. Hervey's Meditations" 75; "On Recovery from Sickness" 68; "On the 17th February a Day Appointed for General Prayer &c" 84; "On the Death of Mr. Hervey" 75, 132–133; "On the Nativity of Christ" 164; "On the Same" 78; "On the Walks of Bath May 1751" 71; "Papal pow'r, or Pagan Night" 86; "A Pastoral Elegy" 71; "Penitence and Hope" 167; "The Pilgrim" 109, 111; "The Pleasures of Spring" 124; "Praise to God for the Blessings of Providence and Grace" 95–96, 164; "The Presence of God, the Only Comfort in Affliction" 176; "The Promised Land" 151; "A Prospect of Life" 109, 115, 118; "Redeeming Love" 98–99; "A Reflection, Occasioned by the Death of a Neighbour" 111; "Refuge in Distress" 109; "Resignation" 141; "Resigning the Heart to God" 83; "Rest and Comfort in Christ Alone" 98; "Retirement and Meditation" 67; "Reviewing My Verses for Publication" 24, 68; "A Rural Hymn" 91; "Self Reflection" 169; "The Sickly Mind" 152; "Silviana" 71; "Submission to God under Affliction" 113; "Support in Trouble" 108; "Thirsting after God" 162–163; "A Thought in Sickness" 110; "To a Friend in Trouble" 114, 116; "To a Friend on His Marriage Oct. 6 1743" 77; "To Amira on Her Mother's Illness" 150–151; "To Amira on the Sudden Death of Her Mother" 108, 141, 153; "To Delia Pensive" 138–139; "To Florio" 87; "To Lysander" 24, 74; "To Melinda" 21; "To Mr. Hervey on His Theron and Aspasio" 75; "To Myra" 146; "To Philander" 139–141; "The Transforming Vision of God" 167; "A Walk in a Churchyard" 134; "The Wonders of Redemption" 163–164; "Written in a Painful Illness" 114, 141–142, 165; "Wrote in an Ill State of Health in the Spring" 110–111; untitled (STE 3/1/1, no. 57) 87, 114, 153; untitled (STE 3/1/4, no. 18) 164; untitled (STE 3/1/4, no. 21) 109; untitled (STE 3/1/5, no. 5) 112–113, 176; untitled (STE 3/3/1, pp. 3–4) 19; untitled (STE 3/3/1, pp. 20–24) 22, 71; untitled (STE 3/3/1, p. 88) 76; untitled (STE 3/3/1, p. 104) 74; untitled (STE 3/3/6, no. 26) 71; untitled (STE 3/3/6, no. 28) 18–19; untitled (STE 3/3/6, no. 36) 71

Steele, Anne, works in prose "Acquaintance with God the Supreme Good" 152; "Comfort Under the Painful Sense of Frailty, in the Unchangeable Goodness of God" 85; "Friendship" 85; "God's Omnipresence" 83; "The Journey of Life" 109; "Longing for the Manifestations of Divine Love" 168; "Of the Knowledge of Ourselves" 85; "Thoughts in Sickness, and on Recovery" 94, 109–110

Steele, Anne Cator 10, 12–13, 15–18, 23, 24, 74–75, 103–104, 105, 106–108, 109, 122, 141, 150, 153, 178, 180, 181, 182

Steele, Anne Froude 10, 12, 16, 103, 111, 178

Steele, Henry 13–15, 18, 178, 180, 181

Steele, Martha Goddard 105, 178

Steele, Mary Bullock 21, 75, 107, 108, 109, 137–141, 178, 181, 182

Steele, Thomas (brother) 10, 103, 178, 180

Steele, William (brother) 1, 5, 6, 10, 12, 15, 16, 18, 21, 22, 23, 24, 26–27, 28, 83, 85, 105, 106–107, 108, 116, 137–140, 144, 146, 178, 180, 181, 182, 184, 185

Steele, William (father) 10, 12, 13, 14–15, 16, 36, 60, 103, 104, 108, 116–117, 157, 178, 180, 181, 182

Steele-Smith, Hugh 5, 6, 23, 105, 106

Steiner, George 81, 82

Stennett, Joseph 17, 58

Stennett, Samuel 58, 62, 64, 144
Stephen, Leslie 121
Sterne, Laurence 118
Sternhold, Thomas 37, 43, 91
  see also *Whole Booke of Psalmes*
stillness 147
Stoicism 148
Sutton, Katherine 52, 57
Swift, Jonathan 40, 184

Tate, Nahum 37, 43, 58, 64
  see also *New Version of the Psalms of David*
Taylor, Mary Scott 22, 145–146, 184, 185
Teresa of Avila 148
Thomas, Gilbert 49
Thomson, James 19, 38, 100, 184
Todd, Janet 30, 33, 35, 39, 41, 46, 48, 50, 119, 122, 125, 161–162, 163, 165
Tomkins, Anne Steele 6, 105, 178
Toplady, Augustus 64
transcendence of God 79, 114, 115–116, 146, 148, 149–150, 168–169, 177
Trapnel, Anna 52, 57
Turner, Daniel 59–60, 157

van Buren, Paul 158
Vaughan, Henry 86
Vickery, Amanda 120–121, 142–143

Wakeford, Hannah Towgood 22, 179
Wakeford, Joseph 22, 23–24, 26, 68, 76, 121, 178, 179, 181, 182
Wakeford, Mary Steele 10, 13, 17–18, 21, 22, 24, 68–71, 75, 83, 103–104, 108, 121, 141, 150–151, 153, 178, 179, 180, 181, 182
Wakeford, Samuel 13, 108, 179, 182
Wallin, Benjamin 17
Watson, J.R. 7, 30, 31, 33, 34, 41, 42, 43–44, 45, 46, 47, 48, 50, 59, 91, 119, 123, 124, 125, 127, 128–129, 131, 155, 156, 159, 163, 165, 166, 169
Watts, Ann Chalmers 90
Watts, Isaac 2, 17, 29, 33, 36, 37–42, 43–47, 48–50, 52–55, 56, 58, 59, 60, 63, 64, 75, 82, 86, 89–91, 96, 115, 116, 121, 122, 124–126, 127, 138, 156–157, 163, 165, 172, 184
  Horae Lyricae 35, 37, 39, 53
  hymn theory 35, 37–41, 90
  Hymns and Spiritual Songs 37, 38, 39–40, 48, 86, 96, 122, 125, 127, 165
  and psalmody 37–39, 42
  Psalms of David 37, 39, 41, 90
  "Short Essay Toward the Improvement of Psalmody" 38, 40
Watts, Isaac, hymns and poems
  "The Church the Garden of Christ" 86;
  "Crucifixion to the World, by the Cross of Christ" ("When I Survey the Wondrous Cross") 96, 124–127; "A Happy Resurrection" 165; "Man Frail and God Eternal" ("Our God, our Help in Ages past") 41–42
Watts, Michael 14, 51
Watts, Susanna 145
Wesley, Charles 2, 29, 33, 36, 42, 43–47, 48–50, 56, 60, 64, 91, 122, 124–126, 128, 129, 158, 161, 163, 169, 170, 172, 184
  conversion 45, 124
Wesley, Charles, hymns and poems
  "Hymn I" ("O for a thousand tongues to sing") 170; "Hymn XXIX" ("Where shall my wandering soul begin?") 124–126; "Hymn 64" ("Lo, he comes with clouds descending") 45–46
Wesley, John 26, 35, 37, 42, 43, 46, 55, 60, 64, 75, 147, 161, 166
  Collection of Hymns, for the Use of the People Called Methodists 35, 46, 48, 124–126, 170
  Collection of Psalms and Hymns 37, 42
  hymn theory 35
Western Association of Particular Baptist Churches 16, 26–27, 180
Whitefield, George 37, 55, 59–60, 64, 76, 181
  and Baptists 59–60
Whitley, W.T. 57, 60
Whole Booke of Psalmes 37, 91
Williams, Helen Maria 185
Williamson, Marilyn 77
women's experiences 18–19, 23, 51–52,

55–56, 76–77, 120–123, 145, 172
and pseudonyms 5, 52, 55, 77

Young, Edward 19–20, 68–69, 74–75, 82,
118–120, 132, 144, 184
Complaint, or Night-Thoughts 19–20,
25, 68–69, 75, 118, 132, 144, 184
Resignation 144
Young, Robert 57, 60, 63

Zinzendorf, Count Nicolaus 46

www.ingramcontent.com/pod-product-compliance
Lightning Source LLC
Chambersburg PA
CBHW070251230426
43664CB00014B/2485